Philosophy of
The Himalayan Master
Yogiraj Gurunath Siddhanath

Comparative Analyses With
Modern Western and Eastern Philosophies

Rudra Shivananda

Alight Publications
2024

Philosophy of the Himalayan Master Yogiraj Gurunath Siddhanath

By Rudra Shivananda

First Edition Published in November 2024

Alight Publications

PO Box 277

Live Oak, CA 95953

email: alightpub@gmail.com

Philosophy of the Himalayan Master Yogiraj Gurunath Siddhanath© 2024 by Runbir Singh.

All rights reserved. No part of this publication may be reproduced, stored in a retrieval system or database, or transmitted in any form or by any means electronic, mechanical, photocopying, recording, or otherwise without the prior written approval of the author or publisher.

Hardcover ISBN: 978-1-931833-67-7

Softcover ISBN: 978-1-931833-68-4

Printed in the United States of America

To That Presence that transcends words and Illuminates our Souls

Table of Contents

Preface /8

Introduction
    Overview of Gurunath's Philosophy /12
    Early influences and Spiritual Awakening /24
    Gurunath's Unique Work in the Modern World /26
    Gurunath's Vision for World Peace /28
    Indian and Western philosophical traditions
        Greek Philosophical Focus /29
        What about the Stoics and Descartes? /32
        Western Philosophy and Existentialism /35

Comparison of Gurunath's Philosophy with Gorakshanath and Shankaracharya
    Influence of Shiva-Goraksha-Babaji /39
    Influence of Adi Shankaracharya /55

Comparative Analysis with Philosophy of Plotinus /65

Comparison with the Mahasiddha Padmasambhava (Guru Rinpoche) /81

Mystic Convergence

Comparing with two Medieval Mystics
Gurunath and Meister Eckhert /91
Gurunath and Ibn Arabi /99

Comparing with Contemporary Western Philosophies
Overview of Contemporary Western Philosophy /103
Historical Context of Indian Philosophy /106
Core tenets of Gurunath's Philosophy /108
The Value of Studying Western Philosophy /111
Themes in Contemporary Western Philosophy /115
Comparing with Edmond Husserl's phenomenology /119
On Henri Bergson's Philosophy of Vital Evolution /122
On Metaphysics and Epistemology / 125
On Ethics and Moral Philosophy /129

The Concept of Self and Consciousness /135
The self in relation to others and the Universe /143
The Journey of the self /146

On Consciousness and Reality /149
Practical implications in everyday life /152

Future Directions and Potential Integration with Modern Western Thought /155

Philosophical Implications for Modern Society /159

Synthesis and Future Directions /163

Revelations from Gurunath's Philosophy

Ultimate Reality is Nothingness .167

On Nature and the Universe /171

The Cycles of Material and Spiritual Evolution /174

Practical Spirituality /190

On Healing and Transformation /193

The Transformative Power of the Master's Presence /198

On Karma and Chakras /200

Self-Realization through Kriya Yoga /202

Alchemy of Total Transformation /203

The Process of Kundalini Awakening /204

Achiieving Self-Realization /205

Gurunath's vision of the Three Gunas /206

Conclusion /217

Appendix

Glossary of Western Philosophy /222

Glossary of Eastern Philosophy /276

More Books by Rudra Shivananda /313

About the Author /320

Yogiraj Gurunath Siddhanath:

"Consciousness is the final state of Knowingness
we call omniscience. The association of your individual
Consciousness with your mind purifies the mind to equal purity
as your Conciousness hence a merger takes place.
Your Consciousness taking along with it the essence of mind,
merges into its own unlimited Conciousness.
Having reached the Enlightenment of Absolute Knowingness,
you have now transcended the universal fabric of mind.
You have gone beyond the space-time continuum of relativity,
into Reality. You can overlord the rules of Creation.
Such a Being; who can master Time (Kaal) is indeed worthy
of the name Mahan-Kaal (The Great Beyond Time), with
your center everywhere and circumference nowhere."

Preface

Yogiraj Gurunath Siddhanath is not a philosopher and he is not a teacher. By his Presence, whether through his voice, image, video or in person, he has been able to transform many spiritual seekers. He has ignited the spark of divinity in tens of thousands of those who have approached him.

The spiritual path is a long and meandering one that can be difficult even for those who have been awakened - there are many pitfalls due to personal, family and world karmas. The purpose of this book is to provide a basis, a foundation for those who are hungering for the guidance of a true spiritual Master who has plumbed the depths and heights of the path towards freedom and liberation from our own self-imposed prison of ignorance of the Self.

Gurunath, as he is most often called by his students, emphasizes the primacy of experience - the real spiritual experiences that he calls 'Anubhuti'. It is from his experiences that he is able to verify and agree to certain philosophical frameworks. However, it is because he is not a didactic philosopher, that he is just as comfortable invoking Satchidananda or Brahman from a Vedantic position as he is to talk in terms of Paramashiva from that of Kashmir Shaivism.

Being a Master whose purpose is to transform his students, his teachings are targetting their needs and capacities at any particular moment of time. It is a challenge to present this teachings from a perspective free from the constraints of individual needs or even group dynamics.

My own interactions with the Master has involved over thirty years of attending his satsangs, retreats and practicing the systems of techniques that he has formulated for achieving Self-Realization in these times. I cannot claim to fully understand such an highly evolved consciousness - at the least in the realms of God and Universal Consciousness - but have endeavored to provide a broad overview of the philosophical bases of his teachings in this book and then follow up with some of his major unique teachings in a second volume. I have included some brief treatment of his teachings which touch on his philosophy presented here.

In ths philosophical portion, I have attempted to provide some comparison and reference to both Western and Indian schools of philosophy. This is not meant to be rigorous scholastic work but more of a support for spiritual students on the path of self actualization. I have not made use of notes and citations but have instead used brief explanations within the text where it may seem necessary and then included a substantial glossary explaining the major philosophers and schools of philosophy that I have used for the comparative analyses.

To the best of my knowledge, Gurunath has primarily studied the teachings of the Nath and Kriya Masters in his youth and attended many of their satsangs. The Nath tradition is especially eclectic and their can be exponents of different philosophies depending on their individual experiences and backgrounds. Some are Vedantists, some Tantrics, some Sufis and some are Shivaites - they all share a veneration for Gorakhnath and Matsyendranath.

It is not possible for me to do justice to describing or circumscribing a dynamic phenomenon such as Gurunath and consequently, for his teachings, I've relied mostly on his own books, such as Wings to Freedom and Babaji The Lightning Standing Still as well as some material from his workshops. I've also needed to fill in some gaps from my discussions with Gurunath spanning over thirty years.

In order to benefit from his philosophy and teachings, I believe it necessary to consider his upbringing, both cultural and academic, followed by the major spiritual influences and experiences. These are sections are brief but sufficient as a background to the rest of the book.

The inclusion of comparative analyses with pertinent Western Philosphies is to help bridge the gap between Eastern and Wester Philosphical traditions and does not reflect any knowledge that Gurunath may have with any of them.

As to who can benefit, it is my intention that everyone who is spiritually inclined and wish to understand the way of a contemporary Master will find it useful. This is especially true for those following a specific spiritual path such as that of the Kriya Yoga given by Gurunath - this will provide a metaphysical map of the goal, the path and the conceptual assumptions for such as practice.

Rudra Shivananda

Introduction

Overview of Gurunath's Philosophy

Yogiraj Gurunath Siddhanath is a spiritual leader and Master (SatGuru) from India, known for his teachings on yoga, meditation, and spirituality. He is often referred to as a Himalayan Yogi, emphasizing his connection to the ancient yogic traditions of the Himalayas. Gurunath traces his lineage to the ancient of days known as Mahavatar Babaji and is recognized for his efforts to bring the knowledge and techniques of Kriya Yoga to a wider audience.

Kriya Yoga, which Gurunath teaches, is an ancient meditation technique that is said to accelerate spiritual growth and bring about a profound state of tranquility and God-realization. It involves specific breathing techniques and other practices designed to harmonize the body, mind, and spirit.

Gurunath has written several books and travels extensively to conduct workshops, retreats, and speaking engagements, sharing his insights and techniques for spiritual development. His teachings often emphasize the importance of self-realization and the interconnectedness of all life. He also speaks about the need for harmony with nature and the cultivation of inner peace.

He has a following of students and practitioners around the world, many of whom attest to the transformative impact of his teachings and practices on their lives. Gurunath's approach is often described as non-dogmatic, encouraging individuals to seek their own personal experience of spirituality.

His teachings are deeply rooted in his personal experiences of spiritual truths, or anubhuti. Gurunath's approach to spirituality is highly experiential, prioritizing direct experience over theoretical knowledge. This direct experience serves as the cornerstone of his teachings and the basis for the philosophical framework he shares with his students.

Basis in Experiential Knowledge

Gurunath's philosophy stems from what he describes as spontaneous revelations and mystical experiences that he has undergone throughout his life. This personal experience, or anubhuti, is emphasized as the ultimate source of truth, transcending the boundaries set by textual or second-hand knowledge. He often mentions how these experiences have provided him with insights into the nature of consciousness, the cosmos, and the processes of spiritual evolution.

Integration with Yogic Philosophy

While Gurunath's teachings are grounded in his personal experiences, they are not isolated from the broader tradition of yoga. He integrates insights from classical yogic texts and philosophies, especially those pertaining to Kriya Yoga and Tantra, to articulate his experiences and shape his teachings. His approach is syncretic, drawing on the rich tapestry of Indian spiritual practices but always returning to the primacy of direct experience as the most reliable source of spiritual knowledge.

Teachings for His Students

From his philosophy, Gurunath has formulated a set of teachings aimed at guiding students on their own paths to self-realization. These teachings revolve around the practice of Kriya Yoga, which he often describes as a "lightning path" to enlightenment. Kriya Yoga involves specific techniques for controlling the breath and the subtle energies within the body, designed to rapidly accelerate the practitioner's spiritual development.

In his teachings, Gurunath frequently emphasizes the importance of direct experience in spiritual practice. He has stated:

"Realization cannot be taught, it must be caught. I can only stir the environment; the awakening has to come from within you."

This statement underscores his belief in the transformative power of personal experience and the limitations of verbal instruction. It highlights his role as a facilitator of spiritual environments where students can themselves have direct experiences of higher consciousness.

Additionally, he often talks about the concept of Satchitananda (Existence, Consciousness, Bliss), a term borrowed from Vedantic philosophy, to describe the nature of the self that one realizes through Kriya Yoga:

"In the bliss of the breath, the divine joy of Being is realized. Therefore, practice your Kriyas; meditate daily. Live in the consciousness of Satchitananda."

This instruction encapsulates his teaching approach—practical, focused on meditation and breathwork, and aimed at realizing the blissful nature of one's own consciousness.

Gurunath's teachings represent a modern interpretation of ancient yogic wisdom, filtered through the lens of his own mystical experiences. His emphasis on anubhuti as the foundation of spiritual knowledge seeks to empower individuals to explore their inner worlds through disciplined practices, leading to personal revelations and spiritual liberation. By fostering an environment conducive to spiritual awakening, he guides his followers toward self-realization, advocating a direct engagement with the divine that is both personal and profound.

Gurunath's experiences and teachings are deeply influenced by his encounters and spiritual relationship with Mahavatar Babaji, whom he identifies with the Mahayogi Gorakshanath, a revered figure in the Nath tradition who was most active around 1000 CE. This connection has significantly framed his yogic philosophy and teachings, blending traditional Nath teachings with the insights and practices of Kriya Yoga.

Connection with Mahavatar Babaji and Gorakshanath

Gurunath posits that Mahavatar Babaji, a legendary immortal yogi said to be a disseminator of Kriya Yoga, is a manifestation of Gorakshanath, the founder of the Nath Sampradaya, which has historically emphasized mastery over the physical and subtle bodies through Hatha Yoga and other tantric practices. This identification ties the esoteric practices of the Nath tradition with the transformative techniques of Kriya Yoga, creating a bridge between ancient yogic wisdom and contemporary spiritual practices.

Notable Aspects of Gurunath's Philosophy and Teachings

1. Integration of Nath and Kriya Yoga Practices: Gurunath's philosophy integrates the rigorous discipline and body-transforming techniques of the Nath tradition with the subtler, energy-manipulating techniques of Kriya Yoga. This synthesis aims to accelerate spiritual evolution, promoting rapid progress toward liberation and enlightenment. Gurunath emphasizes the continuity of these traditions, suggesting that the teachings of Babaji/Gorakshanath represent an unbroken transmission of spiritual wisdom.

2. Emphasis on Direct Experience: Gurunath's experiences with Babaji deepen his emphasis on anubhuti (direct experience) as the core of spiritual learning and practice. He often speaks of his personal encounters with Babaji in both physical and astral forms, which not only validate his teachings but also serve as a testament to the potential for achieving higher states of consciousness accessible through yogic discipline.

3. Teaching of Universal Brotherhood: One of the key messages Gurunath attributes to Babaji is the concept of love and universal brotherhood. He often quotes Babaji's teachings about the unity of all beings and the necessity of love as the basis for real spiritual community and growth. This reflects both a traditional yogic emphasis on compassion and a modern interpretation suited to global spirituality.

4. Focus on Transformation and Healing: Gurunath frequently discusses the healing power of Kriya Yoga, both physically and spiritually. He describes these practices as

tools for purifying the body and mind, ultimately leading to the revelation of the divine self within. This therapeutic aspect is often linked to his experiences with Babaji, who is portrayed as both a healer and a guide for humanity's spiritual evolution.

Gurunath often shares vivid descriptions of Babaji's teachings and his own experiences with him, using these narratives to underline the mystical and accessible nature of his teachings. He describes Babaji/Gorakshanath as not just a teacher of a particular set of techniques but as a living presence that continues to guide and awaken the divine potential within every individual.

The profound impact of Gurunath's spiritual experiences with Babaji as Gorakshanath is evident in the unique blend of Nath and Kriya Yoga practices in his teachings. This integration, along with the emphasis on direct spiritual experience and a universal, compassionate approach to spirituality, characterizes his contribution to contemporary yoga and spiritual practice. Gurunath's teachings, therefore, not only reflect his personal spiritual journey but also offer a modern interpretation of ancient wisdom, aimed at healing, transformation, and the realization of one's highest potential.

Gurunath's narrative as an avatar, including being a reincarnation of Shri Yukteswar Giri, is a significant aspect of his teachings and spiritual philosophy. It places him in a lineage of revered spiritual masters and connects his teachings to a historical and mystical tradition of transmitting spiritual knowledge. The concept of the avatar—meaning "descent," referring to a divine being manifesting in human form—is used within many Indian spiritual traditions to indicate a divine incarnation sent to earth for the spiritual upliftment of humanity.

Avatar Concept in Gurunath's Teachings

1. Continuity of Divine Mission: Gurunath positions himself within a continuum of Cosmic beings whose avatars return in various ages to aid in human evolution and the restoration of dharma (cosmic order and right conduct). By identifying as the reincarnation of Shri Yukteswar, Gurunath aligns his teachings with those of Paramahansa Yogananda and the broader Kriya Yoga tradition, emphasizing a direct transmission of spiritual knowledge from master to disciple.

2. Spiritual Authority and Legacy: By representing such a lineage, Gurunath enhances his spiritual authority, presenting his teachings as not only based on personal spiritual experience but also rooted in a deep, time-honored tradition. This connection underscores the value of lineage as a testament to the efficacy of spiritual transmission.

3. Empowerment Through Association: There is spiritual reassurance and empowerment in the concept that a Master is a divine incarnation with a historical mandate. This belief can deepen commitment to the practices taught and their overall spiritual journey, fostering a community united by a shared trust in the Master's divine role.

Gurunath often discusses his past lives and avatarhood in a way that highlights his spiritual mission and the continuity of his consciousness through different bodies. For instance, he might say:

- On Continuity of Consciousness: "As I was in past ages, so I am now again here to guide you. My spirit, unbound by time and form, continues its journey to awaken the divine in every heart."

- On his role as a Guide: "In each life, my purpose has been to lead souls to liberation. As Shri Yukteswar guided Yogananda, so too am I here to help you find your path to enlightenment."

Unlike empty statements, Gurunath can show his previous life connections with his students as well as casual participants at his satsangs through his Shivapat transmission. When he shares his superconscious states with his audience, they go into a heightened state of awareness and often see the Master's many past lives.

For followers, Gurunath's identification as an avatar of Shri Yukteswar—and by extension, as part of the lineage involving Lahiri Mahasaya and Babaji—provides a potent narrative of spiritual depth and continuity. It frames his teachings within a cosmic drama of recurring divine intervention in human affairs, which can be profoundly motivating and affirming for his students.

The avatar concept in Gurunath's teachings serves multiple roles: it establishes a direct link to revered figures in the spiritual tradition of Kriya Yoga, asserts his teachings' authenticity, and enhances his authority and appeal as a spiritual guide. This belief system not only helps to situate his teachings within a grand spiritual narrative but also promotes a deep and enduring engagement among his followers, who view him as a divine figure with a transcendent purpose. Such beliefs and teachings encourage a committed and cohesive spiritual community centered around his persona and spiritual mission.

Gurunath's teachings revolve primarily around the practice and philosophy of Kriya Yoga, along with broader spiritual principles. Here's a summary of his core teachings:

- Kriya Yoga: Central to his teachings, Kriya Yoga is a meditation technique aimed at accelerating spiritual growth. It involves specific breathing exercises and energy control methods. This practice is believed to help in harmonizing the body, mind, and spirit, leading to higher states of consciousness and self-realization.

- Self-Realization and Enlightenment: Gurunath emphasizes the importance of self-realization, which he describes as understanding and experiencing one's true divine nature. He teaches that enlightenment is attainable by all and is the ultimate goal of human life.

- Harmony with Nature: He often speaks about the significance of living in harmony with nature. This includes respecting all forms of life and recognizing the interconnectedness of all beings.

- Inner Peace and Healing: Gurunath's teachings also focus on achieving inner peace. He advocates that inner peace is essential for individual well-being and is a prerequisite for world peace.

- Universal Love and Compassion: He stresses the importance of universal love and compassion towards all beings, teaching that love is the essence of our true nature.

- Non-Dogmatic Approach: Gurunath is known for a non-dogmatic approach to spirituality. He encourages individuals to seek their own experiences and understanding of spiritual truths, rather than blindly following doctrines or dogmas.

- Global Consciousness: He speaks about the rise of global consciousness and the need for a collective awakening to address the challenges facing humanity.

- Integration of Spirituality and Daily Life: Gurunath advocates for integrating spiritual practices into everyday life, emphasizing that spirituality is not separate from daily activities but is a way of living.

His teachings are often characterized by a blend of ancient yogic wisdom and practical advice for modern living, aimed at aiding individuals in their spiritual journey while contributing positively to the world around them.

In the landscape of modern philosophy, the fusion of Eastern spiritual wisdom and Western analytical rigor presents a unique opportunity for intellectual and spiritual enrichment. The first part of this book seeks to explore this intersection by delving into the Gurunath's philosophy – he is considered a prominent figure in Indian spirituality, and comparing them with contemporary Western philosophical thought.

Gurunath stands as a beacon of Himalayan wisdom, advocating for a path of self-realization through the ancient practice of Kriya Yoga. His philosophy, deeply rooted in the traditions of Indian mysticism, offers a profound understanding of the self, consciousness, and the universe. In contrast, Western philosophy, with its diverse schools of thought from rationalism to existentialism, provides a rich tapestry of ideas concerning knowledge, ethics, and the nature of reality.

This book aims to bridge these two worlds. It is not just an academic comparison but a journey into the heart of what it means to be human in a complex and interconnected universe. We will explore how Gurunath's spiritual insights align, contrast, and potentially enrich Western philosophical discourses. This endeavor is especially pertinent in an era where global challenges demand a synthesis of different perspectives and wisdoms.

Our methodology is comparative and integrative. We seek to understand each philosophy in its own right, and then bring them into dialogue with each other. This approach is rooted in the belief that Eastern and Western philosophies, often seen as divergent, can illuminate each other in meaningful ways.

The key philosophical questions we address include: How do Gurunath's teachings on consciousness and Self, compare with Western notions of identity and mind? What can Western philosophy learn from Eastern approaches to ethics and spirituality? And how can these diverse philosophical traditions guide us in addressing contemporary global issues?

By the end of this exploration, we aim to offer readers not only a deeper understanding of Yogiraj Gurunath Siddhanath's teachings and contemporary Western philosophy but also a new perspective on how these two worlds can come together to offer insightful answers to some of the most pressing questions of our time.

This is in tune with Gurunath's emphasis on spiritual practice instead of spiritual study and action with awareness in the world instead of withdrawal from the environment.

Yogiraj Gurunath Siddhanath:

"There never has been, nor will there ever be a time when man's own nature shall cease to demand its best and foremost attention to unraveling the Truth. *Yoga* is the most excellent way of doing so, commending itself to the foremost minds of the east and the west. Men of marvelous mental power and intense heroism of ancient India were the outcome of the teachings of *yoga*.

It is true that *yoga* is the science of all sciences because it deals with the very essence of the evolution and well being of humanity. It is the one and only science offering the knowledge and practice of total transformation. This is the transformation from man the brute, to man the man, to man the God. It is for this reason that the supreme love, the love for the divine and love for humanity, may be experienced through *yoga*."

Early Influences and Spiritual Awakening

Gurunath was born on May 10th, 1944 into an aristocractic family connected with the rulers of Gwalior. They had ancestral palaces and homes in various places which over time were given away after the independence of India in 1947.

Some notable early spiritual influences:

1. Before his birth, his mother regularly went to one of the temples built by his grandfather in honor of Gorakhnath and used to take the holy ash from the fire-ceremonies with water as a tonic.

2. Gurunath's mother was a profound astrologer and foretold to him as a child that he would grow up to be a great yogi who would teach all over the world.

3. As a child of three or four, Gurunath would spontaneously go into deep states of meditation. These meditative states became more and more profound as he grew older.

4. His grandfather regularly entertained visiting yogis, philosophers, astrologers and miracle workers, all of whom, Gurunath was able to watch and have discourse with.

5. Educated in Sherwood College [Nainital], he met and spent time in the Himalayas with the great Nath Yogis, who would come down to teach as well as test those who were ready for the higher initiations.

6. He was initiated into Kriya Yoga by Swami Hariharananda and also spent time with Swami Satyanananda to further his practice. These two were great yogis in the tradition of Swami Shri Yukteswar and were fellow disciples of Paramhansa Yoganananda.

7. His spiritual transformation was completed by his deep and personal experience with Mahavatar Babaji (Shiva-Goraksha-Babaji) – the same immortal Being introduced by Paramhansa Yogananda in his classic, 'Autobiography of a Yogi'. His experiences with Babaji has been documented in his book, 'Wings to Freedom' as well as presented in various Youtube videos.

8. Gurunath also had profound experiences with the Divine Mother aspects -- notably with Ananandamayi Ma, whom he acknowledged as an avatar. Ma resided often in her Ashram in Puneand was accessible to the young Gurunath.

9. As Gurunath matured and after his experiences with Babaji, he also had experiences in the higher reaches of the Himalayas, in what he calls, 'The Land of the Hamsas,' interacting with great Beings who work behind the scenes for the betterment of Humanity.

Gurunath's Unique Work In This Modern World

Gurunath is a direct disciple of Babaji and with his blessings has founded the Siddhanath Yoga Parampara, a spiritual lineage that encompasses all his teachings.

He teaches various ancient forms of Yoga founded by the Nath Tradition, such as Mahavatar Babaji Kriya Yoga. He transforms those who come to him by bestowing powerful Shaktipat transmissions and unique 'thought free' states of consciousness.Gurunath empowers them to gradually go into Samadhi (awareness of one's own Self), experiencing the depths of Eternal Being.

Gurunath is unique in that as far as can be known to us, he is the only widely accessible Master who gives authentic experiences of Shaktipat Kundalini energy transmission for spiritual and healing transformation essential to the awakening and continued evolution of humanity. The sincere will receive these dimensions of the Guru's consciousness through direct experience as to what true yoga is rather than through intellectual exploration.

He is also sharing in his public talks, his consciousness of Natural Enlightenment, transforming the ripples of thought in the mind lake of the audience into a waveless lake of Soul Awareness -- a no-thought state. The experience of Gurunath's Consciousness as the Guru guides the seeker in transforming his thought-filled finite mind into infinite consciousness free of thoughts. This process he calls "Shivapat".

Gurunath understands that the mind's I-ness will resist its soul consciousness expanding into super consciousness out of fear of losing its ego identity, and reveals the truth that "the individual mind loses its identity only to partake of its vaster identity as infinite awareness, the drop merges into the ocean not to lose itself but to become of it."

A third powerful experience that Gurunath offers to those who come into his presence is called Panapat. This can only be fully appreciated by those who have been initiated into Kriya Yoga. However, all sincere spiritual seekers can experience how the Master 'breathes through their breath' making each breath deeper and longer.

In sharing these experiences with each individual seeker personally and with thousands of receptive people the world over simultaneously, Gurunath is attempting to demonstrate what all the scriptures claim - "that at the level of pure consciousness all Humanity is One."

A fourth experience that Gurunath often shares with his students is called the "Flight of the White Swan," during which he takes them into ever wider states of consciousness .

He teaches that way of the white swan is the evolution of human consciousness - "In the human brain exists the lateral ventricles in the shape of a 'swan in flight' with its head pointing to the back as though the swan is flying faster than light back to the future."

Gurunath's Vision for World Peace

If World Peace is to Herald the Dawn of a New Age,
Let us all realize that:
Humanity Our Uniting Religion
Breath Our Uniting Prayer and
Consciousness Our Uniting God

Indian and Western philosophy

For our purpose of understanding the philosophy of a modern yogi, we must first distinguish Indian philosophy from Greek (Western) philosophy primarily through their approaches to existential questions, their methodologies, and the practical application of philosophical insights. Here are some key distinctions:

Greek Philosophical Focus

1. Existential Focus vs. Abstract Inquiry

- Indian Philosophy: It is deeply existential, focusing on the individual's situation, and seeks to address the practical aspects of living. For instance, the practice of Yoga in Indian philosophy is not just a physical exercise but a comprehensive discipline that encompasses mental and spiritual well-being, aiming to achieve self-realization and enlightenment. This approach underscores the individual's quest for truth and the practical application of philosophical insights to improve one's life.

- Greek Philosophy: While Greek philosophy does explore existential themes, especially in the works of Socrates, who emphasized ethical living and the importance of knowing oneself, it predominantly pursues abstract inquiry and objective knowledge. Early Greek philosophers like Thales and Anaximander were more concerned with understanding the nature of the universe, or "arche" (the principle of all things), than with the individual's place or role within it. This objectivist approach often leads to a more theoretical and less practical application of philosophical principles.

2. Practical Quest for Truth vs. Theoretical Speculation

- Indian Philosophy: Philosophy is seen as a matter of life and death, with a strong emphasis on practical wisdom and guidelines for living. The Bhagavad Gita, for instance, is a philosophical discourse that takes place on a battlefield and addresses the moral and existential dilemma faced by Arjuna, thus directly linking philosophical insights with practical life decisions.

- Greek Philosophy: Although Greek philosophy, especially in the Socratic tradition, does concern itself with how one should live, it often veers towards more speculative inquiries about the nature of reality, knowledge, and existence. Plato's theory of Forms, for example, posits that non-material abstract forms (or ideas) represent the most accurate reality, which, though it has moral and ethical implications, leans towards metaphysical speculation.

3. Integration with Religion and Spirituality

- Indian Philosophy: It is closely integrated with spiritual practices and religious beliefs. The Upanishads, a series of philosophical texts, form the theoretical foundation of Hindu spiritualism, blending philosophical inquiry with religious devotion and spiritual practice. This seamless integration reflects a holistic approach where philosophy is not separate from one's spiritual and religious life.

- Greek Philosophy: Initially, Greek philosophy was closely tied to mythology and religion, but as it evolved, especially with figures like Plato and Aristotle, it became more secular and distinct from religious practice. The focus shifted towards rationalism, ethics, and politics, often exploring these areas independently of religious beliefs. For instance, Aristotle's ethics and politics are grounded in rational principles of the good life and the nature of the polis (city-state) rather than religious doctrine.

4. Concern for Individual Destiny

- Indian Philosophy: It maintains a consistent focus on the individual's destiny and the practical means to achieve a state of enlightenment or liberation (Moksha). Practices like meditation and Yoga are intended to help individuals transcend their limitations and understand their true nature, as seen in the philosophical teachings of the Vedanta.

- Greek Philosophy: While individual ethics and the good life are central themes, especially in the works of Socrates, Plato, and Aristotle, the emphasis is more on understanding universal principles and virtues that can guide human behavior. The Stoics, for instance, focused on personal virtue and wisdom as a means to achieve tranquility, but their view of destiny was more about accepting one's place in the natural order rather than achieving personal liberation.

It is fair to conclude that Indian philosophy is characterized by a deeply existential and practical approach, closely tied to spiritual and religious practices, and aimed at the individual's liberation or enlightenment. In contrast, Greek philosophy, despite its exploration of ethical and existential themes, tends towards more abstract speculation and is more distinctly separated from religious practice, focusing on universal truths and principles.

What about the Stoics and Rene Descartes?

Although the Stoics start with individual decision making and René Descartes starts with individual thought, they both come up short in addressing the existential condition of the individual and their contributions to the broader philosophical discourse.

Shortcomings of the Stoics

- Abstract Idealism vs. Practical Reality: The Stoics are engrossed in their emphasis on an abstract ideal of a wise man, which seemed unattainable in practical terms. Their ethical teachings, while of high standard, lacked a robust explanation of the individual's place in the cosmos. This gap made their ethical doctrines seem detached from the concrete realities of human life, necessitating a reliance on religious grounds for justification.

- Inadequate Addressing of Human Freedom: Stoicism focused on human freedom within a cosmos believed to be governed by deterministic laws. The Stoics advocated for inner tranquility achieved through the control of one's own mind, despite external circumstances.

However, this philosophy is seen as offering little in the way of practical guidance for achieving autonomy or mastery over one's fate, presenting a rather passive approach to dealing with life's challenges.

- Ethics Requiring Religious Justification: Because the Stoics' ethical system lacked a comprehensive account of the individual's cosmic significance, it ultimately leaned on religious justifications. Their moral philosophy, therefore, required a backdrop of faith to hold its ground, which Christianity later provided, adopting much of Stoicism's ethical framework but aligning it with Christian dogma.

Shortcomings of Descartes

- Overemphasis on Doubt and Rationalism: Descartes' methodological doubt, which led to his famous dictum "I think, therefore I am" (Cogito, ergo sum), has an over reliance on rationalism. While he aimed to establish a firm foundation for knowledge, his approach neglects the direct, lived experience of being. His philosophy suggests that self-awareness or the experience of existence is secondary to the thinking process, a perspective that arguably overlooks the richness of human experience beyond cognition.

- Objectivistic View of the World: Due to his own religious beliefs, Descartes moved quickly from the certainty of his own existence to establishing the existence of an external world and God, primarily through reasoning. This approach perpetuates an objectivistic view of the world, treating the individual as a minor element within a grand mechanical universe. Such a view diminishes the significance of personal experience and the existential reality of the individual.

- Contribution to the Impersonal View of Man: By outlining a mechanical picture of the universe where humans are seen as incidental, Descartes inadvertently contributed to an impersonal view of humanity. This perspective, laid the groundwork for a civilization and philosophical tradition that often overlooks the individual's existential plight, favoring abstract, universal principles over personal, lived experience.

In summary, the Stoics, while offering valuable ethical insights, failed to provide a practical framework for individual autonomy within a deterministic cosmos. Descartes, on the other hand, grounded his philosophy in abstract rationalism and an objectivistic worldview, neglecting the immediate, subjective experience of existence and reducing the individual to a cog in the vast machinery of the universe. From a yogic perspective both approaches are seen as overlooking the existential dimensions of human life, emphasizing abstract ideals or rationality at the expense of addressing the lived experiences and concerns of individuals.

There is greater convergence between Indian Philosophy and Western thought when we examine existential themes such as the search for truth, the nature of existence, freedom, and transcendence, beginning with Kierkegaard.

Western Philosophy and Existentialism

- Kierkegaard's Contribution: Søren Kierkegaard, a Danish philosopher, is highlighted for his critique of Hegelian philosophy and the broader inadequacies of modern philosophical and religious thought. Unlike Hegel, who emphasized a speculative, abstract approach to understanding reality, Kierkegaard argued for a personal, subjective approach to truth. He believed that truth is not something to be found in objective analysis or in the dogmas of religion but is a personal matter that becomes apparent in the "moment of choice" when an individual decides to believe in God or not. This decision, for Kierkegaard, is not a one-time act but a continuous, repeated affirmation of faith, embodying a personal struggle and commitment.

- Existentialism's Humanism: Existentialism, particularly the works of Jean-Paul Sartre, emphasizes its nature as a "humanism." Existentialism posits that philosophy should be about the individual's personal quest for truth and how it impacts their way of life. This contrasts with the view of philosophy as merely an objective inquiry. Existentialism highlights the uniqueness of individual existence, the concept of "being-in-the-world," and the idea that existence precedes essence. For example, Sartre's notion that "existence precedes essence" suggests that humans first exist, encounter themselves, and emerge into the world to define their essence. There is no predetermined essence or nature that humans must fit into; instead, individuals create their essence through their actions and choices.

Indian Philosophy and its Emphasis on the Individual

- Integration of Philosophy and Religion: Unlike Western philosophy, which often sees a division between the secular and the sacred, Indian philosophy has traditionally integrated philosophical inquiry with religious and spiritual practice. This integration is seen in the way philosophical concepts are reflected in religious texts, myths, and practices, and vice versa.

- Yoga as a Philosophical Practice: Yoga is presented as a practical discipline that serves both as a means of philosophical investigation and a method for achieving transcendence. Through yoga, individuals can directly experience the truths discussed in philosophical texts, moving beyond intellectual understanding to a direct, experiential knowledge of reality. Yoga practices, such as meditation, aim at transcending the limitations of individuality and experiencing a higher state of consciousness.

- Phenomenological Approach: Indian philosophy often adopts a phenomenological approach, focusing on consciousness and its relation to the world. This approach is less concerned with external objective reality and more with the processes occurring within an individual's consciousness. For instance, the Advaita Vedanta school emphasizes the non-duality of Atman (the self) and Brahman (the ultimate reality), suggesting that the ultimate truth lies in the realization of one's own consciousness as being identical with the universal consciousness.

Both Western existentialism and Indian philosophy grapple with the nature of existence, the search for authenticity, and the individual's quest for transcendence. However, they approach these themes differently. Western existentialism emphasizes personal responsibility, the absurdity of existence, and the individual's freedom to create their essence through choices and actions. Indian philosophy, on the other hand, offers a more integrated view that includes practical disciplines like Yoga for transcending individual limitations and realizing a higher, more unified state of being.

These philosophical traditions provide valuable insights into the human condition, suggesting that a comprehensive understanding of existence might benefit from a dialogue between these diverse perspectives.

Comparison of Gurunath's Philosophy with Gorakhnath and Shankaracharya

Rudra Shivananda

Influence of Shiva-Goraksha-Babaji on Gurunath's Philosophy

The philosophy of Gorakhnath offers profound insights into the nature of reality, consciousness, and the path to liberation. Gorakhnath, the immortal Mahayogi, is considered a pivotal figure in the Nath tradition, embodying a synthesis of yogic practices and philosophical depth. His teachings, marked by their clarity and depth, offer a guide to transcending the limitations of the mundane world through the realization of the self's innate divinity. Gurunath has identified Gorakhnath as the same being that gave Kriya Yoga to Lahiri Mahasaya, that is Mahavatar Babaji. In the Nath tradition, Gorakhnath is revered as the avatar of Lord Shiva. Consequently, Gurunath calls this timeless Being, Shiva-Goraksha-Babaji.

It has to be noted that although the same Being, the Gorakhnath of 1000 CE and the Babaji of 1860 provide different emphasis and appear to be teaching different systems of yoga – that of Hatha Yoga and Kriya Yoga. However, at their essence, Gurunath has shown them to be a continuum if not the same.

The Nature of Reality: Shiva and Shakti

Gorakhnath's philosophy elucidates the dynamic interplay between Shiva and Shakti, the fundamental cosmic principles representing consciousness and energy, respectively. "Shiva without Shakti is shava (a corpse) and Shakti without Shiva has no place to reside," he states, highlighting the inseparability and mutual dependence of consciousness and energy. This union of Shiva and Shakti in the human body is the essence of Gorakhnath's teachings, illustrating the potential for each individual to realize their inherent divine nature.

The Path of Yoga

Central to Gorakhnath's philosophy is the practice of yoga as a means to achieve spiritual liberation. Unlike the purely ascetic or renunciatory paths, Gorakhnath's yoga is an integration of physical discipline, breath control, and meditation, aimed at awakening the latent spiritual energy within (Kundalini) and guiding it through the chakras to unite with the supreme consciousness. "The body is the temple, the asanas are the prayers, and the breath is the divine word," he posits, emphasizing the holistic nature of yoga as a transformative practice.

Mastery over the Mind

For Gorakhnath, mastery over the mind is a fundamental tenet. He teaches that the mind, often clouded by desires and illusions (Maya), is the root cause of suffering and bondage. Through the disciplined practice of yoga and meditation, one can transcend the mind's limitations, experiencing a state of pure consciousness or Samadhi. "Control the mind, and you will see the Moon and the Sun seated in the same chariot," Gorakhnath advises, suggesting the luminous clarity and unity of experience attainable through such mastery.

The Guru-Disciple Relationship

The relationship between the Guru and the disciple is of paramount importance in Gorakhnath's philosophy. The Guru is not merely a teacher but a spiritual guide who initiates the disciple into the mysteries of the self and the universe. "The Guru is the boatman who helps cross the ocean of existence," Gorakhnath declares, highlighting the essential role of the Guru in the spiritual journey. It is through the grace of the Guru that the disciple can navigate the path of yoga and attain the ultimate realization.

The Goal of Liberation

The ultimate goal of Gorakhnath's teachings is liberation (Moksha) from the cycle of birth and death (Samsara). This liberation is not an escape from the world but a realization of one's true nature as part of the universal consciousness. "In the heart of the yogi, all distinctions merge, and there remains no more the duality of the seer and the seen," he elucidates, describing the state of oneness that characterizes liberation. This realization brings about a profound peace and joy, free from the vicissitudes of worldly existence.

Gorakhnath's philosophy, with its emphasis on the union of Shiva and Shakti, the practice of yoga, mastery over the mind, the importance of the Guru-disciple relationship, and the goal of liberation, offers a comprehensive path to spiritual awakening.

In a similar way, Gurunath's teachings are profound yet practical, aiming to inspire and guide seekers on their journey towards self-realization. In the words of Gurunath, the path he delineates is not merely a set of practices but a way of life, a transformation of being that reveals the inherent divinity within all.

Pinda-Brahman

Gurunath has personal experience of the the Pinda Brahman philosophy of Gorakhnath, illustrating the microcosm-macrocosm relationship within the spiritual context. This philosophy posits that the entire universe (Brahmanda), or cosmic reality (Brahman), is reflected within the individual (Pinda), encapsulating the principle "as above, so below." Gorakhnath, through this philosophy, emphasizes the interconnectedness and essential unity between the individual self and the cosmic reality.

Core Concepts

- Unity of Individual and Cosmos: Gorakhnath teaches that the individual body (Pinda) is a microcosmic reflection of the entire universe (Brahmanda). This concept suggests that all elements and principles governing the cosmos are present within the individual, making the body a sacred space where one can realize universal truths.

- Realization of the Inner Universe: The philosophy encourages practitioners to explore their inner universe through meditation and yogic practices. Gorakhnath asserts, "Within this body lies the entire creation; know this, and you know Brahman." This exploration leads to the realization that the individual soul (Atman) and the universal soul (Brahman) are one and the same.

- Path of Yoga as Unification: The practice of yoga, according to Gorakhnath, is the method by which one can experience the unity of Pinda and Brahman. Through disciplined practice, the yogi awakens the Kundalini energy, guiding it through the chakras to achieve a state of Samadhi, where the individual consciousness merges with the cosmic consciousness.

- Transcendence of Dualities: In realizing the unity of Pinda and Brahman, the practitioner transcends dualities and distinctions between the self and the other, the inner and the outer, the microcosm and the macrocosm. Gorakhnath teaches, "In the heart of a true yogi, where the light of self-realization shines, there lies the confluence of the individual and the infinite."

- Practical Implications for Spiritual Practice: This philosophy underscores the importance of the body and the internal world in the spiritual quest. It suggests that enlightenment and the realization of ultimate reality are not to be sought solely in external rituals or pilgrimage but within one's own being.

The Pinda Brahman philosophy of Gorakhnath is a powerful reminder of the sacredness of the individual as a complete universe unto themselves. It offers a holistic view of spirituality, where the journey towards cosmic realization begins and ends within the individual.

Consequently, Gurunath not only elevates the human body to a temple of divine presence but also offers a direct path to liberation through the recognition of one's inherent unity with all existence. This philosophy serves as a cornerstone of his philosophy, guiding seekers towards the realization that **the ultimate truth lies within**, waiting to be discovered through the mirror of their own being.

The "Goraksha Shataka," from Gorakhnath stands as a beacon in the vast landscape of yogic literature. Comprising a hundred verses (Shataka means 'hundred'), this text distills the essence of yogic wisdom, offering seekers a guide to understanding the profound practices and principles of yoga. Gorakhnath, through the "Goraksha Shataka," navigates the intricate pathways of spiritual awakening, articulating a vision of yoga that is as transformative as it is transcendent. This text formed the core and inspiration for the much later Hatha Yoga Pradipika of Yogi Swatmarama.

The "Goraksha Shataka" begins with an exposition on the foundational principles of yoga. It elucidates the importance of the Yamas and Niyamas, the ethical precepts that lay the groundwork for a life conducive to spiritual exploration. Gorakhnath asserts, "True yoga begins not with the body but with the mind," emphasizing the necessity of purity, truthfulness, contentment, and self-discipline as the bedrock upon which the yogic journey is built.

Gorakhnath dedicates a significant portion of the text to the practice of Asanas, the physical postures of yoga. He posits, "The body is the temple of the spirit, and asanas are its foundation stones." Each posture is presented not merely as a physical exercise but as a means to cultivate stability, health, and equilibrium, preparing the body for the deeper practices of meditation and pranayama.

The text intricately explores Pranayama, the regulation of breath, as a vital tool for mastering the life force (Prana) that animates all existence. Gorakhnath describes, "As the wind moves a boat on water, so does prana move the body." He offers detailed techniques for controlling and directing prana, highlighting the transformative potential of breathwork in achieving higher states of consciousness.

Pratyahara, the withdrawal of the senses, and Dharana, focused concentration, are presented as essential steps in the internalization of awareness. Gorakhnath likens Pratyahara to "a turtle withdrawing its limbs," a metaphor for the retreat of consciousness from the external to the internal. Dharana, then, is the sharpening of this inward focus, laying the groundwork for deep meditation.

The pinnacle of Gorakhnath's exposition is the exploration of Dhyana (meditation) and Samadhi (spiritual absorption), the final limbs of yoga. He articulates, "In Dhyana, the mind is like a flame in a windless place," illustrating the profound stillness and clarity that meditation brings. Samadhi, the ultimate goal of yoga, is described as a state of complete union with the Divine, where the individual self dissolves into universal consciousness. Gorakhnath assures, "In Samadhi, the yogi finds the treasure of treasures, the self in the Self."

Throughout the "Goraksha Shataka," the importance of the Guru is reiterated. Gorakhnath venerates the Guru as the key to unlocking the mysteries of yoga, stating, "The Guru is the boatman across the ocean of existence." The text underscores that while the practices of yoga are profound and potent, the guidance of an enlightened Guru is indispensable in navigating the path to liberation.

The "Goraksha Shataka" is not merely a manual of yogic practice but a sacred text that invites the seeker into the heart of spiritual awakening. Gorakhnath, with his characteristic clarity and depth, offers a roadmap that is as relevant today as it was centuries ago. His teachings remind us that the journey of yoga is a journey of return—to the essence of who we are, beyond the confines of body and mind, in the eternal embrace of the divine. Through the "Goraksha Shataka," Gorakhnath continues to guide seekers on this timeless path, illuminating the way with the light of his wisdom.

The "Goraksha Rahasya" (The Revelation of Gorakhnath) is a profound text that delves into the esoteric practices and philosophical underpinnings of the Nath tradition, a lineage of Indian yogic and spiritual thought attributed to the revered sage Gorakhnath. At its core, the "Goraksha Rahasya" is an exploration of the mysteries of existence, the nature of the self, and the ultimate reality. Gorakhnath, through this text, invites the seeker to delve into the depths of their being, to uncover the truth that lies veiled by ignorance and illusion.

The Unification of Shiva and Shakti

One of the central themes of the "Goraksha Rahasya" is the unification of Shiva (consciousness) and Shakti (energy), symbolizing the non-dual nature of reality. Gorakhnath elucidates, "Just as the sun is reflected in countless droplets of water, so is Shiva reflected in every particle of creation, animated by Shakti." This metaphor captures the essence of the text's teaching: that the division between the individual and the cosmos is an illusion, and in realizing the unity of Shiva and Shakti within, one awakens to their true nature. *This is the cornerstone of the Kriya technique that is given by Gurunath, called the Shiva-Shakti Kriya Pranayama.*

The Journey through the Chakras

A significant portion of the "Goraksha Rahasya" is devoted to the journey through the chakras, the energy centers within the subtle body. Gorakhnath presents the chakras as gateways to higher consciousness, each representing a different aspect of human experience and spiritual awakening. He guides the practitioner through practices aimed at purifying and activating these centers, facilitating the ascent of Kundalini Shakti from the base of the spine to the crown of the head. "The ascent of Kundalini is the ascent of consciousness, from the confines of the ego to the boundless expanse of the divine," Gorakhnath declares, highlighting the transformative power of this process. *In the Siddhnath Kriya tradition taught by Gurunath, this journey through the chakras is given importance by the technique called Omkar Kriya.*

The Role of the Guru

The "Goraksha Rahasya" emphasizes the indispensable role of the Guru in the spiritual journey. Gorakhnath describes the Guru as the living embodiment of the divine, whose grace is key to the disciple's awakening. "In the presence of the Guru, ignorance dissolves, just as darkness vanishes at the break of dawn," he states, underscoring the Guru's role in dispelling the darkness of ignorance and leading the disciple to the light of knowledge and realization. ***Gurunath exemplifies this role of the Guru.***

The Path of Hatha Yoga

Gorakhnath also explores the path of Hatha Yoga as a means to prepare the body and mind for higher spiritual practices. He elucidates the importance of asanas (postures), pranayama (breath control), and mudras (gestures) in harmonizing the physical and subtle bodies. "Hatha Yoga is the foundation upon which the temple of realization is built," he asserts, advocating for a balanced approach to spiritual practice that includes attention to the physical body.

According to Gurunath, the "Goraksha Rahasya" is not just a text but a living transmission of the spiritual heritage of Gorakhnath. It offers a comprehensive guide to understanding the mysteries of life, the universe, and oneself. Through its teachings on the unification of Shiva and Shakti, the journey through the chakras, the role of the Guru, and the practice of Hatha Yoga, the text serves as a roadmap for the spiritual aspirant. Gorakhnath, with profound wisdom and compassion, invites each seeker to embark on this sacred journey, promising that at its end lies not just self-realization, but the realization of the Self in all.

Since Gurunath is teaching in modern times, there are subtle changes to the philosophical and practical approaches from that of the medieval Gorakhnath.

Realization of the Self

Yogiraj Gurunath Siddhanath emphasizes the realization of the Self as an experiential understanding of one's true nature beyond the physical form. "We are not mere bodies of flesh and bone," Yogiraj posits, "but are, in essence, luminous beings of light, embodiments of pure consciousness." His teachings often revolve around the experiential aspect of spirituality, urging seekers to transcend the mind's limitations through direct experience.

Gorakhnath, on the other hand, lays a foundational emphasis on the attainment of self-realization through the mastery of the body and mind, utilizing the sometimes extreme tools of Hatha Yoga. "The body is the bow, Asanas are the arrows, and the soul is the target," he elucidates, highlighting the instrumental role of physical discipline in achieving spiritual liberation. Gorakhnath's approach is methodical, emphasizing the step-by-step awakening of the Kundalini energy to realize the Self.

The Path of Yoga

Both Yogiraj and Gorakhnath advocate yoga as a supreme path to enlightenment, yet their approaches illuminate different facets of this ancient discipline.

Yogiraj's teachings are deeply rooted in the practice of Kriya Yoga, a potent meditative technique aimed at accelerating spiritual growth, re-introduced in modern times by Mahavatar Babaji. "Kriya Yoga is the jet plane route to God-realization,"

Yogiraj often says, underscoring the efficacy and directness of this path. His approach is marked by simplicity and directness, appealing to the seeker's heart and intuition.

Medieval Gorakhnath presents a comprehensive system of Hatha Yoga, emphasizing the importance of purifying the body and mind as precursors to spiritual awakening. His philosophy is encapsulated in the adage, "First the body, then the spirit." Gorakhnath's teachings are detailed, covering a wide range of practices from asanas to pranayama, leading the practitioner gradually towards higher states of consciousness.

It should be pointed out that Gurunath has decoded the Goraksha Shataka to unveil practices that correspond to that of Kriya Yoga also.

The Concept of Maya

The concept of Maya, or illusion, is another area where Yogiraj and Gorakhnath offer illuminating insights.

Yogiraj speaks of Maya as the divine play of consciousness, an expression of the cosmic dance between Shiva and Shakti. He views the world not merely as an illusion to be transcended but as a manifestation of the divine to be realized and embraced. "In every leaf, in every drop of water, the entire cosmos can be seen, if only one looks with the eyes of love," he teaches, inviting a perception of unity in diversity.

Medieval Gorakhnath, while acknowledging the illusory nature of the material world, focuses on transcending Maya through the realization of the Self. He regards the world as a stage for the soul's journey towards liberation, a labyrinth that the yogi navigates with the light of wisdom. "Maya ensnares those who are asleep to their true nature, but for the yogi, it is but a thin veil that is easily torn asunder," Gorakhnath asserts, emphasizing liberation through knowledge and self-mastery.

The Role of the Guru

Both spiritual masters hold the Guru in high esteem, though their emphasis on the Guru-disciple relationship varies.

Gurunath sees the Guru as an embodiment of grace, a divine catalyst for the awakening of the disciple. "The Guru is not outside you; he is the spark within that ignites the fire of self-realization," he reflects, highlighting the inner dimension of the Guru.

Gorakhnath presents the Guru as the indispensable guide on the path of yoga, the one who provides the map, the tools, and the wisdom to navigate the path of liberation. "Without the Guru, the path is treacherous and the way unclear; with him, every step is assured and every obstacle surmountable," he states, underscoring the external role of the Guru in the disciple's spiritual journey.

Gurunath and Gorakhnath, through their teachings, offer rich, albeit distinct, tapestries of spiritual wisdom. Yogiraj's emphasis on direct experience, the heart's primacy, and the divine play within Maya contrasts with Gorakhnath's methodical approach, the mastery of body and mind, and transcendence of illusion. Yet, at their core, both paths converge on the ultimate goal

Unity of Gorakhnath and Babaji

In the annals of spiritual history, few figures captivate the imagination and stir the soul as do **Gorakshanath and Mahavatar Babaji.** Gurunath offers a compelling narrative that bridges centuries and traditions, positing that these two luminaries are, in fact, manifestations of the same eternal spirit. This assertion not only challenges conventional narratives but also invites us to reconsider the nature of spiritual lineage and identity.

Unveiling the Unity

Gurunath's exploration into the confluence of Gorakshanath and Mahavatar Babaji is not merely academic but is rooted in profound spiritual insight and personal experience. "In the realm of the eternal, time and names are but veils that thinly disguise the essence of the divine," Yogiraj elucidates, suggesting that the spiritual essence transcends temporal and nominal distinctions.

The Legacy of Gorakshanath

Gorakshanath, a founder of the Nath tradition, is renowned for his contributions to yoga and spiritual philosophy. His teachings, emphasizing the transcendence of the physical to realize the union with the divine, laid the groundwork for myriad spiritual practices across India. Yogiraj points to Gorakshanath's emphasis on the realization of the self beyond the confines of the material, quoting, "The body is the temple, the breath its hymn, the self its deity."

The Mystique of Mahavatar Babaji

Mahavatar Babaji, a figure shrouded in mystery, emerges in more recent spiritual narratives, most notably in the accounts of Paramahansa Yogananda. Babaji is depicted as an ageless yogi, guiding disciples in Kriya Yoga, a path to self-realization and liberation. Gurunath shares, "Babaji, like a river that flows timeless, brings the ancient wisdom to the present, revitalizing the eternal truth."

Bridging Two Masters

Gurunath provides detailed accounts and teachings that highlight the thematic and philosophical continuities between Gorakshanath and Mahavatar Babaji. He draws parallels in their teachings on the importance of breath control, meditation, and the awakening of the Kundalini energy as means to spiritual enlightenment. "As Gorakshanath unveiled the path of transcendent yoga in ages past, so does Babaji reveal the same truths to the modern seeker," Yogiraj observes, pointing to the singularity of their mission.

Personal Revelations

Gurunath's assertions are bolstered by his personal spiritual experiences, which he shares with both depth and humility. He recounts meditative visions and encounters where the spiritual unity of Gorakshanath and Mahavatar Babaji was revealed to him, not through intellectual deduction, but through direct spiritual communion. "In the silence of deep meditation, the veils lifted, and I saw the light that illuminates both Gorakshanath and Babaji as one," Yogiraj shares, providing a testimony that transcends scholarly debate.

Implications for Spiritual Seekers

The proposition that Gorakshanath and Mahavatar Babaji are one and the same person has profound implications for spiritual seekers. It suggests that the spiritual path is not linear but cyclical, with masters returning in various forms to guide humanity. This understanding deepens the mystery of the guru-disciple relationship, emphasizing the eternal nature of spiritual guidance.

Gurunath's exploration into the unity of Gorakshanath and Mahavatar Babaji serves as a bridge across time, bringing together ancient wisdom and modern spiritual inquiry. Through detailed examples and quotes in his book "Babaji The Lightning Standing Still" Gurunath invites us to look beyond the surface of historical and spiritual narratives, to perceive the underlying unity that binds all seekers and masters. In doing so, he not only enriches our understanding of these two great beings but also illuminates the path for those who tread the journey of self-realization.

The Influence of Shankaracharya

Adi-Shankaracharya, with his profound insight and unparalleled intellect, redefined the contours of Indian philosophy, presenting Vedanta in its most quintessential form. Through his teachings, he navigated the complex interplay of the material and the spiritual, offering a path that leads beyond the ephemeral to the eternal.

Non-Duality (Advaita Vedanta)

At the heart of Shankaracharya's philosophy is the principle of Advaita, or non-duality, which asserts the oneness of the individual soul (Atman) with the ultimate reality (Brahman). This concept challenges the illusion of separation, positing that the diversity observed in the material world is merely a veil obscuring the underlying unity. Shankaracharya elucidates, "Brahman is the only truth, the world is illusion, and there is ultimately no difference between Brahman and individual self." This radical assertion invites the seeker to transcend the limitations of individual identity and experience the boundless nature of pure consciousness.

Maya: The Illusion of the Material World

Integral to understanding non-duality is the concept of Maya, which Shankaracharya describes as the cosmic illusion that makes the one Brahman appear as many, and the eternal appear transient. Maya is not merely a philosophical abstraction but a practical reality that ensnares beings in the cycle of birth, death, and rebirth. Through the lens of Maya, Shankaracharya offers a nuanced perspective on existence, urging the seeker to discern the impermanent from the permanent, and the real from the unreal.

The Path of Knowledge (Jnana Yoga)

Shankaracharya champions the path of Jnana Yoga as the direct route to liberation. This path is characterized by the rigorous inquiry into the nature of the self, leading to the discernment (viveka) between the eternal Atman and the transient world. The practice of Jnana Yoga demands an unwavering commitment to truth, supported by the cultivation of dispassion (vairagya) towards worldly attachments. Shankaracharya's methodical approach to spiritual inquiry has illuminated the minds of seekers, offering a clear, cogent path to enlightenment.

The Role of the Guru

In the journey to self-realization, Shankaracharya underscores the indispensable role of the Guru. The Guru is not merely a teacher, but a living embodiment of the truth, whose guidance dispels the darkness of ignorance. In the presence of a true Guru, the scriptures come alive, and the abstract becomes intimate. Shankaracharya's own life, a testament to the transformative power of spiritual mentorship, inspires seekers to approach a Guru with humility and openness.

Shankaracharya's contributions to Vedanta philosophy are not just intellectual innovations but are profound spiritual truths that continue to resonate with seekers of truth across ages. His teachings, characterized by depth, clarity, and an unwavering focus on the ultimate goal of liberation, invite us to embark on a journey within. In this journey, the distinctions between the knower, the known, and the process of knowing dissolve, revealing the luminous essence of pure consciousness that is the heart of Vedanta.

By synthesizing the essence of the Upanishads, Shankaracharya provided not only a philosophical framework but also a practical guide for those aspiring to tread the path of spiritual awakening. In the clarity of his vision and the purity of his message, seekers find a source of perennial wisdom, guiding them beyond the transient to the transcendent.

Distinctiveness of Gurunath's approach to Vedanta

Similarly to Shankaracharya, Gurunath has adopted various aspects of Vedanta philosophy that conform to his spiritual experiences and offer profound insights into the nature of reality, self, and the universe. He navigates the depths of consciousness, yet illuminates the path of realization in distinctively nuanced ways.

Oneness of Self and the Universe

Shankaracharya's non-dualistic Vedanta, or Advaita Vedanta, posits the fundamental unity of the individual soul (Atman) with the ultimate reality (Brahman). He articulates a vision of oneness where the multiplicity of existence is seen as an illusion (Maya), a veil obscuring the singular truth of Brahman. "Brahman is the only truth, the world is illusion, and there is ultimately no difference between Brahman and the individual self," Shankaracharya elucidates, inviting the seeker to transcend perceived separations.

Gurunath, echoes this eternal truth through his teachings on the unity of consciousness. However, Yogiraj enriches this perspective with his experiential insights, emphasizing the dynamic interplay between consciousness and creation. While acknowledging the illusionary nature of the material world, he also celebrates the divine play (Lila) within Maya, encouraging a harmonious existence that honors the sanctity of life and the natural world. Gurunath asks his students to take good care of the body vehicle.

The Path to Liberation

For Shankaracharya, liberation (Moksha) is achieved through the path of knowledge (Jnana Yoga), where rigorous self-inquiry leads to the realization of the self's identity with Brahman. This path demands a detachment from the transient pleasures of the world, guided by the principles of discrimination (Viveka) and dispassion (Vairagya).

Gurunath, while valuing the path of knowledge, places a significant emphasis on the transformative power of love and direct spiritual experience. His teachings incorporate Kriya Yoga as a practical method for accelerating spiritual evolution, integrating breath control, meditation, and energy work to awaken higher states of consciousness. Gurunath's approach is holistic, addressing the spiritual aspirant's entire being—mind, body, and soul—underscoring the importance of direct experience and inner transformation as pathways to realizing one's divine nature.

On Role of the Guru

In Shankaracharya's tradition, the Guru is revered as an indispensable guide on the spiritual path. The Guru not only elucidates the scriptures but also embodies the living truth of Vedanta, acting as a mirror reflecting the disciple's true self beyond the egoic mind. Shankaracharya's own life, marked by his profound teachings and debates, exemplifies the Guru as a beacon of wisdom, guiding seekers toward liberation.

Gurunath extends the concept of the Guru beyond the traditional role, emphasizing the Guru as a catalyst for spiritual awakening and a conduit of grace (Shaktipat). Through his presence and teachings, he facilitates a direct transmission of spiritual energy, accelerating the disciple's journey inward. He embodies the principle that the Guru is not just a teacher but a spiritual Presence that awakens the latent divinity within each seeker.

Integration with the World

Shankaracharya's Advaita Vedanta, while celebrating the non--dual nature of reality, often emphasizes renunciation as a means to transcend the illusion of the material world. This path of renunciation is seen as a withdrawal from worldly attachments to realize the self's unity with Brahman.

Conversely, Gurunath advocates for a life of dynamic engagement with the world. His teachings encourage living in the awareness of oneness while actively participating in the world's affairs. For him, enlightenment is not an escape from the world but a deeper engagement with it from a place of realized unity and compassion. His philosophy suggests that true realization encompasses both the transcendent and the immanent, inviting a balanced existence that honors the spiritual within the material.

It can be seen that although grounded in the Sanatana Dharma of Advaita, Gurunath offers a distinct pathway to spiritual realization. Shankaracharya's Vedanta appeals to the intellect, emphasizing knowledge and renunciation as keys to liberation. **Gurunath's teachings, in contrast, speak to the heart and** *soul, advocating for a path that integrates spiritual practice with active participation in the world – the role of the householder yogi.*

Both paths converge on the fundamental truth of non-duality, yet they unfold in complementary ways, embodying the vastness and diversity of spiritual exploration. In their teachings, seekers find profound guidance for the journey inward, each offering a unique perspective on how to navigate the terrain of consciousness and ultimately realize the unity of all existence.

Refer to the table in the following three pages for some the salient features of Gurunath's philosophy as compared to Patanjali, Shankaracharya and Abhinavagupta.

Aspect	Yogiraj Gurunath Siddhanath	Patanjali	Shankaracharya	Abhinavagupta
Core Philosophy	Non-duality of spirit and matter. Synthesis of self-realization through Kundalini awakening and the guidance of a living master	Duality of Spirit and Matter. Focus on the cessation of mental fluctuations (chitta vritti nirodha) for achieving peace and self-knowledge	Advaita Vedanta: Absolute non-dualism; asserts that Brahman (Absolute) is the only reality, and the world is an illusion (Maya)	Non-dualism where Shiva and Shakti are one, with the emphasis on Spanda (divine vibration) as the nature of consciousness
Objective	Self-realization, liberation from karma, and evolution toward a state of pure consciousness in union with the Divine (Shivashakti)	Kaivalya (liberation) through achieving a state beyond mental fluctuations and identifying with the Purusha (pure consciousness)	Moksha (liberation) through realization of Brahman, transcending the illusion of individuality and the phenomenal world	Realization of oneness with Shiva through the recognition of one's true nature as universal consciousness

Key Methods	Kriya Yoga, Pranayama, Kundalini awakening, Shivapat (grace transmission), and focuses on energy-based practices that lead to a thoughtless state (No-Mind)	Ashtanga Yoga (eight limbs), including Yama, Niyama, Asana, Pranayama, Pratyahara, Dharana, Dhyana, and Samadhi – Kriya Yoga procedure	Jnana Yoga (knowledge-based path), including self-inquiry (Neti-Neti), contemplation on Upanishadic texts, and realization of the Atman as Brahman	Tantra, Mantra, Meditation on Spanda (vibration), and self-recognition to realize Shiva consciousness
View on Consciousness	Consciousness as pure awareness (Param Shiva) that, through self-realization, unifies with the cosmic vibration (Spanda) of Shakti; differentiates between lower mind (manas) and higher consciousness (chit-shakti)	Consciousness is Purusha, the pure witness, separate from Prakriti (nature). Liberation arises when Purusha realizes its true nature beyond mental fluctuations	Pure, non-dual consciousness is Brahman, and the individual self (Atman) is one with Brahman; consciousness in the waking, dream, and deep sleep states leads to Turiya, the transcendent state	Consciousness as the dynamic, vibrating essence of Shiva, the source of creation, sustenance, and dissolution

Path to Liberation	Liberation through Kundalini awakening, leading to thoughtless consciousness; emphasis on the master's grace as essential for spiritual evolution	Liberation achieved through disciplined practice of Yoga, culminating in Samadhi. Ishvara is the undisturbed Purusha and guides those that are enmeshed in Prakriti.	Liberation is achieved through self-inquiry, discerning the real (Brahman) from the unreal (world), and realizing one's identity with Brahman	Liberation through recognition of one's true nature as Shiva - a shift in perception revealing the divine in every aspect of existence
Unique Contributions	Emphasis on direct experience of the Divine -Babaji as the eternal yogic guide; blends Kriya Yoga and Spanda principles with a modern perspective on evolution and the soul's cry for liberation	The systematization of the yogic path (Ashtanga Yoga) with a psychological and moral framework; also influenced later yogic and meditative practices worldwide	Development of Advaita Vedanta, emphasizing the illusory nature of the world and the identification of Atman with Brahman, laying the foundation for non-dualistic philosophy in India	Abhinavagupta's works provide a detailed Tantric and non-dual interpretation within Kashmir Shaivism

Comparative Analysis with the Philosophy of Plotinus

Plotinus (204/5–270 CE) was an ancient philosopher and the founder of Neoplatonism, a major school of thought that had a lasting influence on Western philosophy, Christian theology, and Islamic thought. His ideas can be found primarily in his work, the Enneads, a collection of his teachings compiled by his student Porphyry. Plotinus built upon the metaphysical framework of Plato but introduced original elements, creating a unique philosophy that seeks to explain the nature of reality, the soul, and the path to spiritual ascent.

1. The One (The Good)

At the core of Plotinus' philosophy is The One, which he also calls The Good. It is the ultimate reality, beyond being, intellect, and the material world. The One is completely transcendent, without attributes, limits, or multiplicity—it is the absolute unity from which all existence flows. Plotinus describes it as pure simplicity and beyond human comprehension, beyond even concepts like existence or essence. It is the source of all things, yet it is undivided and unaffected by what it creates.

• The One is ineffable: Since the One is beyond all categories of thought and language, it can only be approached through mystical intuition rather than rational discourse.

• Self-sufficient and perfect: The One is complete in itself, lacking nothing. It doesn't desire or will anything because it is already perfect.

2. Emanation

From the One, all of reality emanates. This process of emanation is central to Plotinus' metaphysics and contrasts with the idea of creation ex nihilo. The One, in its superabundant perfection, overflows naturally, producing the rest of existence in a hierarchical order. This process is spontaneous and necessary, not a deliberate act.

The levels of emanation proceed in a descending order of perfection:

2.1. Nous (Intellect)

The first emanation from the One is Nous, often translated as Intellect or Divine Mind. While the One is beyond thought and being, the Nous represents the realm of ideas and forms. It is a reflection of the One, but unlike the One, it is dual in nature—it involves both thinking and the objects of thought.

• Nous contains the Platonic Forms: These are the archetypes or eternal realities upon which the physical world is modeled.

• Unity in multiplicity: While Nous is one entity, it contains within it a multiplicity of ideas, and it contemplates both itself and the One. It is the realm of pure thought and being.

2.2. Soul (Psyche)

The next level of emanation is the Soul, which is responsible for life, movement, and existence in the material realm. The Soul bridges the gap between the intellectual world of Nous and the physical world. It has a dual nature:

• Higher Soul: Contemplating the Nous, staying in touch with the eternal and immutable.

• Lower Soul: Involved with the material world, bringing order and life to the cosmos.

The Soul is what animates the universe (the World Soul), and individual souls emanate from it, inhabiting bodies in the material world. This descent into matter is not inherently evil, but it leads to a degree of forgetfulness of the soul's divine origins.

3. The Material World

The lowest emanation is the material world, which is furthest from the One and represents the greatest degree of multiplicity and imperfection. Matter, in itself, is not evil for Plotinus, but it is associated with privation or lack—it lacks the fullness of the One, and so it is subject to change, decay, and fragmentation.

In the material realm, the soul becomes embodied and thus subject to the limitations of time, space, and physical desires. However, Plotinus maintains that matter is still an emanation from the One, though it represents the lowest degree of being.

4. The Soul's Ascent

For Plotinus, human beings are essentially souls temporarily residing in bodies. The ultimate goal of life is for the soul to return to the One by turning inward and transcending the material world. This is the process of spiritual ascent, which follows a path through:

• Virtue: Ethical living purifies the soul and turns it away from material desires.

• Philosophical contemplation: The practice of philosophy leads the soul to contemplate higher realities, moving beyond the senses and intellect to the truth of the Forms in the Nous.

• Mystical union: The final step is the soul's union with the One, beyond even Nous and the realm of forms. This is an ecstatic experience where the soul transcends individuality and achieves complete unity with the divine.

Plotinus describes this process as a return to the undivided unity of the One, in which the soul overcomes its fragmentation and multiplicity. The soul, in this state, experiences the ultimate peace and fulfillment, as it has returned to its source.

5. Evil and the Problem of Dualism

Plotinus does not believe in a dualistic opposition between good and evil as in some Gnostic systems. Evil, in his view, is not a positive force but rather a lack of good or a privation. It arises from the soul's descent into materiality and forgetfulness of its divine origin, but it has no real existence on its own. The farther something is from the One, the more it is marked by imperfection and privation, which we perceive as «evil.»

6. Beauty and Aesthetics

Plotinus also emphasizes the importance of beauty, which he sees as a reflection of the divine order. Beauty in the material world is a manifestation of the higher, divine Forms. The experience of beauty can help lead the soul upward, as it reminds the soul of the perfection and unity of the higher realms.

• Inner beauty: True beauty is not just physical but is rooted in the soul. It reflects harmony, order, and closeness to the One.

7. Influence on Later Thought

Plotinus' philosophy had a profound influence on early Christian thinkers, especially in developing the concept of God as a transcendent, ineffable being. His ideas also shaped mystical traditions in both Christianity (e.g., Pseudo-Dionysius) and Islam (through Sufi metaphysics). In the Renaissance, Plotinus' works were rediscovered and influenced thinkers such as Marsilio Ficino and the Cambridge Platonists.

In summary, Plotinus' philosophy is a metaphysical system that describes a hierarchical reality emanating from the One, with a focus on the soul's return to unity through contemplation and virtue. His ideas offer a vision of spiritual ascent, where the goal is to overcome multiplicity and division, achieving union with the source of all things.

The philosophies of Yogiraj Gurunath Siddhanath's Kriya Yoga-centric Advaita and Plotinus' Neoplatonism both emphasize a metaphysical journey of the soul from the realm of multiplicity to unity with the divine source. Despite emerging from different cultural and historical contexts—one from the yogic traditions of India, and the other from the Hellenistic philosophical world—these philosophies share some striking similarities, particularly in their notions of the soul's ascent, the role of meditation or contemplation, and the idea of a transcendent, unchanging source. However, they also have important differences rooted in their metaphysical frameworks, spiritual practices, and goals.

1. The Ultimate Source: The One vs. Advaita Brahman/Shiva

Plotinus' One:

• Transcendence: Plotinus' One is beyond all categories of being, intellect, and language. It is a state of absolute simplicity, devoid of qualities, yet it is the source from which all levels of existence emanate.

• Impersonal: The One is beyond personal attributes and cannot be grasped by the mind or through conventional categories of thought.

• Unity in Multiplicity: The entire universe emanates from the One, descending into increasing degrees of complexity and imperfection as it moves further from the One. The process of emanation leads to Nous (Intellect) and the World Soul, but the One remains unaffected by this outflow.

Yogiraj Gurunath's Brahman/Shiva:

• Transcendence and Immanence: In the Advaita tradition,

Brahman or Shiva is both transcendent and immanent. It is the non-dual reality (Advaita) that pervades everything. Brahman is formless and beyond qualities, but it also manifests as the world of forms through the interplay of the three gunas (Sattva, Rajas, Tamas).

• Brahman as Consciousness: According to Yogiraj Gurunath's teachings, Brahman or Shiva is consciousness itself—Chit—and it is also pure bliss (Ananda) and existence (Sat). The material world is a manifestation of this underlying consciousness, not a separate creation.

• Shiva as the First Cause: Unlike the impersonal One of Plotinus, Yogiraj's teaching presents Shiva as an active, personal principle that is not just the ultimate reality but also the source of creation, preservation, and destruction, interacting with the world through Shakti (divine energy).

Comparison:

• Both systems agree on the existence of an ultimate source that transcends the material and intellectual realms, but while Plotinus' One is entirely impersonal, Yogiraj's Brahman/Shiva integrates a more personal aspect, particularly through its manifestation as Shiva and the dynamic interplay with Shakti.

• The process of emanation in Plotinus' thought is somewhat passive—an overflow from the One—whereas in Yogiraj's philosophy, Brahman's interaction with Shakti creates the world, embedding it with the qualities of consciousness, and offering a dynamic vision of creation.

2. The Process of Emanation and Creation

Plotinus:

• Hierarchical Emanation: Plotinus describes a threefold process of emanation: the One, followed by Nous (the realm of ideas and pure intellect), and then the World Soul, which animates the material world. Each emanation reflects a lower degree of reality, with the material world being the furthest removed from the One.

Yogiraj Gurunath:

• Interplay of Gunas: Yogiraj's cosmology describes creation as a result of the interplay of the three gunas—Sattva, Rajas, and Tamas. He explains how these gunas correlate to the building blocks of the material universe (Sattva as electrons, Rajas as protons, and Tamas as neutrons), yet all these elements arise from the non-dual Brahman/Shiva.

• Kriya and Vibration: Central to Yogiraj's teachings is the idea that vibration (Spanda) plays a fundamental role in creation. Through Kriya Yoga, the practitioner taps into this primal energy or vibration, realizing their oneness with the divine and bypassing the cosmic layers that veil the true self.

Comparison:

• In both systems, the material world represents a departure from the highest reality and is seen as a lesser reflectionof the divine. Plotinus' concept of Nous and Soul creating the material world is echoed in the idea that Shiva and Shakti create the cosmos through a hierarchical descent.

• Plotinus' hierarchical emanation is static and involuntary, while Yogiraj's emphasis on the dynamic interplay of the gunas and vibration gives a more active and cyclical flavor to the process of creation and dissolution.

3. The Nature of the Soul and Its Descent

Plotinus:

• The World Soul: For Plotinus, the World Soul animates the

cosmos, and individual souls are aspects of this world soul. However, as souls descend into the material world, they become fragmented and subject to ignorance, leading to a sense of separateness from the One.

• The Fall of the Soul: The soul's descent into matter involves forgetting its true nature, and its life in the physical body is marked by imperfection and desire. However, the soul is always connected to its divine origin and can ascend back to the One through contemplation and virtue.

Yogiraj Gurunath:

• Jivatman and Paramatman: According to Yogiraj, the Jivatman (individual soul) is a reflection of the Paramatman (supreme soul). It descends into the cycle of birth and death (samsara) due to the accumulation of karma and identification with the ego. However, through Kriya Yoga and the purification of the body and mind, the soul can realize its oneness with Brahman.

• Forgetfulness and Karma: The soul forgets its divine nature due to ignorance (avidya) and is caught in the web of desires and karmic actions, similar to Plotinus' idea of the soul becoming fragmented in the material realm.

Comparison:

• Both philosophies describe a descent of the soul into the material world, leading to forgetfulness of its true divine nature.

• Plotinus' soul descends out of a natural process of emanation, while in Yogiraj's system, the soul's descent is often linked to the bonds of karma, necessitating practices like Kriya Yoga to ascend.

4. Spiritual Ascent and Liberation

Plotinus:

• Contemplation and the Return to the One: Plotinus teaches that the soul's return to the One occurs through virtue, philosophical contemplation, and ultimately mystical union. The soul must transcend its attachment to the body and the physical world, rising through the Nous (realm of intellect) to experience the One directly.

Yogiraj Gurunath:

• Kriya Yoga and the Ascent to Brahman: In Gurunath's system, the spiritual ascent occurs through the practice of Kriya Yoga, which involves pranayama (breath control), meditation, and inner focus. The goal is to raise the Kundalini energy up the spine, purifying the chakras, and leading to Shivapat, a direct experience of divine consciousness, similar to the mystical union described by Plotinus.

• Shivapat and No-Mind: Gurunath also emphasizes the experience of No-Mind, a thoughtless state where the practitioner transcends all dualities and attains the direct transmission of Shiva's consciousness (Shivapat). This is the realization of the non-dual state, akin to the mystical union with the One in Plotinus.

Comparison:

•Both systems describe mystical ascent as the process of returning to the ultimate reality, whether it is the One or Brahman/Shiva.

•Plotinus emphasizes contemplation and intellectual ascent, while Yogiraj focuses on the energetic and experiential aspects of ascent through Kriya Yoga and the awakening of Kundalini.

5. Role of the Physical and Ethical Practices

Plotinus:

• Virtue and Philosophy: The soul ascends primarily through moral purification and philosophical contemplation. The body is seen as a hindrance, and virtue serves to detach the soul from material desires.

Yogiraj Gurunath:

• Kriya as the Path: While ethical conduct is important, the central practice for spiritual ascent in Gurunath's system is Kriya Yoga. It is a complete system involving breathing techniques, meditation, and mantra, designed to purify the body, mind, and soul, leading to spiritual liberation (moksha).

Comparison:

• While Plotinus emphasizes philosophical thought and virtue, Gurunath emphasizes yogic practices like Kriya Yoga as the direct means to liberation, focusing on spiritual energetics rather than purely intellectual contemplation.

• Both Plotinus and Yogiraj Gurunath Siddhanath offer profound systems that describe the soul's journey from the multiplicity of the material world back to unity with the divine source. However, the pathways they emphasize and the nuances of their metaphysical systems differ in important ways:

6. Mediators of Spiritual Ascent: Intellect vs. Guru

Plotinus:

• Nous (Intellect) as the Bridge: In Plotinus' system, the Nous (Divine Intellect) plays a critical role in the soul's ascent. The intellect is both the tool and the realm through which the soul contemplates higher realities and ultimately reaches the One. The forms and ideas residing in Nous are reflections of divine truth, and the soul must align itself with this intellectual vision to ascend.

Yogiraj Gurunath:

• Guru and Shivapat: In the yogic tradition of Yogiraj, the Guru plays a central role in guiding the practitioner through the spiritual ascent. The direct transmission of spiritual energy (Shivapat) from the Guru helps awaken the Kundalini and accelerate the soul's journey back to Shiva or Brahman. The Guru's grace is seen as essential in transcending karmic bonds and achieving liberation.

• Kundalini Energy as a Mediator: Unlike Plotinus' intellectual focus, Gurunath's system emphasizes the Kundalini energy as the vital force that rises through the body's chakras, dissolving karmic knots (granthis) and leading to direct realization of the divine.

Comparison:

• Plotinus stresses the intellect as the primary mediator for the soul's ascent, while in Gurunath's system, the Guru and Kundalini are critical facilitators.

• In Plotinus, spiritual progress is largely an individual intellectual and contemplative effort, whereas in Yogiraj's philosophy, the Guru-disciple relationship and the transmission of Shaktipat or Shivapat are central to accelerating spiritual progress.

7. The Ultimate Experience: Mystical Union vs. No-Mind and Shivapat

Plotinus:

• Mystical Union with the One: The ultimate goal in Plotinus' philosophy is a mystical union with the One, in which the soul transcends individuality, intellect, and all dualities. This experience is often described as ecstatic and beyond ordinary thought, where the soul becomes one with the One in a state of pure simplicity and unity.

Yogiraj Gurunath:

• No-Mind and Shivapat: In Gurunath's teachings, the ultimate experience is the state of No-Mind (thoughtless awareness), which occurs when the practitioner transcends the ego and dualistic thinking. This experience is facilitated by the Shivapat, the transmission of divine consciousness from the Guru, leading to the realization of oneness with Shiva. Unlike Plotinus' intellectual ascent, this state is reached through energetic and meditative practices that dissolve the mind's activity entirely, allowing for direct perception of non-duality (Advaita).

Comparison:

• Both traditions describe an ultimate state beyond intellect and duality, but while Plotinus' union with the One is a result of intellectual contemplation, No-Mind in Gurunath's system is achieved through energetic awakening and meditative absorption. Plotinus' experience emphasizes unity and simplicity, while Gurunath's experience focuses on bliss, thoughtlessness, and the dissolution of the ego.

8. Views on the Material World

Plotinus:

• Matter as Imperfect but Not Evil: Plotinus views the material world as the lowest level of emanation, representing imperfection and multiplicity. While it is a lesser reflection of the divine, it is not inherently evil. Rather, evil arises from privation, the absence of good or unity with the One. The material world is a necessary stage in the soul's journey, though it is ultimately to be transcended.

Yogiraj Gurunath:

• Material World as Maya: In Advaita philosophy, which underlies Gurunath's teachings, the material world is seen as Maya—an illusion that veils the true, non-dual nature of reality. While the material world is not evil, it is illusory, and attachment to it keeps the soul in the cycle of samsara (birth and death). The goal is to see through this illusion and realize the underlying oneness of Brahman that pervades all existence.

Comparison:

• Both systems view the material world as imperfect and something to be transcended, but Plotinus emphasizes the inherent imperfection of multiplicity, while Yogiraj's philosophy frames the material world as illusory, a veil over the true nature of reality.

9. Path to Liberation: Kriya Yoga vs. Contemplation

Plotinus:

• Philosophical Contemplation: The path to liberation in Plotinus' philosophy is through philosophical contemplation, moral virtue, and the soul's purification from attachment to material desires. The intellect plays a key role in helping the soul ascend through the hierarchy of being, from the material realm to the realm of Nous, and ultimately to the One.

Yogiraj Gurunath:

- Kriya Yoga: In Gurunath's system, the primary path to liberation is through the practice of Kriya Yoga, which involves techniques like pranayama (breath control), meditation, and mantra repetition. These practices purify the body, mind, and soul, allowing the practitioner to transcend the ego, dissolve karmic knots, and realize the oneness of Brahman. Kriya Yoga is seen as an accelerated path to liberation, fast-tracking the soul's progress compared to purely contemplative or intellectual paths.

Comparison:

- Plotinus' path is based on contemplative philosophy and ethical living, while Yogiraj emphasizes the energetic and experiential practices of Kriya Yoga. Both systems aim to transcend the material world and reunite the soul with its divine source, but their methods are distinct—one intellectual, the other yogic and energetic.

A Comparative View

Both Plotinus and Yogiraj Gurunath Siddhanath offer metaphysical systems that describe a journey of the soul from the multiplicity and imperfection of the material world to unity with the divine source. In both systems, the material world represents a fall from unity, and the soul must undertake a process of ascent to return to its true, higher nature. However, their methodologies differ significantly:

- Plotinus' system is rooted in intellectual contemplation and the idea that the soul ascends through philosophical inquiry and virtue. His vision of the One is entirely impersonal and beyond all attributes, and the journey back to the One is primarily through the intellect and Nous.

- Yogiraj Gurunath Siddhanath's Kriya Yoga philosophy, on the other hand, emphasizes experiential practices, particularly the raising of Kundalini energy and the Guru's grace. The divine source, Brahman/Shiva, is non-dual but also immanent, interacting with the world through Shakti. The ultimate experience in Gurunath's philosophy is not just unity but a state of thoughtless awareness (No-Mind) and direct, blissful realization of oneness with Shiva.

Despite these differences, both philosophies converge on the idea that the soul is fundamentally divine and must undergo a process of purification and ascent to reunite with the ultimate source, experiencing the highest truth, bliss, and peace that transcend the ordinary, fragmented experience of life in the material world.

Comparison with the great Buddhist Mahasiddha Padmasambhava

Padmasambhava, also known as **Guru Rinpoche**, is regarded as one of the most significant figures in Tibetan Buddhism. He is credited with bringing Vajrayana Buddhism to Tibet during the 8th century, establishing it as the foundation of Tibetan spirituality. His name means "Lotus-Born," referencing his legendary birth from a lotus flower in Lake Dhanakosha in the region of Oddiyana (present-day Swat Valley, Pakistan). Padmasambhava is considered a fully enlightened being, often depicted as an emanation of the Buddha Amitabha.

Life and Journey to Tibet

According to tradition, Padmasambhava was invited to Tibet by King Trisong Detsen to subdue local demons and obstacles that were hindering the construction of the first Buddhist monastery in Tibet, Samye. Padmasambhava is known for his mastery of tantric practices, which allowed him to pacify and convert negative forces, transforming them into protectors of the Dharma (Buddhist teachings). Along with his consort Yeshe Tsogyal, he is said to have concealed numerous termas (spiritual treasures) throughout Tibet, to be revealed by later masters when needed.

Philosophy and Teachings

Padmasambhava's teachings are foundational to Tibetan Buddhism, particularly within the Nyingma school, which views him as its founder. His philosophy centers around Vajrayana Buddhism, a path of esoteric teachings that emphasize the use of rituals, mantras, and meditative practices to achieve enlightenment within a single lifetime.

Key elements of his philosophy include:

1. Vajrayana Buddhism: This path, also known as the Diamond Vehicle, is known for its use of powerful tantric methods. Vajrayana practices are considered advanced and offer a fast track to enlightenment, though they require proper initiation and guidance.

2. Non-Dualism: Padmasambhava's teachings, influenced by both Indian Mahayana Buddhism and indigenous Tibetan Bön practices, emphasize the non-dual nature of reality. This non-duality refers to the ultimate state where distinctions such as subject and object, self and other, are dissolved in the realization of the innate purity and emptiness of all phenomena.

3. Dzogchen: A significant teaching attributed to Padmasambhava is Dzogchen, or the "Great Perfection." Dzogchen presents the view that the true nature of the mind is inherently pure, luminous, and devoid of conceptual thoughts. The practice of Dzogchen involves recognizing and abiding in this natural state, leading to spontaneous liberation without the need for extensive practices or effort.

4. Integration of Tantric Methods: Padmasambhava taught that through visualization, mantra recitation, and the use of mandalas, practitioners can transform their ordinary experiences into expressions of enlightenment. This involves the visualization of oneself as a deity, reciting sacred mantras, and developing deep concentration to unite with the wisdom of the enlightened beings.

5. The Power of Adversity: A key element of Padmasambhava's teachings is the transformation of obstacles into opportunities for spiritual growth. His life exemplified how negative forces, when approached with wisdom and skill, can be converted into aids on the path to enlightenment.

6. Compassion and Skillful Means: Like other Buddhist

teachings, Padmasambhava emphasized the importance of compassion for all sentient beings and the use of skillful means (upaya) to help others realize the truth of their nature.

Through his introduction of Vajrayana Buddhism, Padmasambhava not only transformed Tibetan spirituality but also left behind a legacy of profound practices aimed at realizing the nature of mind and achieving liberation. His influence continues to shape Tibetan Buddhism to this day.

The philosophies of Padmasambhava and Yogiraj Gurunath Siddhanath both aim at the ultimate realization of one's true nature and liberation, but they approach this from slightly different cultural, historical, and spiritual contexts. Below is a comparative exploration of their philosophies.

1. Path to Enlightenment: Vajrayana vs. Kriya Yoga

- Padmasambhava: As a key figure in Tibetan Buddhism, particularly in the Vajrayana (Tantric) tradition, Padmasambhava taught that enlightenment could be achieved within a single lifetime through the use of esoteric practices, including mantras, visualization, and rituals. Vajrayana emphasizes the transformation of ordinary experiences into opportunities for awakening by engaging with the subtle energies of the body and mind through methods like deity yoga and the use of mandalas.

- Yogiraj Gurunath Siddhanath: Gurunath teaches Kriya Yoga, an ancient yogic science focusing on the pranayama (breath control) technique that accelerates spiritual evolution by clearing karmic patterns and opening subtle energy channels. Through controlled breath, the life-force (prana) is directed to ascend the spinal column, bringing the practitioner into states of higher consciousness. Like Vajrayana, Kriya

Yoga also offers a fast track to enlightenment, but it is done by working directly with the breath and the nervous system (pranic energy) rather than visualizations or rituals.

2. View on Reality: Non-Dualism in Different Traditions

• Padmasambhava: His teachings, especially in Dzogchen, are deeply rooted in the non-dual view that all phenomena, including mind and matter, are ultimately empty of inherent existence. Dzogchen emphasizes recognizing the natural state of the mind, which is pure, luminous, and free from dualistic thinking. Liberation, in this view, comes from recognizing that the mind is already enlightened and resting in that state.

• Yogiraj Gurunath Siddhanath: Yogiraj's teachings also emphasize non-dualism, particularly in his view of Shiva-Shakti—the union of divine consciousness (Shiva) and cosmic energy (Shakti). The practices of Kriya Yoga aim to bring about the realization that the individual soul (Atman) is one with the universal consciousness (Brahman). In this context, the dissolution of the ego through Kriya practices leads to a state of thoughtlessness or No-mind, aligning closely with the non-dual experience of the Self as one with the Divine.

3. Role of Karma and Purification

• Padmasambhava: In Vajrayana Buddhism, karma is acknowledged, and many of Padmasambhava's teachings focus on purifying negative karma through tantric rituals, mantras, and visualizations. The idea is to transform delusions and karmic obstructions into wisdom by invoking enlightened deities and working with the subtle energies of the mind and body.

• Yogiraj Gurunath Siddhanath: Gurunath emphasizes karmic purification through Kriya Yoga practices, particularly the process of pranayama and meditation, which burn off past karmic impressions (samskaras) stored in the astral spine. Kriya Yoga is designed to remove karmic knots (granthis) and elevate the practitioner to higher states of consciousness by clearing the energetic channels (nadis) within the subtle body.

4. Role of the Guru

• Padmasambhava: In Tibetan Buddhism, the guru or spiritual teacher plays a central role as the guide who introduces the disciple to the nature of their own mind. Padmasambhava himself is regarded as the "Second Buddha" and a living embodiment of awakened wisdom. His relationship with his followers is one of a guru-disciple dynamic, where he uses skillful means (upaya) to lead his students to liberation.

• Yogiraj Gurunath Siddhanath: Gurunath places great emphasis on Shivapat, a direct transmission of energy from the guru to the disciple. He sees the guru as a channel of divine grace, capable of awakening the disciple's latent spiritual potential. Like Padmasambhava, Gurunath stresses the importance of the guru in guiding the disciple to higher consciousness, but the focus in Kriya Yoga is on internal realization through energetic awakening rather than ritualistic or symbolic methods.

5. Subtle Energy and the Body

• Padmasambhava: Vajrayana Buddhism, particularly in its tantric practices, works with the subtle body, including channels (nadis), winds (prana), and chakras. Practitioners use visualization and breathing techniques to control these energies and open the central channel (avadhuti), similar to some yogic practices but within a Buddhist framework of emptiness and compassion.

• Yogiraj Gurunath Siddhanath: The subtle body in Kriya Yoga is also of critical importance, where prana is consciously moved through the spinal chakras to achieve higher states of consciousness. Kriya breath techniques open the Sushumna channel to facilitate the rise of Kundalini energy, leading to enlightenment. Gurunath's approach is very hands-on, with an emphasis on physiological and energetic transformation through direct practice.

6. Goal of Spiritual Practice

• Padmasambhava: The ultimate goal of Padmasambhava's teachings is to recognize and rest in the innate nature of the mind, which is already enlightened. Dzogchen practitioners aim to achieve spontaneous liberation by realizing the mind's original purity, without the need for elaborate practices once this realization occurs.

• Yogiraj Gurunath Siddhanath: The goal in Kriya Yoga is to merge the individual soul (Atman) with the universal consciousness (Brahman), realizing the state of divine unity (Shiva consciousness). This leads to liberation (moksha) from the cycle of birth and death. While Yogiraj also teaches that the true Self is already divine, the emphasis is on working systematically to clear karmic obstructions and realize this state through energetic practices.

Summary:

• Padmasambhava operates within the Vajrayana framework, using tantric rituals, deity yoga, and Dzogchen's non-dual view of mind to achieve liberation. His path incorporates rich symbolism and rituals aimed at transforming ordinary experiences into opportunities for awakening.

• Yogiraj Gurunath Siddhanath offers Kriya Yoga, which focuses on the internal energetic transformation of the practitioner through pranayama and meditation, aiming to directly experience and merge with divine consciousness.

While both paths are seen as fast tracks to enlightenment, Padmasambhava's teachings emphasize the role of visualization, ritual, and compassion in transforming reality, whereas Gurunath's teachings emphasize breath control, energetic awakening, and karmic purification to reach a thoughtless state and ultimate liberation.

About Nothingness and Emptiness

The comparison between Padmasambhava's philosophy of Shunya (emptiness) and Yogiraj Gurunath Siddhanath's concept of Nothingness reveals subtle yet significant differences in how each spiritual tradition approaches the nature of reality, consciousness, and liberation. Both concepts point to a transcendental state beyond duality, but their contexts and implications differ based on the metaphysical frameworks of Tibetan Buddhism and Kriya Yoga.

1. Shunya (Emptiness) in Padmasambhava's Philosophy

• Shunya (often referred to as Sunyata) is a central tenet of Mahayana Buddhism, especially in the teachings of Padmasambhava. In this context, Shunya refers to the emptiness of inherent existence in all phenomena. According to this view, everything that exists does so in dependence upon causes, conditions, and interrelations; therefore, nothing possesses an independent, permanent essence.

• Shunyata as Non-Duality: In the teachings of Dzogchen, which Padmasambhava propagated, Shunyata is not a nihilistic void, but rather a realization of the non-dual nature of reality. It is the recognition that there is no separation between subject and object, self and other. Everything is a manifestation of a single, indivisible reality that is empty of independent existence but simultaneously full of radiant awareness and potential. The mind, when seen in its true nature, is empty, luminous, and self-liberating. This is known as Rigpa, or the recognition of one's intrinsic awareness.

- Practical Implication of Shunyata: Shunya is experienced through meditative realization where one sees beyond dualistic thought and conceptions. By recognizing the empty, open, and impermanent nature of all things, a practitioner transcends suffering and reaches a state of liberation. The key insight is that emptiness is inseparable from awareness—emptiness is not a void, but the very nature of enlightenment itself, beyond conceptual elaboration.

2. Nothingness in Yogiraj Gurunath Siddhanath's Teachings

- Nothingness in the context of Yogiraj Gurunath Siddhanath's teachings refers to a state of absolute thoughtlessness which he refers to as Consciousness, also sometimes described as No-mind or the Void. This concept points to a direct experience of consciousness beyond mental activity, concepts, or forms. Yogiraj speaks of reaching a state where the mind, freed from thoughts, concepts, and egoic identity, merges into the primordial state of stillness or nothingness.

- No-Mind and the Void: In Kriya Yoga, this state of Nothingness is cultivated through practices like pranayama and meditation. As one progresses, the mind enters a deep silence where even the subtlest mental activity ceases, and the practitioner experiences the pure presence of the Self (Atman) or Shiva consciousness. This nothingness is not a lack, but rather the dissolution of egoic consciousness into the eternal, formless essence of the Divine. It is beyond space, time, and the dualities of existence.

- Beyond Duality in Nothingness: Yogiraj describes this state of Nothingness as the experience of being "nowhere" and "everywhere" simultaneously, a transcendent state where the individual realizes their true nature as part of the infinite, formless Divine. While it is called "nothingness," it is also seen as plenitude, because it contains all possibilities in an unmanifested form, and from it emerges all creation.

3. Key Similarities: Shunya and Nothingness

• Non-Duality: Both Shunya and Nothingness are rooted in the understanding that duality is an illusion. In Padmasambhava's Shunya, all phenomena are seen as empty of inherent existence, dissolving the dualistic distinction between self and other, subject and object. In Gurunath's Nothingness, duality is also transcended, where the distinction between the ego and the Divine vanishes, and the practitioner realizes their oneness with the eternal essence.

• Beyond Mental Constructs: Both concepts describe a state of transcendence beyond thought and conceptualization. In Shunya, all conceptual fabrications are seen as empty, and the practitioner moves beyond the grasping mind to see the natural luminosity of awareness. In Nothingness, the practitioner's mind becomes silent and thoughtless, merging into the absolute stillness where the ego dissolves.

• Liberation through Direct Realization: In both traditions, the realization of Shunya or Nothingness leads to spiritual liberation. For Padmasambhava, the realization of emptiness liberates one from samsara (the cycle of birth and death). For Gurunath, the experience of Nothingness brings about liberation from the karmic cycle and the realization of one's unity with Shiva consciousness.

4. Key Differences: Context and Implications

Metaphysical Framework:

• Shunya (Buddhist): In Mahayana Buddhism, particularly in Dzogchen, Shunya emphasizes the lack of inherent, independent existence in all phenomena, focusing on the interdependence and emptiness of both the self and the world. The realization of Shunyata leads to liberation by understanding that everything is transient, interrelated, and void of a fixed essence.

- Nothingness (Yogic): In Gurunath's teachings, Nothingness is more closely aligned with the realization of the eternal, formless Divine (Shiva or Brahman). While the ego and mind are seen as transient, there is an ultimate, formless reality (Brahman or Shiva) which one realizes by entering a state of complete stillness or nothingness. This has a more cosmic dimension, implying not just the emptiness of form but the direct experience of divine consciousness.

Approach to Practice:

- Shunya (Padmasambhava): The realization of Shunyata comes through the recognition of Rigpa, or pure awareness, which is intrinsic to the nature of mind itself. This often involves practices such as analytic meditation, contemplation, and advanced tantric visualizations aimed at deconstructing all mental fabrications and realizing the empty yet luminous nature of reality.

- Nothingness (Gurunath): The realization of Nothingness comes through the energetic practices of Kriya Yoga, particularly the breath control (pranayama) that leads to the stopping of mental fluctuations. This is more direct and experiential, as the practitioner focuses on controlling and transcending the breath and mind to enter a state of No-mind, leading to the experience of the void beyond thought.

Emptiness vs. Fullness:

- Shunya (Buddhist View): Emptiness in Buddhism is not a nihilistic void but is often paradoxically described as full of potential. It refers to the lack of inherent essence but simultaneously recognizes the interdependent, luminous, and boundless nature of all phenomena. Shunya reveals the interconnectedness and inseparability of all existence.

- Nothingness (Yogic View): Gurunath's Nothingness may appear as a void or empty space, but it is described as being filled with conscious potential. It is an experience of divine plenitude, where one merges into the eternal, formless consciousness of the universe (Shiva consciousness). This nothingness is often seen as the womb of creation from which all arises.

Summary:

• Padmasambhava's Shunya focuses on the emptiness of inherent existence in all phenomena, guiding practitioners to realize that reality is empty of a fixed, independent self but simultaneously full of luminous awareness. It is a path of deconstructing duality and recognizing the natural state of the mind.

• Yogiraj Gurunath Siddhanath's Nothingness refers to a state of absolute stillness and thoughtlessness, where the practitioner experiences the void beyond the ego and mind, merging with the formless essence of the Divine. It is a direct, experiential realization of Shiva consciousness, beyond time, space, and form.

In essence, both Shunya and Nothingness point to a transcendental reality beyond dualistic thought, but while Shunya emphasizes the emptiness and interdependence of all things, Nothingness in Gurunath's teachings highlights the silent stillness of consciousness and its direct unity with the Divine.

Mystic Convergence
Comparing Gurunath's Philosophy with two medieval mystics

Gurunath and Meister Eckhart

Comparing the ontologies of Yogiraj Gurunath Siddhanath and Meister Eckhart involves exploring the conceptual frameworks and metaphysical understandings of reality as presented by these two spiritual figures from very different cultural and historical backgrounds.

Gurunath is a living master from India who teaches Kriya Yoga and a philosophy grounded in the realization of the Self as part of a greater universal consciousness. His teachings emphasize the direct experience of the divine within oneself, suggesting that enlightenment and the realization of one's divine nature are accessible to all through the practice of yoga and meditation.

His ontology is deeply rooted in the Sanatana Dharma and yogic traditions, which posit that the ultimate reality (Brahman) is omnipresent and manifests as individual souls (Atman). The goal of spiritual practice, according to Gurunath, is to experience the unity of Atman and Brahman, thereby overcoming the illusion of separation (Maya) and realizing one's true divine nature.

Meister Eckhart, on the other hand, was a Christian mystic and theologian from the late 13th and early 14th centuries, whose teachings focus on the direct experience of God. Eckhart's ontology can be described as Neoplatonic with Christian overtones, emphasizing the unity and simplicity of God. He taught that God is the ground of all being and that creation is an expression of the divine overflow of God's love. Eckhart spoke of the soul's ability to directly experience God through detachment from the world and the ego, a process he termed as "the birth of the Word in the soul." This mystical union with God leads to an understanding of the fundamental oneness of all creation in God, transcending the distinctions between creator and creation.

Comparative Analysis of Ontology

- Foundation: Both Gurunath and Meister Eckhart teach that the ultimate reality is a singular divine presence (Brahman in Vedantic terms, God in Christian mysticism) that is accessible to human experience.

- Method of Realization: Both emphasize direct, personal experience as the means to spiritual realization. Siddhanath promotes Kriya Yoga as a practical method for achieving this realization, while Eckhart speaks of inner detachment and the cultivation of a state of receptiveness to the divine presence.

- Concept of the Divine: While Gurunath's teachings are based on Vedantic/Nath concepts of divinity, emphasizing the non-duality of Jiva (the soul) and Atman/Brahman/Paramashiva (the ultimate reality), Eckhart's Christian perspective focuses on the unity with God achieved through the process of inner purification and detachment from worldly desires.

- Spiritual Goal: Both aim for the individual's realization of oneness with the divine, though the paths they describe are influenced by their respective traditions. For Gurunath, it is the realization of one's true self as part of the universal consciousness. For Eckhart, it is the mystical union with God, where the individual soul transcends its separate identity.

In summary, while Gurunath and Meister Eckhart come from distinct spiritual traditions, their ontologies share a common core in the belief in a fundamental unity between the individual and the divine. Their teachings both navigate the path towards this realization, albeit through different practices and conceptual frameworks, reflecting their diverse cultural and religious backgrounds.

Comparative Analysis of Epistemology

Epistemology, the branch of philosophy concerned with the nature and scope of knowledge, varies significantly across different spiritual traditions. When comparing the epistemologies of Gurunath and Meister Eckhart, we delve into how each understands the means by which knowledge of the divine or ultimate reality is acquired, justified, and validated.

Yogiraj Gurunath Siddhanath's epistemology is deeply rooted in the yogic and Vedic traditions of Sanantana Dharma. He emphasizes experiential knowledge or direct experience (Aparoksha Anubhuti) as the primary means of gaining true understanding. In his teachings, the practice of Kriya Yoga is central. Kriya Yoga is a set of meditative practices that facilitate the practitioner's ability to perceive and realize their innate divinity and oneness with the cosmos. Gurunath teaches that through the regular practice of these techniques, one can achieve self-realization and enlightenment. This direct, experiential knowledge transcends intellectual understanding or scriptural study, as it involves an inner awakening to one's true nature, which is seen as a part of the universal consciousness.

Example: A practitioner of Kriya Yoga, under Gurunath's guidance, might experience moments of profound inner peace and glimpses of non-duality, where the separation between the self and the universe dissolves. These experiences are considered valid means of knowledge, as they directly reveal the nature of reality.

Meister Eckhart's epistemology, while emerging from within the Christian mystic tradition, also emphasizes experiential knowledge, but with a strong theological and philosophical overlay. Eckhart believed in the possibility of direct experience of God, which he described as the "spark" or "ground" of the soul. This direct experience is beyond the grasp of intellect or sensory perception and is accessible through a process of detachment from the material world and the ego.

For Eckhart, true knowledge of God is achieved through an inner experience of unity with the divine, which transcends rational thought and empirical observation.

Example: In his sermons, Eckhart often spoke of the soul's journey towards God, describing moments of mystical union where the individual soul experiences a direct encounter with the divine essence. Such moments are considered true knowledge of God, accessible not through intellectual reasoning but through the soul's inner purification and opening to the divine presence.

Comparative Analysis

- Source of Knowledge: Both Gurunath and Eckhart prioritize experiential knowledge over other forms of knowing. However, Gurunath emphasizes the role of specific yogic practices as the means to achieve this knowledge, while Eckhart focuses more on a general process of inner purification and detachment from the ego.

- Nature of Ultimate Reality: While both figures aim for the realization of a union with the ultimate reality, Gurunath's teachings are framed within the context of Yogic metaphysics, which sees the ultimate reality as a universal consciousness. Eckhart, operating within a Christian framework, describes the ultimate reality as God, with whom the soul can achieve mystical union.

- Role of Practices: For Gurunath, specific techniques (Kriya Yoga) are prescribed as the practical means to attain enlightenment. In contrast, Eckhart's approach is less prescriptive about specific practices and more focused on the inner attitude of detachment and surrender to God. It should be pointed out that in the Yogic tradition, especially those based on Patanjali's yoga sutras, detachment (Vairagya) and surrender to the Divine (Ishvar Pranidhana) play an important part.

- Validation of Knowledge: In both traditions, the validation of spiritual knowledge comes from the transformative impact it has on the individual's life. For followers of Gurunath, this may manifest as increased peace, joy, and a sense of oneness with all beings. For Eckhart's followers, it might manifest as a deepening love for God, detachment from worldly things, and a life lived in accordance with divine will.

Despite these differences, the core epistemological stance of both Yogiraj Gurunath Siddhanath and Meister Eckhart is that true knowledge is inherently experiential and transcendent, going beyond mere intellectual understanding or empirical evidence. This shared emphasis on the experiential, direct encounter with the divine or ultimate reality highlights a commonality across spiritual traditions, even as the specific paths to this knowledge diverge due to their distinct religious and cultural contexts. Both Masters advocate for a transformative journey inward, suggesting that the deepest truths about existence and our place in the universe are discovered through personal, inner experience rather than external observation or analysis. This approach underlines a universal quest for understanding and connection with a greater reality, a theme that resonates across many spiritual and philosophical traditions.

Gurunath and Ibn Arabi

Comparing the ontology and epistemology of Yogiraj Gurunath Siddhanath and Ibn Arabi offers a fascinating glimpse into the spiritual and philosophical underpinnings of two influential figures from distinct traditions—Sanatana Dharma and Sufism, respectively. Both figures explore profound questions about the nature of reality, the divine, and the path to spiritual knowledge, albeit from within their cultural and religious contexts.

Ontology

We've already examined Gurunath's ontology, grounded in the concepts of Yoga and Advaita Vedanta. He emphasizes the non-dual nature of reality, where individual souls (Atman) are essentially one with the universal consciousness or Brahman. The physical world and the separation we perceive are considered manifestations of Maya (illusion), and the ultimate goal is to realize the Atman's unity with Brahman.

The goal of life is to transcend the ego and individual consciousness to experience this fundamental oneness, thus overcoming the illusion of separation.

Ibn Arabi, a Sufi mystic and philosopher, proposed a sophisticated ontology known as the "Unity of Being" (Wahdat al-Wujud). He posited that all existence is a manifestation of the single divine reality or God, and everything in the universe reflects the divine attributes. According to Ibn Arabi, while the essence of God is beyond comprehension, His manifestations in the world allow us to glimpse the divine presence.

Ibn Arabi's concept of the "Perfect Man" (al-Insān al-Kāmil) illustrates how the human being can embody the divine attributes and serving as a comprehensive representation of the divine essence.

Comparative Analysis of Ontology:

- Both Gurunath and Ibn Arabi emphasize a fundamental unity underlying apparent diversity and multiplicity in the universe.

- While Gurunath's ontology is rooted in the Vedantic understanding of Brahman and Atman, Ibn Arabi's is framed within Islamic Sufism, focusing on the relationship between the divine and its manifestations.

- Both ontologies challenge the ordinary perception of separation between the divine and creation, though they use different conceptual frameworks to articulate this unity.

As we have stated previously, Gurunat advocates for direct experiential knowledge (Aparoksha Anubhuti) as the means to spiritual realization. Through the practice of Kriya Yoga, individuals can directly experience the unity of Atman and Brahman, transcending intellectual understanding and empirical knowledge.

Example: The practice of Kriya Yoga includes specific breathing techniques that facilitate altered states of consciousness, enabling practitioners to experience spiritual truths directly.

Ibn Arabi also emphasized the importance of direct, mystical knowledge of God, which transcends rational thought and empirical evidence. This knowledge is accessible through spiritual intuition (Dhawq) and contemplation, leading to an experiential understanding of the divine presence in all things.

Example: Ibn Arabi described the concept of "taste" (dhawq) in spiritual experiences, where the mystic directly perceives the divine reality, bypassing intellectual reasoning.

Comparative Analysis of Epistemology:

- Both mystics underscore the limitations of intellectual reasoning and sensory perception in grasping spiritual truths, advocating for a direct, experiential approach to knowledge.

- Gurunath's approach is rooted in yogic practices that facilitate experiential knowledge of the divine within, while Ibn Arabi's method involves mystical intuition and contemplation to experience the divine in all aspects of creation.

- The goal of both epistemologies is to transcend the ordinary modes of understanding to achieve a direct, experiential realization of the divine or ultimate reality.

In summary, while Yogiraj Gurunath Siddhanath and Ibn Arabi come from different spiritual traditions, their ontologies and epistemologies share striking similarities. Both advocate for the realization of an underlying unity behind the apparent multiplicity of the world and emphasize the importance of direct, experiential knowledge of the divine. Their teachings reflect a profound quest for spiritual understanding and enlightenment, offering paths that, while distinct in practice and cultural context, converge on the essential unity of all existence and the possibility of direct, personal realization of this truth.

Comparing with Contemporary Western Philosophy

Rudra Shivananda

Overview of Contemporary Western Philosophy

In providing a background for a comparative study with the philosophy of Yogiraj Gurunath Siddhanath, an overview of contemporary Western philosophy is essential. Contemporary Western philosophy, broadly spanning from the late 19th century to the present, is characterized by diverse and often competing schools of thought, each addressing fundamental questions about knowledge, existence, ethics, and the human condition.

- Late 19th and Early 20th Century Foundations: This era marked a transition from traditional philosophical concerns towards more diverse and complex ideas. Philosophers like Friedrich Nietzsche challenged existing moral and religious norms, while pragmatists like William James focused on the practical applications of thought.

- Existentialism and Phenomenology: Emerging in the 20th century, existentialism, led by figures like Jean-Paul Sartre and Martin Heidegger, delved into human freedom, individuality, and the subjective experience of being. Phenomenology, pioneered by Edmund Husserl, focused on the structures of experience and consciousness.

- Analytic Philosophy: Dominant in the Anglo-American academic world, analytic philosophy emphasizes clarity, logic, and scientific rigor in philosophical discourse. Key figures include Bertrand Russell, Ludwig Wittgenstein, and more recently, Saul Kripke and Judith Jarvis Thomson, who have contributed significantly to areas like philosophy of language, logic, metaphysics, and ethics.

- Postmodernism and Critical Theory: Postmodern thinkers like Michel Foucault, Jacques Derrida, and Jean-François Lyotard critiqued the notions of absolute truth and objective reality, focusing on power structures, language, and cultural constructs. Critical theory, associated with the Frankfurt School, addresses issues of capitalism, modernity, and socio-political structures.

- Ethics and Political Philosophy: Contemporary discussions in ethics and political philosophy range from the works of John Rawls and his theory of justice to debates in bioethics, environmental ethics, and the philosophy of human rights. This reflects a growing concern with social and ethical issues on a global scale.

- Philosophy of Mind and Consciousness: This area has seen significant developments, particularly with the rise of cognitive science and neuroscience. Philosophers like Daniel Dennett and David Chalmers explore consciousness, the nature of the mind, and the mind-body problem.

- Science, Technology, and Society: Contemporary philosophy also engages deeply with the implications of scientific discoveries and technological advancements. This includes discussions on artificial intelligence, bioethics, and the philosophy of science.

In comparison, Gurunath philosophy, rooted in the ancient traditions of Indian spirituality, offers a contrasting yet potentially complementary perspective. His emphasis on inner experience, spiritual practices, and the quest for enlightenment provides a different lens through which to view the human experience. The following sections will explore these differences and intersections in greater detail, hopefully, providing a modern framework to understand the timeless wisdom inherent in Gurunath's philosophy and teachings to the Western mind.

Historical Context of Indian Philosophy

To adequately compare Gurunath's teachings with contemporary Western philosophy, it's essential to understand the historical context of Indian philosophy. Indian philosophy, with its rich and diverse traditions, offers a profound insight into the human condition, ethics, metaphysics, and the nature of reality. It spans several millennia and encompasses a wide range of beliefs and practices.

- Vedic and Upanishadic Period (1500 BCE - 500 BCE): Indian philosophy's roots are in the Vedas, ancient sacred texts that offer rituals, hymns, and incantations. The Upanishads, which followed the Vedas, mark a significant shift towards introspection and metaphysical questions. They explore themes like Brahman (universal soul), Atman (individual soul), karma (action and consequence), and moksha (liberation).

- Classical Philosophical Schools (500 BCE - 1100 CE): This period saw the development of six major orthodox (āstika) schools of Hindu philosophy - Nyaya, Vaisheshika, Samkhya, Yoga, Mimamsa, and Vedanta - and several heterodox (nāstika) schools like Buddhism, Jainism, and Charvaka. Each school had distinct views on metaphysics, epistemology, and ethics, but shared a common goal of understanding the nature of reality and achieving spiritual liberation.

- Medieval Period (1100 CE - 1800 CE): This era witnessed the rise of various sub-schools and commentaries on classical texts. Key figures like Adi Shankaracharya

(Advaita Vedanta), Ramanuja (Vishishtadvaita Vedanta), and Madhva (Dvaita Vedanta) contributed significantly to Vedanta philosophy. Bhakti and Sufi movements emphasizing devotion and personal experience of the divine also became prominent.

- Modern Period (1800 CE - Present): The encounter with Western culture and philosophy during the British colonial period led to new interpretations and syntheses of Indian philosophy. Figures like Swami Vivekananda, Rabindranath Tagore, and Sri Aurobindo sought to reconcile Eastern spirituality with Western rationalism and science. There was a renewed interest in ancient texts and practices, alongside engagement with contemporary issues.

- Contemporary Indian Philosophy: Today, Indian philosophy is a blend of traditional teachings and modern interpretations. It continues to engage with global philosophical discourse, addressing contemporary issues through the lens of ancient wisdom. Yogiraj Gurunath Siddhanath is a part of this ongoing tradition, bringing the insights of Kriya Yoga and Himalayan wisdom to a global audience.

We can explore how Gurunath's teachings, deeply embedded in this rich historical context, interact with contemporary Western philosophical thought. This comparison not only highlights the uniqueness of each tradition but also offers a deeper understanding of their potential to complement and enrich each other in addressing the fundamental questions of life and existence.

Core Tenets of Yogiraj Gurunath Siddhanath's Philosophy - Kriya Yoga and Spiritual Practices

In this chapter, we delve into the fundamental aspects of Yogiraj Gurunath Siddhanath's teachings, focusing on the principles of Kriya Yoga and his approach to spiritual practices. Siddhanath's philosophy is deeply rooted in the ancient wisdom of the Himalayan masters, and he articulates it with a clarity and depth that makes it accessible to a contemporary audience.

Kriya Yoga: The Science of Self-Realization

- Definition and Importance: Kriya Yoga, as taught by Gurunath, is often described as "a spiritual science of self-realization." It is a meditation technique that focuses on controlled breathing patterns to accelerate spiritual growth. Gurunath emphasizes its transformative power: "Kriya Yoga is not only for achieving spiritual enlightenment but also for bringing about a profound balance and harmony in all aspects of human life."

- Techniques and Practices: The practice involves specific techniques of breath control (pranayama), concentration (dharana), and meditation (dhyana). Gurunath often refers to these techniques as tools for awakening the spiritual energy within: "Through the regular practice of Kriya Yoga, one can awaken the dormant energies within, facilitating a journey towards inner peace and enlightenment."

- Philosophical Underpinnings: The philosophy behind Kriya Yoga is grounded in the concept of the inner self (Atman) and its union with the universal consciousness (Brahman). Siddhanath articulates this connection: "In the stillness of meditation, one realizes that the individual self and the Universal Self are one."

Spiritual Practices and Principles

- The Path of Self-Realization: Gurunath's teachings focus on the journey towards self-realization. He describes this path as an inward journey: "The true journey is inward, where one discovers the vastness of one's own soul, a limitless expanse of consciousness."

- Harmony with Nature and Universal Consciousness: A key aspect of his philosophy is living in harmony with nature and recognizing the interconnectedness of all life. He states, "Our connection with nature is not just physical but deeply spiritual. In respecting nature, we acknowledge the divine in all forms of life."

- Role of the Guru: Gurunath emphasizes the importance of the guru-disciple relationship in the spiritual journey. He believes that a true guru guides the disciple not just through teachings, but by example: "A guru is not merely a teacher but a living embodiment of wisdom, guiding the seeker through the light of his own experience."

- Integration with Daily Life: Siddhanath advocates for integrating spiritual practices into everyday life. He suggests that spirituality is not separate from daily activities but is a way of life: "Spirituality is not confined to moments of meditation; it is a continuous flow of awareness and love in all actions and thoughts."

In summary, Gurunath's teachings on Kriya Yoga and spiritual practices offer a comprehensive philosophy spiritual growth, emphasizing the importance of self-realization, harmony with the universe, and the practical application of spiritual principles in daily life. These teachings provide a pathway for individuals seeking inner peace and a deeper understanding of their true nature.

Rudra Shivananda

The value of studying Western Philosophy

The limitations of Western philosophical systems when measured against the profound heights of Vedanta do not imply that there is no merit in the insights of Western thinkers. In the vast expanse of intellectual endeavor, the contributions of Kant, Locke, Husserl, Hegel, and Whitehead rise as monumental peaks, akin to towering spires of human thought—each reflecting a different facet of the boundless Reality. These luminaries, though limited by the very structure of Western philosophical frameworks, have nonetheless rendered invaluable service to the collective evolution of human understanding.

Immanuel Kant, the founder of modern critical philosophy, stands at a pivotal junction in the history of thought, much like the seers of the East, who have laid bare the limitations of empirical faculties. Kant's critique unveils the insufficiency of the senses and the mind to apprehend the noumenal Reality. In the same way that Gurunath (from the Vedanta position) speaks of avidya (ignorance) clouding our perception of Brahman, Kant, too, asserts that our faculties, constrained by space and time, cannot grasp the transcendent Reality. His insistence on the need for an 'intellectual intuition,' a higher mode of knowledge beyond the categories of thought, mirrors the Yogic insight into the direct experience of the Atman, free from the veils of mental constructs. Yet, for all his brilliance, Kant remained entangled in the world of phenomena, unable to transcend the duality that Vedanta pierces through in its realization of the non-dual Brahman.

Kant's ethical philosophy, however, retains echoes of the Vedantic concern with Dharma. His postulation of God, freedom, and immortality based on the moral imperative within man brings to mind the svadharma (one's righteous duty) in the Bhagavad Gita. Yet, Kant's God remains a postulate, a construct of reason and morality, far removed from the living experience of Brahman that Gurunath urges us to realize in direct communion.

Georg Wilhelm Friedrich Hegel, with his grand vision of dialectical progression, presents a vision of Reality that comes closer to the Vedantic synthesis. Hegel's Absolute, which unfolds through a dynamic interplay of thesis, antithesis, and synthesis, echoes the Vedantic understanding of the evolution of consciousness through the interplay of the three gunas—Sattva, Rajas, and Tamas. His doctrine of internal relations, where everything is interconnected and nothing is excluded, mirrors the integral vision of Kashmir Shaivism, where the Spanda (vibration) is seen as the pulsation of the Divine within every aspect of creation.

Hegel's Absolute, however, though immanent in all stages of development, falls short of the unchanging, timeless Brahman of Vedanta. The Absolute Idea in Hegel reaches its culmination in Spirit, but it is still bound by the necessity of dialectical progression. Vedanta, in contrast, reveals the Self as beyond all change, nirvikara, ever-present, untouched by the flux of becoming. Hegel's genius lies in his recognition of the interconnectedness of all things, a realization that can pave the way for universal love and harmony, yet, unlike the realized Gurunath, Hegel remains within the framework of intellectual speculation, never touching the shores of that silent, still ocean of undifferentiated consciousness.

Alfred North Whitehead's process philosophy, with its focus on the dynamic flow of events and the interpenetration of all entities, takes a bold step into the recognition of the cosmic play of energies. His concept of "actual occasions" as drops of experience aligns with the Vedantic understanding of the universe as a dance of energies within the field of consciousness. However, where Whitehead's metaphysics remains rooted in the flux of becoming, Vedanta reveals the substratum of pure

Being, upon which this cosmic play takes place. Whitehead's brilliant critique of the mechanistic worldview of science resonates with the Vedantic rejection of the reality of Maya, the illusory appearances of the phenomenal world, but he too stops short of the ultimate realization that the Upanishads proclaim: Tat Tvam Asi—Thou art That.

If Kant reminds us to humble our intellect before the mystery of the unknown, and Hegel to embrace the whole of existence in its unfolding, Whitehead points toward the flow of life as a process of becoming. Yet, Gurunath speaks a truth beyond all becoming: the One Reality that ever Is, beyond time, beyond space, beyond thought.

In this grand symphony of thought, the Western thinkers have each played their part, much like the rishis of the Vedas, each voicing a note in the infinite scale of Truth. Schopenhauer, with his penetrating insight into suffering, echoes the Buddha's cry of dukkha—the inherent suffering in existence. Nietzsche's will to power, though often misunderstood as a cry for domination, reflects the ego's search for its lost wholeness, a search that, when purified, leads to the realization of the Atman, the true source of strength.

Bergson's intuition as the key to knowledge brings him close to the Vedantic insistence on viveka (discrimination) and direct experience of Truth. His critique of the intellect's limitations aligns with Gurunath's understanding that the mind cannot grasp the infinite. Yet, even here, intuition, for Bergson, is still a faculty, while for Gurunath, intuition becomes direct perception to the very unveiling of the Self.

These great minds, while bound by the limitations of their respective cultural and intellectual milieus, offer us profound insights into the nature of Reality, much as the great Acharyas of India—Shankaracharya, Ramanujacharya, and Madhvacharya—have offered varied interpretations of the eternal Truth. The non-dual yogi, with his rootedness in the unitary experience of the Self, can see in these Western philosophers the play of thought at various levels of Reality, each contributing to the grand mosaic of human understanding.

The marriage of Eastern wisdom and Western logic, when undertaken with humility and reverence for the vastness of Truth, can pave the way for the dawn of a new era in human understanding—one where the unity of the Self is recognized in the multiplicity of thought, where the Absolute embraces all relative manifestations, and where the intellect bows before the radiant light of undifferentiated consciousness, the Brahman that alone is.

Themes in Contemporary Western Philosophy

In this chapter, we explore the key themes in contemporary Western philosophy, drawing parallels and noting contrasts with Yogiraj Gurunath Siddhanath's teachings. This comparison provides a rich tapestry of ideas, illustrating how different philosophical traditions address similar existential queries.

Rationalism and Empiricism

- Western Perspective: Rationalism, exemplified by René Descartes' famous dictum "Cogito, ergo sum" (I think, therefore I am), places emphasis on reason as the primary source of knowledge. Empiricism, on the other hand, as argued by John Locke and David Hume, asserts that knowledge comes primarily from sensory experience.

- Comparison with Gurunath's Teachings: He emphasis on inner experience and intuition as paths to knowledge presents an interesting juxtaposition. While differing from the empirical reliance on external sensory experience, it shares similarities with rationalism's focus on internal processes. However, Gurunath transcends mere rationality, suggesting a deeper, spiritual source of knowledge: "True knowledge arises from the depths of inner silence, beyond the grasp of reason alone."

- Similarities and Differences: The primary difference lies in the source and nature of knowledge – sensory and rational in Western philosophy, and intuitive and transcendental in Gurunath's teachings.

Existentialism and Postmodernism

- Western Perspective: Existentialists like Sartre and Camus explore themes of individual freedom, responsibility, and the subjective human experience. Postmodernists challenge absolute truths, focusing on relativism and the construction of reality through language and social context.

- Comparison with Gurunath's Teachings: Gurunath acknowledges the individual's quest for meaning but views it through the lens of spiritual awakening and self-realization. He states, "Our existential dilemma is not just about making choices in the external world but understanding our true nature."

- Similarities and Differences: Both perspectives value individual experience, but Siddhanath's approach is more spiritually oriented, emphasizing a universal truth beyond subjective realities.

Ethics and Political Philosophy

- Western Perspective: Contemporary Western ethics grapple with issues like human rights, justice, and the good life. Political philosophy debates governance, freedom, and societal organization.

- Comparison with Gurunath's Teachings: His focus on universal love and compassion aligns with Western ethics' concern for human welfare and dignity. He advocates, "True ethics arise from the realization of oneness, where the well-being of others is seen as intrinsic to our own."

- Similarities and Differences: The common ground lies in the emphasis on ethical living and societal welfare. However, Gurunath's approach is rooted in spiritual understanding as opposed to Western philosophy's often secular framework.

Philosophy of Mind and Consciousness

- Western Perspective: Contemporary debates involve understanding consciousness, the mind-body problem, and the nature of self. Thinkers like Daniel Dennett and David Chalmers offer differing views on these topics.

- Comparison with Gurunath's Teachings: His insights into consciousness and self-awareness offer a mystical perspective, emphasizing the unity of individual and universal consciousness. "Consciousness is not just a function of the brain; it is the essence of our being, connecting us with the universal."

- Similarities and Differences: While both traditions explore consciousness, Western philosophy often adopts a more analytical and scientific approach, whereas Gurunath's perspective is experiential and spiritual.

In conclusion, contemporary Western philosophy and Yogiraj Gurunath Siddhanath's teachings, while different in their approaches and underlying assumptions, both engage deeply with the fundamental questions of existence, knowledge, ethics, and consciousness. This brief comparative analysis not only highlights their distinct features but also reveals potential areas where they can inform and enrich each other.

We can now examine in greater detail those Western philosophical traditions that are still meaningful in our modern era.

Analysis of Edmund Husserl's Phenomenology and Yogiraj Gurunath Siddhanath's Philosophy

In this section, we delve into a comparative analysis between the phenomenology of Edmund Husserl and the teachings of Yogiraj Gurunath Siddhanath. This comparison brings into focus the convergence and divergence between Western phenomenological methods and Eastern spiritual insights.

Edmund Husserl's Phenomenology

- Foundations: Husserl's phenomenology is a philosophical approach that focuses on the structures of consciousness and the phenomena that appear in acts of consciousness. It seeks to describe the lived experience without preconceived notions or biases.

- Intentionality and Consciousness: A key concept in Husserl's work is the idea of intentionality, the notion that consciousness is always consciousness of something. Husserl states, "All consciousness is consciousness of something," highlighting the relational aspect of human experience.

- Epoché and Reduction: Husserl proposes the method of epoché, a suspension of judgment about the natural world, followed by phenomenological reduction, which aims to reveal the essence of experiences.

Gurunath's Spiritual Philosophy

- Inner Experience and Consciousness: He emphasizes the importance of inner experience in understanding the self and the universe. His teachings revolve around direct spiritual experiences, transcending the ordinary conscious state.

- Unity of Consciousness: Gurunath speaks of the interconnectedness of individual consciousness with universal consciousness. He suggests a holistic view: "In the depth of meditation, one realizes that the individual awareness and the cosmic consciousness are but reflections of the same truth."

- Meditation and Self-Realization: The practice of Kriya Yoga and meditation in Gurunath's philosophy is aimed at achieving a state of self-realization, where one transcends the ego and experiences a state of oneness with all existence.

Comparative Analysis

- Approach to Consciousness: Both Husserl and Gurunath place significant emphasis on consciousness. However, while Husserl's focus is on the structures and phenomena of consciousness as experienced from a first-person perspective, Gurunath's focus is on transcending individual consciousness to experience a higher state of universal awareness.

- Methodology: Husserl's phenomenological method involves a systematic approach to describe experiences, attempting to bracket out biases and assumptions. Gurunath, on the other hand, advocates for a more experiential and spiritual approach through meditation, where knowledge is attained through personal spiritual experiences, first through intuition and then direct awareness.

- Intentionality vs. Transcendence: Husserl's idea of intentionality suggests a directedness of consciousness towards objects, whereas Gurunath's teachings suggest a transcendence of the subject-object dichotomy, leading to an experience of non-dual consciousness.

- Objective vs. Subjective Realities: Husserl seeks to uncover the essence of experiences within the framework of subjective reality. In contrast, Gurunath points towards a universal truth that transcends subjective experience, suggesting a more holistic and interconnected reality.

In conclusion, while Husserl's phenomenology and Siddhanath's spiritual philosophy both offer profound insights into human consciousness and experience, they differ significantly in their methodologies, objectives, and ultimate understanding of consciousness. Husserl's work contributes to a deeper understanding of subjective experience, while Siddhanath provides a pathway to transcendental experiences and spiritual enlightenment. This comparative analysis not only highlights the richness of both approaches but also illustrates the diverse ways in which consciousness can be explored and understood.

Comparing Henri Bergson's Philosophy of Vital Evolution with Yogiraj Gurunath Siddhanath's Philosophy

In this section, we explore the philosophical parallels and divergences between Henri Bergson's philosophy of vital evolution and Yogiraj Gurunath Siddhanath's spiritual teachings. This comparison sheds light on how different philosophical traditions approach concepts of evolution, consciousness, and life.

Henri Bergson's Philosophy of Vital Evolution

- Élan Vital (Life Force): Bergson introduces the concept of élan vital as a creative and unifying life force driving evolutionary processes. In «Creative Evolution», Bergson posits, "Life is a continuous creation of unforeseeable novelty."

- Time and Consciousness: Bergson emphasizes the importance of duration (la durée), a concept of time that is fluid and subjective, as opposed to the mechanistic and linear time of classical science. He asserts that true understanding of life and consciousness comes from an intuition of this duration.

- Critique of Mechanistic Evolution: Bergson challenges the purely mechanistic view of evolution, arguing that evolution is creative and cannot be fully explained by simple Darwinian mechanics.

Yogiraj Gurunath Siddhanath's Spiritual Philosophy

- Universal Consciousness and Evolution: Gurunath's teachings encompass the idea of a universal consciousness that pervades all existence, guiding spiritual evolution. He often states, "The evolution of the soul is a journey of consciousness from the finite to the infinite."

- Inner Experience and Time: Similar to Bergson's concept of duration, Gurunath emphasizes the non-linear nature of spiritual experiences. He suggests that in deep meditation, the conventional sense of time dissolves, revealing a timeless dimension of existence.

- Spiritual Evolution as Unfolding Awareness: Gurunath's perspective on evolution is spiritual rather than biological. He views evolution as the unfolding of spiritual awareness, leading to an expanded consciousness.

Comparative Analysis

- Concept of Life Force: Both Bergson's élan vital and Gurunath's universal consciousness propose a vitalistic aspect to life and evolution. However, while Bergson's élan vital is a force behind biological evolution, Gurunath's universal consciousness is more about spiritual awakening, while the life-force or Prana is more of instrument of this process.

- Understanding of Time and Consciousness: Both philosophers challenge the conventional understanding of time, but their approaches differ. Bergson's emphasis is on understanding consciousness through the intuition of real time, whereas Gurunath focuses on transcending time in spiritual experiences.

- Evolutionary Processes: Bergson's critique of mechanistic evolution aligns somewhat with Gurunath's view of spiritual evolution. However, Bergson still grounds his theory in the physical realm, while Gurunath's teachings are rooted in the metaphysical realm of spiritual growth and enlightenment.

- Integration of Spirituality and Science: Both Bergson and Gurunath attempt to integrate scientific understanding with deeper, often spiritual insights. Bergson does this by philosophically interpreting evolution, while Gurunath integrates spirituality directly with personal experience and consciousness.

In conclusion, while Henri Bergson and Yogiraj Gurunath Siddhanath approach life, evolution, and consciousness from different perspectives, their philosophies converge on several key points, such as the importance of a non-materialistic view of evolution and a deeper understanding of time and consciousness. This comparison not only highlights the richness of their individual philosophies but also illustrates how Eastern and Western thoughts can intersect, offering a more holistic understanding of life and evolution.

Comparative Analysis: Metaphysics and Epistemology

In this chapter, we delve into a detailed comparison between the metaphysical and epistemological aspects of Yogiraj Gurunath Siddhanath's teachings and those of contemporary Western philosophy. This analysis aims to uncover both convergences and divergences, offering a nuanced understanding of these philosophical traditions.

Metaphysics: The Nature of Reality

Yogiraj Gurunath Siddhanath's View:

- Non-Dualism: Gurunath's metaphysical view is deeply influenced by the non-dualistic (Advaita) philosophy of the Upanishads. He states, "In the ultimate reality, there is no distinction between the self and the universe, it is a state of absolute oneness."

- Spiritual Monism: His teachings often reflect a monistic view where the ultimate reality (Brahman) is seen as the sole existential entity, with the individual soul (Atman) being identical to it.

Contemporary Western Metaphysics:

- Pluralistic Approaches: Western metaphysics does not adhere to a single view but includes pluralistic approaches ranging from materialism, dualism to idealism.

- Existence and Reality: Key themes include the nature of existence, the reality of abstract entities, and the mind-body problem. Philosophers like Daniel Dennett advocate for a more materialistic understanding of consciousness, while others like David Chalmers propose dualistic views.

Epistemology: The Theory of Knowledge

Yogiraj Gurunath Siddhanath's Perspective:

- Intuitive Knowledge: Gurunath emphasizes that true knowledge is beyond intellectual understanding and is accessed through intuitive experiences. "Knowledge of the self is not a conceptual understanding but a direct experience attained through deep meditation."

- Inner Wisdom: He advocates for a direct, experiential form of knowing that arises from inner spiritual practices.

Western Epistemology:

- Rationalism and Empiricism: Western epistemology often balances between rationalism, which values reason as the source of knowledge, and empiricism, which emphasizes sensory experience.

- Analytic Tradition: The analytic tradition focuses on logical analysis, language, and scientific methods as means to acquire knowledge.

Comparative Analysis:

- Nature of Reality: Gurunath's non-dualistic approach contrasts with the pluralistic and often materialistic views prevalent in Western metaphysics. While he speaks of a unified reality, Western philosophy explores a multiplicity of explanations about the nature of reality.

- Sources of Knowledge: Gurunath emphasizes intuition and inner experience as sources of knowledge which differs significantly from the Western focus on reason and sensory experience. This difference highlights an experiential versus analytical approach to understanding truth.

- Reality and Consciousness: The perception of consciousness in Gurunath's teachings as an integral part of the universal reality contrasts with Western debates on the nature of consciousness and its relation to the physical world.

- Synthesis and Insights: This comparative analysis reveals that while Western philosophy offers rigorous analytical tools and diverse perspectives, Yogiraj Gurunath Siddhanath provides a holistic and spiritually enriched view of reality and knowledge. The synthesis of these views can offer a more comprehensive understanding of reality, encompassing both the material and spiritual dimensions of existence.

In summary, this chapter provides a detailed examination of how Yogiraj Gurunath Siddhanath's metaphysical and epistemological views contrast with and complement contemporary Western philosophy. This comparison not only highlights the rich diversity in philosophical thought but also suggests potential areas of integration that can enrich our understanding of reality and knowledge.

Yogiraj Gurunath Siddhanath:

*"In relation to the external world,
the mind – manasi perceives and presents,
the Ego – ahamkara arrogates,
the intelligence – buddhi discriminates, decides and acts."*

Comparative Analysis: Ethics and Moral Philosophy

In this chapter, we explore the ethical and moral dimensions of Yogiraj Gurunath Siddhanath's teachings in comparison to contemporary Western philosophical thought. This analysis will highlight the similarities and differences in their approaches to ethical questions and moral living.

Yogiraj Gurunath Siddhanath's Ethical Philosophy

- Universal Love and Compassion: Central to Gurunath's teachings is the principle of universal love and compassion. He emphasizes, "True spirituality manifests as unconditional love and compassion towards all beings."

- Ethics of Self-Realization: Gurunath advocates that ethical living is intrinsically linked to self-realization. As one progresses spiritually, ethical behavior naturally unfolds: "As we realize our inner divinity, we naturally embrace virtues like truth, non-violence, and compassion."

- Harmony with Nature: Reflecting the ancient Indian principle of 'Ahimsa' (non-violence), Gurunath stresses living in harmony with nature and all forms of life. "Living in harmony with nature is not just an environmental imperative but a moral duty."

Contemporary Western Ethics

- Diverse Ethical Theories: Western ethics encompasses a range of theories, including utilitarianism, Kantian ethics, virtue ethics, and more. Each offers a different approach to defining right and wrong.

- Ethics of Duty and Rights: Kantian ethics, for instance, emphasizes duty and the moral law, with Kant stating, "Act only according to that maxim whereby you can at the same time will that it should become a universal law."

- Moral Pluralism and Relativism: Contemporary Western ethics also grapple with moral pluralism and relativism, reflecting the diverse and often conflicting moral perspectives in modern society.

Comparative Analysis

- Foundations of Ethical Behavior: While Western ethics often bases moral principles on rationality and social constructs, Gurunath's approach is deeply rooted in spiritual understanding and self-realization.

- Universalism vs. Pluralism: Gurunath's emphasis on universal love and compassion aligns with certain Western ethical ideals like human rights and global justice but differs in its spiritual underpinning, rather than societal imperatives.

- Integrating Ethics with Spiritual Practice: Unlike many Western ethical frameworks that separate ethics from personal spiritual practices, Gurunath's teachings integrate the two, suggesting that true ethical behavior is a natural outcome of spiritual awakening.

- Environmental Ethics: Gurunath's stress on harmony with nature finds echoes in Western environmental ethics, but his approach is more holistic, viewing it as a spiritual duty rather than just an ecological necessity.

While Gurunath's ethical teachings and contemporary Western ethics approach moral questions from different vantage points, they share common concerns about compassion, justice, and harmony. Gurunath provides a spiritually integrated perspective to ethics, offering insights that could enrich Western ethical discourse, especially in the realms of environmental ethics and the pursuit of universal compassion.

This section elaborates on the diverse theories and compares them with Yogiraj Gurunath Siddhanath's ethical views.

1. Utilitarianism

- Definition: Utilitarianism, pioneered by philosophers like Jeremy Bentham and John Stuart Mill, is an ethical theory that posits the best action is the one that maximizes utility, generally defined as that which produces the greatest well-being of the greatest number of people.

- Comparison: Gurunath's teachings, while emphasizing universal compassion, do not necessarily align with utilitarianism's focus on the greatest good for the greatest number. His approach is more individualistic, focusing on personal spiritual growth leading to universal compassion.

2. Kantian Ethics (Deontological Ethics)

- Definition: Immanuel Kant proposed an ethics based on duty rather than consequences. Kantian ethics argues that actions are morally right based on their adherence to certain rules or duties.

- Comparison: While Kantian ethics focuses on duty, Gurunath emphasizes the natural unfolding of ethical behavior through self-realization. However, both approaches value intrinsic principles (duty or spiritual truth) over consequentialist outcomes.

3. Virtue Ethics

- Definition: This approach, with roots in Aristotle's philosophy, focuses on virtues and character. It suggests that ethical behavior stems from the development of virtuous characteristics like courage, temperance, and justice.

- Comparison: There is a notable similarity here, as Gurunath's teachings also emphasize the development of inner virtues like compassion and truthfulness as a result of spiritual growth, resonating with the idea of cultivating a virtuous character.

4. Moral Relativism

- Definition: Moral relativism suggests that what is right or wrong varies based on cultural or individual perspectives, denying absolute moral truths.

- Comparison: Gurunath's teachings, rooted in the idea of universal spiritual truths, contrast with moral relativism. He suggests that certain ethical truths are universal, stemming from a deeper spiritual understanding.

5. Social Contract Theory

- Definition: Proposed by philosophers like Thomas Hobbes, John Locke, and Jean-Jacques Rousseau, this theory posits that individual's consent, either explicitly or tacitly, to surrender some of their freedoms and submit to the authority of the ruler (or to the decision of a majority) in exchange for protection of their remaining rights.

- Comparison: Gurunath's teachings do not directly address the idea of social contracts. His focus is more on internal spiritual development rather than societal constructs or agreements.

6. Environmental Ethics

- Definition: This field of ethics explores the moral relationship between humans and the environment, emphasizing our ethical obligations to protect and preserve the natural world.

- Comparison: Gurunath's emphasis on harmony with nature aligns closely with environmental ethics. He advocates for a deep, spiritual connection with nature, which is similar to the deep ecological perspectives in Western environmental ethics.

In summary, while Western ethical theories offer various frameworks based on consequences, duties, virtues, social contracts, or cultural contexts, Yogiraj Gurunath Siddhanath's ethical perspective is rooted in spiritual self-realization and inner transformation. The key differences lie in the foundational premises: Western ethics often rely on rational, social, or utilitarian principles, whereas Gurunath's approach is intrinsically linked to spiritual growth and universal consciousness. However, there are similarities as well, especially in the emphasis on virtues and environmental ethics, suggesting areas where Eastern spiritual insights can enrich and expand Western ethical thought.

Yogiraj Gurunath Siddhanath:

"As we evolve, the fusion of our positive awareness

with that of nature's, cultivates an

improved and balanced eco-system.

Help to evolve Nature with your Nature, because

Nature is the Nature of Man"

The Concept of Self and Consciousness

The exploration of the self and consciousness forms a crucial intersection between Yogiraj Gurunath Siddhanath's philisophy and contemporary Western philosophy. It is a challenge to unravel the intricacies of these concepts, comparing the Eastern spiritual insights with Western philosophical thought.

Understanding the Self

In exploring the concept of the self, we encounter one of the most profound philosophical questions: Who am I? This question penetrates the core of human existence, and its interpretation varies significantly across different philosophical traditions.

Eastern Perspective: Yogiraj's View on Self

- Gurunath offers a perspective deeply rooted in the ancient wisdom of the Himalayas. According to him, the self is not merely an individual entity but a part of the universal consciousness. He states, "The self is an ocean of consciousness, not confined to the body but connected to the infinite." This view aligns with the Advaita Vedanta philosophy, which sees the individual self (Atman) as essentially one with the universal self (Brahman).

Western Perspective: Theories of Self in Western Philosophy

- Western philosophy presents diverse views on the self. Descartes' cogito ergo sum (I think, therefore I am) posits self-awareness as the foundation of existence. In contrast, Hume argues that the self is nothing but a bundle of perceptions, with no underlying substance. Modern Western philosophy, influenced by psychological and neuroscientific insights, often views the self as a construct, evolving and defined by personal and social contexts.

Comparative Analysis

- The primary contrast lies in the perception of the self's nature. Gurunath's teachings, emphasizing a spiritual and universal dimension, contrast sharply with the more materialistic and individualistic perspectives common in Western thought. However, both traditions acknowledge the complexity and depth of the self, seeking to understand its role in human experience and consciousness.

As we proceed, we will delve deeper into these concepts, exploring consciousness, the relationship of the self to others and the universe, the journey of the self through life, and the practical implications of these philosophical insights. The goal is not only to compare and contrast these viewpoints but also to find potential areas where they may complement and enrich each other, providing a more holistic understanding of the self and consciousness.

Consciousness Explored

We will now try to explore the pivotal concept of consciousness, fundamental in understanding Gurunath's teachings and gaining importance in Western philosophy. The understanding of consciousness varies significantly between these traditions, offering rich insights and diverse perspectives.

Gurunath's Teachings on Consciousness

He offers a perspective on consciousness that is deeply rooted in the spiritual traditions of India. His teachings suggest that consciousness is not merely a by-product of the brain but a fundamental aspect of the universe.

- Universal Consciousness: According to Gurunath, consciousness is an all-pervading reality, synonymous with the Brahman of Vedantic philosophy. He often describes it as an infinite expanse, transcending the limitations of time and space: "Consciousness is the eternal backdrop of all existence, the fabric upon which the universe weaves its patterns."

- Individual Consciousness and Self-Realization: Gurunath teaches that individual consciousness is a manifestation of this universal consciousness. He emphasizes the journey of self-realization as a process of awakening to this truth, where the individual realizes their oneness with the universal consciousness.

- Meditative Experience of Consciousness: Central to his teachings is the experience of consciousness through meditation. Gurunath asserts that in deep meditation, one can directly experience this expanded state of consciousness, moving beyond the confines of the ego and the physical body.

Western Philosophical Views on Consciousness

Western philosophy has approached consciousness from various angles, often focusing on its nature, origins, and relationship with the physical world.

- Consciousness as a Physical Process: Many contemporary Western theories, influenced by scientific approaches, view consciousness as a product of brain processes. Philosophers like Daniel Dennett and neuroscientists such as Antonio Damasio propose models where consciousness arises from complex neural activities.

- Philosophical Investigations into Consciousness: Philosophers like David Chalmers have addressed the 'hard problem' of consciousness, questioning how subjective experiences arise from physical processes. Chalmers suggests that conscious experience poses a unique challenge for physicalist explanations.

- Phenomenological Approaches: Philosophers such as Edmund Husserl and later Martin Heidegger and Maurice Merleau-Ponty have explored consciousness through phenomenology, focusing on the lived experience and the intentionality of consciousness.

Comparative Analysis

The exploration of consciousness in Gurunath's teachings and Western philosophy reveals fundamental differences in understanding and approach.

- Materialism vs. Spirituality: Western approaches often lean towards materialism, explaining consciousness through physical processes, while Gurunath's perspective is spiritual, viewing consciousness as an intrinsic aspect of the universe.

- Experiential vs. Analytical Understanding: Gurunath advocates for an experiential understanding of consciousness achieved through meditation and spiritual practices. In contrast, Western philosophy frequently adopts an analytical and theoretical approach, often grounded in empirical research and logical reasoning.

- Unified vs. Fragmented Consciousness: Gurunath's teachings on the universality of consciousness contrast with the Western view, which often sees individual consciousness as separate and distinct.

- Integrative Potential: Despite these differences, there is potential for integration. Gurunath's spiritual insights can offer a deeper, more holistic understanding of consciousness, complementing the detailed, empirical studies of Western science and philosophy.

In summary, the exploration of consciousness in Yogiraj Gurunath Siddhanath's teachings and Western philosophy showcases a fascinating divergence in perspectives. While Gurunath offers a spiritual, holistic view of consciousness as a universal, fundamental aspect of reality, Western philosophy provides a diverse, often materialistic view, focusing on empirical and logical analysis. This contrast not only enriches our understanding of consciousness but also opens avenues for integrating spiritual insights into the broader philosophical discourse.

Considering the similarities between Gurunath's spiritual teachings on consciousness and **contemporary neuroscience** requires bridging two distinct realms: spirituality and science. Despite their different starting points and methodologies, there are intriguing areas where these perspectives intersect or complement each other.

Gurunath's View on Consciousness restated

His teachings describe consciousness as a universal, all-encompassing entity, intrinsic to the fabric of reality. This view posits consciousness not as a by-product of physical processes but as a fundamental aspect of the universe.

- Unified Field of Consciousness: Gurunath often speaks of consciousness as a unified field, connecting all beings and existence. This perspective resonates with some interpretations of quantum physics, which also suggest an interconnected reality.

- Inner Experience and Transformation: His emphasis on meditation and spiritual practices as ways to experience and expand consciousness aligns with the idea that consciousness is malleable and can be transformed through intentional practices.

Neuroscience and consciousness

Modern neuroscience typically views consciousness as a product of brain activity. Researchers explore how neural processes correlate with conscious experiences, aiming to understand the brain's role in generating consciousness.

- Neuroplasticity: Neuroscience has revealed the brain's remarkable ability to change and adapt, known as neuroplasticity. This concept supports the idea that conscious experiences, like meditation, can physically alter brain structures and functions.

- Consciousness as an Emergent Property: Many neuroscientists view consciousness as an emergent property of complex neural networks. This view, while materialistic, acknowledges the intricate and somewhat mysterious nature of how consciousness arises.

Points of Convergence

- Transformational Potential of Consciousness: Both Gurunath's teachings and neuroscience acknowledge the transformational potential of consciousness. Gurunath's meditative practices are aimed at expanding consciousness, similar to how neuroplasticity allows the brain to reorganize and adapt in response to new experiences.

- Subjective Experience: Neuroscience increasingly recognizes the importance of subjective experiences in understanding consciousness. This aligns with Gurunath's focus on personal, inner experiences of consciousness through meditation.

- Interconnectedness: While Gurunath's view of consciousness as a unified field is more metaphysical, some theories in quantum physics, which influence neuroscience, also explore ideas of interconnectedness that resonate with this view.

Differences and Complementary Perspectives

Despite these convergences, significant differences remain. Neuroscience approaches consciousness from a physicalist perspective, seeking to explain it in terms of brain activity and neural processes. In contrast, Gurunath's approach is spiritual, viewing consciousness as a fundamental, universal attribute that transcends physical explanation.

Nevertheless, these two perspectives can be seen as complementary rather than contradictory. Neuroscience provides a detailed understanding of the brain's role in consciousness, while Gurunath's teachings offer a broader, more holistic perspective on consciousness as a universal phenomenon. Together, they can provide a more comprehensive understanding of consciousness, integrating the physical and metaphysical aspects of this profound and elusive phenomenon.

The Self in Relation to Others and the Universe

This section examines the concept of the self, particularly how it relates to others and the universe from both Yogiraj Gurunath Siddhanath's spiritual teachings and Western philosophical perspectives. This exploration offers a deeper understanding of the self, not as an isolated entity but in its broader existential and relational context.

Interconnectedness in Gurunath's Philosophy

Yogiraj Gurunath Siddhanath's teachings emphasize the interconnectedness of the self with the greater universe and other beings. This perspective stems from a deeply spiritual understanding of existence.

- Non-Duality of Self and Universe: Gurunath's teachings, rooted in Advaita Vedanta, propose a non-dualistic view where the individual self (Atman) and the universal consciousness (Brahman) are essentially one. He often states, "The realization that the self is not separate from the universe is the key to enlightenment."

- Universal Love and Compassion: Gurunath emphasizes that this realization of non-separation leads to universal love and compassion. He advocates, "In understanding our oneness with the universe, compassion and love flow naturally towards all beings."

- Harmony with Nature: The teachings also highlight the

importance of living in harmony with nature, seeing it as an extension of the self. "Recognizing the earth as a living, breathing entity, of which we are an integral part, is vital for our spiritual and physical survival," he suggests.

The Concept of Individualism in Western Thought

Western philosophy has traditionally focused more on individualism, exploring the self as a distinct, autonomous entity.

- Individualism and Autonomy: Philosophical traditions in the West, especially since the Enlightenment, have emphasized the importance of the individual, personal autonomy, and self-determination. This is reflected in the works of philosophers like John Locke and Jean-Paul Sartre.

- Social Contract Theory: Theories like those of Thomas Hobbes and Jean-Jacques Rousseau view the self in the context of societal structures, emphasizing the relationship between individual rights and societal obligations.

- Existentialism and the Self: Existentialist philosophers, such as Sartre, explore the self in terms of its existence, freedom, and responsibility, often highlighting the individual's unique position in a seemingly indifferent universe.

Comparative Analysis

- Concept of Self: While Gurunath's teachings offer a view of the self that is intrinsically linked to the universe and other beings, Western philosophy often presents the self as more discrete and autonomous.

- Relational Understanding: Gurunath's approach suggests a more relational understanding of the self, where the individual's actions and consciousness are directly connected to the larger whole. In contrast, Western thought, while acknowledging social and ethical relationships, often maintains a more pronounced distinction between the self and others.

- Ethical Implications: The non-dualistic view in Gurunath's teachings leads to an ethic of universal compassion and environmental stewardship. Western ethics, while diverse, often derive from frameworks emphasizing individual rights, duties, or utility.

- Integration of Perspectives: Both views offer valuable insights: the Eastern approach reminds us of our deeper connection to the world and each other, while the Western perspective underscores the importance of individual agency and autonomy. An integrated view can foster a balanced understanding, recognizing our profound interconnectedness with the universe while honoring individual uniqueness and responsibility.

In conclusion, the exploration of the self in relation to others and the universe in Yogiraj Gurunath Siddhanath's teachings and Western philosophy reveals a rich tapestry of thought. While differing in their primary focus, these perspectives together provide a comprehensive understanding of the self's place in the broader tapestry of existence.

The Journey of the Self

We now explore the concept of the self's journey, a theme central to both Yogiraj Gurunath Siddhanath's teachings and Western philosophy. This journey is not just a metaphorical path but a profound exploration of personal growth, transformation, and the evolution of consciousness.

Spiritual Evolution According to Gurunath

Gurunath presents the journey of the self as a spiritual evolution, a process of awakening and realization of one's true nature and unity with the cosmos.

- Awakening and Self-Realization: In Gurunath's teachings, the journey of the self is primarily about awakening to the true nature of one's existence. He describes this process as a shift from identifying with the ego and the physical body to realizing one's identity as part of the universal consciousness. "The greatest journey a soul undertakes is the journey inward towards its own source," he states.

- Stages of Spiritual Growth: This journey is often described in stages, starting from a state of ignorance or unawareness of one's spiritual nature, progressing through various stages of awakening, and ultimately culminating in enlightenment or self-realization.

- Transformation through Practices: Gurunath emphasizes the role of spiritual practices like Kriya Yoga in facilitating this journey. These practices are tools for transforming consciousness and accelerating spiritual growth. "Through meditation and Kriya Yoga, we cleanse our perception, revealing the luminous essence of the self," he explains.

Western Philosophical Concepts of Personal Growth and Development

In Western philosophy, the journey of the self is often framed in terms of personal growth, self-actualization, and the pursuit of meaning.

- Existential Journey: Philosophers like Jean-Paul Sartre and Albert Camus have explored the journey of the self as an existential quest for meaning in an often absurd and indifferent universe. This journey involves confronting existential angst and embracing freedom and responsibility.

- Psychological and Developmental Models: Psychological theories, such as those proposed by Carl Jung or Abraham Maslow, describe the journey of the self in terms of stages of psychological development, individuation, or self-actualization.

- Ethical and Moral Development: Philosophers like Immanuel Kant and John Stuart Mill view the journey of the self through the lens of ethical and moral development, focusing on the cultivation of virtues, moral reasoning, and the pursuit of the good life.

Comparative Analysis

- Nature of the Journey: Gurunath's view of the self's journey as a spiritual evolution contrasts with the Western focus on existential, psychological, or ethical development. ***The Eastern approach is more about realizing an inherent spiritual truth, while the Western approach often involves constructing or discovering meaning and identity.***

- Role of Practices: While Gurunath underscores specific spiritual practices for the journey, Western philosophy generally lacks prescribed practices, focusing more on intellectual, ethical, or existential exploration.

- End Goals: The end goal in Gurunath's teachings is enlightenment or self-realization, a state of unity with the universal consciousness. In contrast, Western thought often views the journey of the self as ongoing, with goals like self-actualization, moral development, or existential understanding.

- Synthesis of Perspectives: Combining these perspectives can offer a more holistic view of the self's journey, integrating the spiritual awakening of Eastern traditions with the existential, psychological, and ethical insights of Western thought.

In conclusion, the journey of the self, as explored in Yogiraj Gurunath Gurunath's teachings and Western philosophy, presents a multidimensional path of growth, discovery, and transformation. This journey, whether viewed as a spiritual awakening or a process of personal and ethical development, reflects the deep and universal quest for understanding our place in the world and realizing our true potential.

Consciousness and Reality

The exploration of consciousness and reality forms a significant intersection between Gurunath's teachings and Western philosophy. This topic delves into the nature of consciousness and its relationship with the perceived reality, a central theme in both Eastern spiritual traditions and Western philosophical discourse.

Gurunath's Views on Consciousness and Reality

Gurunath's teachings provide a unique perspective on consciousness, emphasizing its fundamental role in shaping reality.

- Consciousness as the Ground of Being: Gurunath views consciousness not merely as a by-product of the brain, but as the very essence of existence. He often states, "Consciousness is the canvas on which the cosmos paints its existence. It is not in us; rather, we are in it."

- Illusion of Separation and Maya: A significant aspect of Gurunath's teachings is the concept of Maya, or illusion, which suggests that the everyday reality we perceive is not the ultimate truth. Instead, it is a limited perspective, clouded by our ego and mind. "The world we perceive through our senses is just the surface layer of a deeper, more unified reality," he explains.

- Realization of Non-Duality: In Gurunath's philosophy, realizing the non-dual nature of consciousness and reality is crucial. This realization transcends the ordinary perception of a separate self and universe, leading to an experience of oneness with all existence.

Western Philosophical Debates on Consciousness and Reality

Western philosophy approaches consciousness and reality from various angles, often with a focus on the nature and mechanisms of consciousness, and its implications for understanding reality.

- Materialist and Dualist Views: Materialist views in Western philosophy, such as those espoused by Daniel Dennett, argue that consciousness arises from physical processes. Dualist views, like those of René Descartes, maintain a distinction between mind and matter.

- Phenomenological and Existential Perspectives: Philosophers like Husserl and Sartre delve into consciousness from a phenomenological and existential standpoint, exploring how consciousness shapes our experience and understanding of reality.

- The 'Hard Problem' of Consciousness: David Chalmers and other contemporary philosophers grapple with the 'hard problem' of consciousness – explaining how and why subjective experiences arise from physical processes in the brain.

Comparative Analysis

- Nature and Source of Consciousness: While Gurunath's teachings view consciousness as a fundamental, universal aspect of reality, Western philosophy often debates whether consciousness is a product of physical processes or a separate entity.

- Perception of Reality: Gurunath's concept of Maya aligns with some Western philosophical ideas about the constructed nature of reality. However, his approach is more holistic, suggesting a spiritual awakening to perceive the true nature of reality, beyond sensory and cognitive limitations.

- Understanding of Self and Universe: The non-dual understanding in Gurunath's teachings contrasts with the dualistic tendencies in much of Western thought, which often separates the self from the universe and consciousness from material reality.

- Integrative Insights: These differing perspectives can be integrated for a more comprehensive understanding of consciousness and reality. Gurunath's insights provide a spiritual dimension to the understanding of consciousness, while Western philosophy offers analytical and empirical approaches to studying its nature and implications.

In summary, the exploration of consciousness and reality in Gurunath's teachings and Western philosophy opens up a vast and profound area of inquiry. This exploration not only highlights the diverse perspectives and understandings of these fundamental concepts but also suggests the possibility of a richer, more integrated understanding that encompasses both spiritual and empirical dimensions.

Practical Implications in Everyday Life

We will now address the practical implications of the philosophical concepts of consciousness and self as explored in Yogiraj Gurunath Siddhanath's teachings and Western philosophy. This section aims to translate these high-level philosophical ideas into tangible effects on everyday life, offering insights into how these theories can influence our daily experiences, interactions, and personal growth.

Application of Gurunath's Teachings

Yogiraj Gurunath Siddhanath's teachings, while deeply spiritual and metaphysical, offer practical guidance for everyday living.

- Mindfulness and Awareness: Gurunath emphasizes the importance of mindfulness and heightened awareness in daily life. Practicing mindfulness, as he suggests, helps individuals stay connected to their inner selves, enhancing clarity and tranquility: "Be present in all you do, and you will find the divine in every moment."

- Compassion and Empathy: By recognizing the interconnectedness of all beings, his teachings naturally lead to a life of compassion and empathy. This perspective encourages individuals to consider the impact of their actions on others, fostering a more harmonious and caring society.

- Stress Reduction through Meditation: Regular practice of meditation and Kriya Yoga, as advocated by Gurunath, can significantly reduce stress and improve mental health. This practice helps individuals find inner peace and balance, positively affecting their emotional well-being.

- Environmental Consciousness: Gurunath's teachings on the unity of all life extend to environmental consciousness. By viewing nature as an extension of oneself, individuals are more likely to engage in sustainable practices and respect for the environment.

Western Philosophical Applications

Western philosophical concepts, while diverse, also have significant practical implications for everyday life.

- Ethical Decision-Making: Western ethics, from utilitarianism to deontological theories, offers frameworks for moral decision-making. These theories can guide individuals in making choices that are not only beneficial for themselves but also considerate of the greater good.

- Critical Thinking and Reasoning: The analytical nature of Western philosophy fosters critical thinking and reasoning skills. This intellectual rigor can be applied in problem-solving and decision-making in various aspects of life, from career to personal relationships.

- Existential Authenticity: Existentialist philosophy, emphasizing personal freedom and responsibility, encourages individuals to live authentically and make choices that align with their true selves, enhancing personal fulfillment and integrity.

- Social and Political Engagement: Theories in social and political philosophy inspire individuals to engage in societal and political issues, advocating for justice, equality, and human rights.

Comparative Analysis

- Inner vs. Outer Focus: Gurunath's teachings often focus on inner transformation as a pathway to improving one's life and the world, whereas Western philosophy frequently emphasizes external actions and intellectual rigor.

- Holistic Well-being vs. Specific Applications: The spiritual practices in Gurunath's teachings aim at holistic well-being, encompassing mental, emotional, and spiritual health. In contrast, Western philosophical applications tend to be more compartmentalized, addressing specific areas of life.

- Integrating Eastern and Western Approaches: Combining the mindfulness and spiritual focus of Gurunath's teachings with the ethical frameworks and critical thinking of Western philosophy can lead to a well-rounded approach to life, balancing inner growth with effective engagement in the world.

In conclusion, both Gurunath's teachings and Western philosophy, despite their differing origins and focuses, offer valuable insights for practical living. Integrating these teachings can enrich our daily experiences, leading to a life of greater awareness, ethical integrity, and holistic well-being. This integration demonstrates how philosophical concepts, when applied, can profoundly impact our everyday lives, enhancing personal growth and contributing to a more mindful and compassionate society.

Future Directions and Potential Integrations

What is the future directions and potential integrations of Gurunath's teachings with Western philosophical thought. This exploration aims to envision how these diverse perspectives can converge, inform, and enrich each other in the future, contributing to both personal development and broader societal progress.

Synthesizing Eastern and Western Views

The synthesis of Eastern spiritual insights and Western philosophical rigor presents a promising frontier for future intellectual and practical endeavors.

- Integrative Approaches to Well-being: Combining the spiritual practices and holistic view of consciousness from Gurunath's teachings with Western psychological and therapeutic methods can lead to more comprehensive approaches to mental health and well-being.

- Enhanced Ethical Frameworks: Incorporating the universal compassion and interconnectedness from Eastern philosophy into Western ethical theories could lead to more inclusive and empathetic ethical frameworks, addressing global challenges like environmental sustainability, social justice, and human rights.

- Interdisciplinary Studies: The integration of these philosophies can stimulate interdisciplinary studies, combining philosophy, psychology, neuroscience, and spirituality. This could lead to novel insights into the nature of consciousness, the self, and the universe.

- Spirituality in Everyday Life: Bringing spiritual practices into the mainstream, informed by both Eastern and Western perspectives, can enhance everyday living, offering tools for stress reduction, self-awareness, and personal growth.

Implications for Future Philosophical and Spiritual Discourses

The dialogue between Gurunath's teachings and Western philosophy is not just of academic interest; it has profound implications for future philosophical and spiritual discourses.

- Expanding Philosophical Horizons: This dialogue can lead to a more global and inclusive philosophical landscape, where diverse perspectives are recognized and valued. It encourages a move away from Eurocentric views, embracing a more holistic understanding of human experience and knowledge.

- Spirituality and Science: The intersection of these philosophies can encourage a closer relationship between spirituality and science, exploring how spiritual practices like meditation impact the brain and consciousness and vice versa.

- Ethical and Societal Transformation: By integrating the spiritual emphasis on inner transformation with the Western focus on societal structures, there is potential for profound ethical and societal change. This could influence everything from education and healthcare to politics and environmental policy.

- Personal and Collective Growth: On a personal level, integrating these teachings can lead to more balanced personal development, harmonizing intellectual, emotional, and spiritual growth. Collectively, this integration can foster a more compassionate, understanding, and interconnected society.

In summary, the future directions and potential integrations of Gurunath's teachings and Western philosophy hold immense promise. They offer pathways to a more integrated, holistic approach to understanding and living, which can significantly contribute to individual well-being and collective advancement. As we continue to explore and synthesize these rich traditions, we open ourselves to a world of deeper understanding, greater compassion, and enhanced potential for both personal and societal transformation.

Yogiraj Gurunath Siddhanath:

"By virtue of being a World Citizen, It is One's inborn right to attain the Consciousness of Natural Enlightenment leading to the realization that your expanded consciousness and Humanity's consciousness is One"

Philosophical Implications for Modern Society

We can briefly explore the broader implications of Yogiraj Gurunath Siddhanath's teachings and contemporary Western philosophy for modern society. This examination highlights how philosophical ideas can influence and shape societal norms, values, and practices. We will explore several key areas where these philosophies intersect with modern life, using quotes and examples to illustrate their relevance and impact.

1. Addressing Global Challenges

Gurunath's teachings and Western philosophy both offer perspectives that can help address global challenges like climate change, social injustice, and the quest for peace.

- Environmental Ethics: Gurunath's emphasis on harmony with nature can inspire more sustainable environmental practices. He states, "Our survival depends on our ability to understand that we are not separate from nature but an intrinsic part of it." This viewpoint aligns with Western environmental ethics, advocating for responsible stewardship of the planet.

- Social Justice and Equity: Western philosophical concepts of justice and equity, as discussed by philosophers like John Rawls, can be complemented by Gurunath's teachings on universal compassion and interconnectedness, promoting a more inclusive approach to societal issues.

2. Influencing Education and Learning

The integration of these philosophical insights can profoundly impact educational systems and learning methodologies.

- Holistic Education: Gurunath's holistic approach to personal growth can inspire educational models that emphasize not only intellectual development but also emotional and spiritual growth. As he suggests, "True education is not just the acquisition of knowledge, but the awakening of consciousness."

- Critical Thinking and Ethics: Western philosophy's emphasis on critical thinking, ethical reasoning, and philosophical inquiry can enrich curriculums, fostering a more thoughtful, questioning, and morally aware generation of students.

3. Shaping Healthcare and Wellness

Both Gurunath's teachings and Western thought have significant implications for healthcare and wellness, particularly in how we understand and treat mental and emotional well-being.

- Mind-Body Connection: Gurunath's teachings on the interconnectedness of mind, body, and spirit align with holistic health approaches in Western medicine. This perspective supports integrative health practices that combine physical care with mindfulness, meditation, and spiritual wellness. Gurunath: "True wellness emerges from within; it is the harmony of body, mind, and spirit."

- Ethical Healthcare: Western bioethics, with its focus on

patient autonomy and rights, can be enhanced by Gurunath's emphasis on compassion and empathy, leading to more humane and ethical healthcare practices.

4. Transforming Business and Leadership

The principles derived from both Gurunath's teachings and Western philosophy can transform business ethics and leadership models.

- Conscious Leadership: Gurunath's focus on inner awareness and ethical conduct can inspire a new model of conscious leadership in businesses. He advocates, "Leadership is not just about guiding others, but about awakening their potential and nurturing their growth."

- Corporate Responsibility: Western philosophical principles of responsibility and fairness can be applied to corporate governance, promoting ethical business practices that consider the welfare of all stakeholders, including the environment and society at large.

5. Advancing Technological Ethics

As technology plays an increasingly dominant role in society, the ethical considerations surrounding it are critical.

- Ethical Use of Technology: Gurunath's teachings on mindfulness and conscious living can inform the ethical use of technology, emphasizing its use in ways that enhance, rather than detract from, human well-being and social connection.

- Philosophy of Technology: Western philosophy offers frameworks for understanding the impact of technology on society and the individual, questioning and guiding the development and application of new technologies in a responsible manner.

Conclusion

In summary, we have illustrated how the blending of Yogiraj Gurunath Siddhanath's spiritual wisdom and contemporary Western philosophical thought can offer valuable insights and practical applications for modern society. From global challenges to individual well-being, the integration of these philosophies provides a rich tapestry of ideas that can help navigate the complexities of the modern world, fostering a more ethical, conscious, and harmonious society.

Synthesis and Future Directions

We can summarize the key findings from the comparative study of Yogiraj Gurunath Siddhanath's teachings and contemporary Western philosophy. We also explore potential future directions for this rich and meaningful dialogue.

Synthesis of Philosophical Examination

The journey through this comparative study highlights the profound depth and breadth of both Gurunath's teachings and Western philosophical thought.

- Unity of Consciousness and Diversity of Thought: Gurunath's perspective on consciousness as a unifying element of the universe complements Western philosophy's diverse inquiries into the nature of consciousness. "In the realm of consciousness, we are all interconnected; our separateness is an illusion," he asserts. This idea finds echoes in Western discussions about the mind-body problem and the nature of personal identity.

- Ethical and Moral Convergence: The ethical teachings of compassion and interconnectedness from Gurunath align with Western philosophy's emphasis on ethics and morality. As he says, "Our actions must be guided by a deep sense of love and responsibility towards all beings," a sentiment that resonates with Western ethical theories advocating for human rights and social justice.

- Philosophical Complementarity: The spiritual and introspective approaches of Eastern philosophy provide a complementary balance to the analytical and often outward-focused methods of Western thought. This synthesis offers a more holistic view of the world and our place in it.

Future Directions

The integration of these philosophies opens up exciting possibilities for future exploration and application.

- Interdisciplinary Research: There is a growing opportunity for interdisciplinary research combining Eastern spiritual insights with Western scientific and philosophical methods. This could lead to new understandings in fields like neurology, psychology, and even quantum physics.

- Global Philosophical Dialogue: As the world becomes increasingly interconnected, the dialogue between different philosophical traditions becomes more important. This book is a step towards a global philosophical conversation that respects and learns from diverse perspectives.

- Practical Applications in Society: The principles discussed here have practical implications in areas like education, healthcare, environmental policy, and business ethics. Implementing these ideas can contribute to a more compassionate, sustainable, and peaceful world.

- Personal Growth and Development: On a personal level, these teachings offer guidance for self-development and spiritual growth. As individuals integrate these ideas into their lives, they contribute to a collective shift towards a more conscious and mindful society.

Conclusion

This exploration of Gurunath's teachings and Western philosophy reveals that, despite their differences, there is much they can offer to each other and to us. In his words, "The journey of understanding is endless, but every step taken in awareness brings us closer to our true self and the universe." As we continue this journey, let us embrace wisdom from all corners of the world, enriching our lives and the society we live in.

The philosophical synthesis of Yogiraj Gurunath Siddhanath's spiritual insights with Western philosophical thought provides a framework of experiential wisdom, offering profound implications for our understanding of consciousness, ethics, and the very fabric of our society. As we move forward, it is with the hope that this dialogue continues to evolve, shedding light on the enduring questions of human existence and guiding us towards a more enlightened and compassionate world.

Revelations from
Gurunath's Philosophy

The Ultimate Reality is Nothingness

The concept that "from the Nothing is the Everything created" is a profound philosophical idea from Gurunath. Very few cultures and belief systems throughout history had made the leap to explore such a concept.

In Hindu philosophy, particularly in the Advaita Vedanta tradition, the concept of Brahman is central. Brahman is considered the ultimate reality, beyond space and time, and is often described as the formless, infinite, and eternal essence from which everything emanates. From the perspective of Advaita Vedanta, the material world is an expression of Brahman, emerging from its unmanifested state, often referred to as "Nothingness."

This Nothingness need to be understood from the perspective of the inadequacy of any tools of description because the Ultimate Reality is beyond mind, concepts, language and in fact beyond time and space itself.

In Taoist philosophy, the concept of Wuji represents the state of emptiness or non-being, which precedes the manifestation of the universe. From Wuji arises Taiji, the ultimate source of all things. This notion suggests that everything originates from a state of emptiness or nothingness.

In Mahayana Buddhism, the concept of Sunyata, or emptiness, is fundamental. Sunyata refers to the ultimate nature of reality, which is devoid of inherent existence. All phenomena are seen as empty of inherent self-nature and arise interdependently. From this perspective, the universe emerges from a state of emptiness or nothingness.

From our modern Perspectives, the concept of Nothingness is beoming more and more congruent with science and Western Philosophy.

In modern physics, particularly in quantum mechanics, there is a notion that the underlying nature of reality is far from solid and deterministic. Quantum mechanics describes the behavior of particles at the subatomic level, where particles can exist in multiple states simultaneously and can be influenced by observation. The concept of the quantum vacuum, which is not truly empty but filled with virtual particles popping in and out of existence, suggests a dynamic and fertile ground from which the universe arises.

In cosmology, theories such as the Big Bang propose that the universe originated from a singularity, a point of infinite density and temperature. However, before the Big Bang, the universe was in a state of singularity, which can be metaphorically likened to nothingness or a state devoid of space and time. From this singularity, the universe expanded and evolved, giving rise to the vast cosmos we observe today.

In contemporary philosophy and metaphysics, there is ongoing exploration of the nature of existence and reality. Some philosophical schools argue for a fundamental ground of being from which all phenomena emerge, similar to Gurunath's concept of primordial nothingness. Others explore the nature of consciousness and its role in shaping reality, suggesting that consciousness itself may be the underlying substrate from which the universe arises.

The idea that "from the Nothing is the Everything created" reflects a deep insight into the nature of reality, transcending cultural and temporal boundaries. Whether expressed through ancient religious and philosophical traditions or modern scientific and metaphysical inquiry, this concept invites contemplation on the ultimate nature of existence. It suggests that the universe, with all its diversity and complexity, emerges from a source that transcends conventional notions of being and non-being, form and formlessness. Embracing this idea can lead to a profound shift in perspective, inviting us to explore the interconnectedness of all things and our place within the vast tapestry of existence.

Gurunath's philosphy encapsulates a profound spiritual perspective, emphasizing the inherent divinity within each individual and the journey towards realizing this divinity. Let's break down the key concepts:

"You are god to the extent that you know god": This statement suggests that our understanding and realization of divinity determine the extent to which we embody that divine essence. It implies that divinity is not something external to us but rather an intrinsic aspect of our being. As we deepen our awareness and connection with the divine, we come to recognize our own inherent godliness.

"You are asleep and ignorant of your divinity": This metaphorical sleep represents a state of unawareness or spiritual ignorance regarding our true nature. In this state, we are disconnected from our divine essence, living our lives in a state of unconsciousness, and therefore unaware of our inherent divinity. This ignorance leads to suffering and a sense of separation from the divine.

"Gurunath has come to awaken the sleeping god": This statement implies that spiritual teachers like Gurunath Gurunath serve as catalysts for awakening individuals to their divine nature. Through their teachings, practices, and guidance, they help individuals transcend their ignorance and realize their inherent divinity. By awakening the sleeping god within, they assist in the journey towards self-realization and spiritual liberation.

In essence, Gurunath's teaching invites individuals to embark on a journey of self-discovery and spiritual awakening. Through practices such as meditation, self-inquiry, and devotion, individuals can gradually awaken to the truth of their divine nature. As they deepen their connection with the divine within, they experience a profound sense of unity, peace, and fulfillment.

As we come full circle and uncover our essential nature, we discover that it is not a 'something' since everything is subject to change. Our true nature is that 'Nothing' that is absolute and unchanging.

Awake, sleeping god,

Know thy divinity's light,

Gurunath guides thee.

In slumber deep, our godly essence hides

Unseen, unheard, beneath the veils of night.

Yet Gurunath, embodiment of wisdom guide,

Awakens souls to bathe in divine light.

On Nature and the Universe

Gurunath's philosophy includes profound insights into the relationship between humanity and nature, the concept of synchronicity, and the idea of a universal consciousness. His teachings emphasize the interconnectedness of all life and the universe, drawing upon his experiences and insights as a Himalayan yogi.

Universal Consciousness and Synchronicity

Gurunath Siddhanath often discusses the idea of synchronicity — meaningful coincidences that occur in one's life, which he views as manifestations of the universal consciousness communicating with the individual soul. He explains this in simple terms: "When you are in sync with the nature of the cosmos, the cosmos speaks to you in the language of events and circumstances."

This notion suggests that there is no such thing as coincidence; instead, there are signs that, if interpreted with awareness, can guide us on our spiritual path.

As an example, if a student of Gurunath shared how, after a deep meditation session, he found a rare flower blooming in his garden, which he took as a sign to continue his meditative practice more seriously. Gurunath will comment that this was an instance of synchronicity, where the universe was affirming the student's spiritual journey.

Interconnectedness with Nature

Gurunath teaches that humans are not separate from nature but are a part of it. This interconnectedness is crucial for spiritual growth. He stresses the importance of living in harmony with the environment and recognizing that every element of nature, from a tiny leaf to a vast ocean, carries divine energy. "See the divine in all," he says, "as all is pulsating with the same life force that pulsates within you."

Healing Walks in Nature

Gurunath often describes his walks in the Himalayas, how the energy of the mountains and the silence of the forests contributed to his spiritual awakening. He encourages his followers to engage in similar practices, such as walking mindfully in natural settings to experience this connection and rejuvenate their spirits.

Gurunath would often lead his students on nature walks during his spiritual retreats and encourage them to connect with nature and sometimes with the stars at night.

Universal Consciousness

At the core of Gurunath's philosophy is the concept of a universal consciousness — an all-encompassing awareness that transcends individual and collective consciousness. He elucidates this idea by stating, "The drop contains the ocean, and the ocean contains the drop. By realizing the nature of the drop, one can understand the nature of the ocean."

This metaphor highlights that by understanding our own consciousness, we can comprehend the universal consciousness.

Gurunath suggests meditations where one visualizes connecting with the stars at night, imagining drawing energy from them, and feeling the vastness of the universe. This practice aims to expand one's awareness to merge with the universal consciousness, helping to realize the unity of all existence.

Reflections on Contemporary Issues

Gurunath also addresses how these spiritual insights can help solve contemporary problems like environmental degradation, social disconnection, and existential crises. He advocates for a spiritual approach to environmental conservation, where understanding our deep connection with nature can lead to more sustainable practices. "When you know that the earth is a part of your own self, you will care for it with as much love as you care for yourself," he advises.

His philosophy seeks to inspire many of his followers to initiate or participate in environmental projects like tree planting drives and wildlife conservation efforts, demonstrating how spiritual insights can translate into practical actions for the betterment of the world.

Gurunath sets an example by planting and cultivating many different plants and trees at his ashram.

The Upward and Downward Cycles of Spiritual Evolution

Gurunath utilizes the framework of mind, samadhi and consciousness as presented in the The Yoga Sutras of Patanjali. Many of the concepts discussed in the Yoga Sutras are known to have as their basis some of the foundation tenets of another philosophical system called Samkhya.

Sankhya is primarily concerned with the "25 categories of existence/evolution – tattvas" . (refer figure on page 186) These tattvas are also incorporated into Vedanta (in world of Maya) and Kashmir Shaivism (which adds additional existents to expand tattvas to 36)

The first two tattvas are purusha and primal nature, prakriti—the dual polarity, viewed as the foundation of all existence. Prakriti, out of which all things evolve, is the unity of the three gunas: sattva, rajas and tamas.

From Gurunath's advaita perspective, these tattvas are relatively real but illusory in absolute terms. However the system of tattvas provide a model for how the spirit has manifested in a material body and more importantly how by reversing the cycle, to achieve liberation from maya and suffering.

The basic aim of Samkhya is to eliminate the three-fold "dukkha" (suffering) that besets humanity:

1. Adhyatmikam (internal)

- Physical – caused by the imbalance of the doshas – vata, pitta, kapha; fever; physical pain

- Mental – separation from loved one; inability to get rid of object of dislike; six enemies (shad-ripu) – lust, anger, greed, infatuation, arrogance, jealousy; fear; grief etc.

2. Adhibhautikam (external) – caused by man, beast, birds, reptiles, plants and other inanimate objects

3. Adhidaivikam (divine) – cyclone, tsunami, fire, plague, flood, famine etc.

Theory of cause and effect (Satkaryavada)

Satkaryavada is one of the main concepts presented in the Samkhya philosophy. According to this theory, the effect is already pre-existent in the cause. For example, milk being the cause, its effect yogurt pre-exists in the milk. Based on a certain specific trigger, the effect gets manifested from the cause. This principle of manifestation from cause to effect is termed as "parinamavada" in Samkhya. The philosophy of evolution of all aspects of this material universe as given in Samkhya is based on this principle.

As an analogy, Gurunath often cites the example of how divinity exists within all of us but we must overcome our karma by practice to be realize our divinity just as oil exists in the seed, but must be pressed to release the oil for use.

Relative duality – Purusha and Prakriti

This universe of animate and inanimate object is the creation of two distinct, independent entities called Purusha and Prakriti. Both these entities are eternal and real. Purusha is pure consciousness whereas Prakriti is the primordial material entity, which has no consciousness of its own. The universe gets manifested from the unmanifest Prakriti through the proximity and conjunction between Purusha and Prakriti - the two work together just as a lame person and a blind person would help each other to arrive at their destination. Having reached the destination, they part ways and become independent of each other. That final state of freedom from each other is termed "Kaivalya" both in the Samkhya Karika as well as the Yoga Sutras of Patanjali.

In the Yoga Sutras, the concept of duality (Purusha and Prakriti) is discussed in many of the sutras, both in chapter 2 and chapter 4. For example:

- Egoism (asmita) is the identification, as it were, of the power of the Seer (Purusha) with that of the instrument of seeing [intellect and the rest] (sutra 2.6)

- The cause of that avoidable pain is the union of the Seer (Purusha) and the seen (Prakriti, or Nature) (sutra 2.17)

Individual Purusha is described as – uncaused; neither produced nor does it produce; attribute-less; absolute; infinite; all-pervasive; inactive; solitary; unsupported; non-emergent; not made of parts; independent; witness only, isolated and free (kaivalya); non-doer (akartrbhava); consciousness (chetana); a free, actionless witness.

In most translations, it is usually referred to as "pure consciousness". In common parlance, Purusha is usually translated as the soul, atman, the Self etc.

Since Prakriti has no consciousness of its own, it uses the reflected consciousness from Purusha so that the intellect, mind, ego and the senses can perform their respective functions.

The multiplicity of Purushas - each individual living entity being its own Purusha is Prakriti is presented as being common to all Purushas.

The concept of Purusha appears in a large number of Patanjali Yoga Sutras. For example, see sutras 1.3 and 2.20. In these sutras, Purusha is referred to as (drashta) or the "seer".

- Then the Seer [Self, Purusha] abides in His own nature (sutra 1.3)
- The Seer (Purusha) is nothing but the power of seeing which, although pure, appears to see through the mind (sutra 2.20)

Prakriti, in its unmanifest form (usually called Mula Prakriti or Pradhana) is independent, uncaused, eternal, and all pervading but has no consciousness of its own. It is the cause of this material creation. However, for creation, it uses the proximity and conjunction with Purusha whose consciousness gets reflected into Prakriti to help with the creation.

There is a thought provoking definition of Prakriti in sutra 2.18:

> The seen (Prakriti) is of the nature of the three gunas: illumination (sattva), activity (rajas) and inertia (tamas); and consists of the elements and sense organs, and its purpose is to provide both experiences and liberation to the Purusha.

Manifestation of the Material Universe

Everything in this material universe is a composite of three gunas – sattva (purity), rajas (action) and tamas (dullness). The unmanifest Prakriti is the combination of these three gunas present in a state of perfect balance or equilibrium. Samkhya Karika, however, gives no indication as to what this "perfect balance" implies. At some point in time (we can call it "time $t = 0$"), due to the proximity between Purusha and Prakriti, this balance is disturbed in favor of rajas and the dominance of rajas leads to the evolution of this material world, including the human being. This state of imbalance which leads to evolution is termed Vikriti. The gunas should not be considered as qualities or attributes of Prakriti but as its very form itself.

Even though at times the gunas may seem antagonistic to each other, they normally work in cooperation with each other:

Sattva is light and illuminating, rajas is exciting and restless, and tamas is heavy and enveloping. They work in conjunction with each other just like oil, wick and the flame work together in a lamp to create light.

An intrinsic quality of the gunas is that they are always in a state of constant flux. If one of the gunas, say sattva, is dominant at a given instance of time, at the very next moment one of the other gunas, rajas or tamas may assume dominance.

It's these gunas that are responsible for developing raga (attachment) and dvesha (aversion) in humans which propel one to action. These actions which can be punya (good or benevolent), apunya (bad or evil) or a mix of these two, result in this perpetual cycle of birth, death and rebirth (called "samsara").

Gunas are mentioned by Patanjali in many sutras:

- When there is non-thirst for even the gunas (constituents of nature) dues to the realization of Parusha (true Self), that is supreme non-attachment (sutra 1.16)

- Thus, the supreme state of Independence (kaivalya) manifests while the gunas reabsorb themselves into Prakriti, having no more purpose to serve the Purusha. Or to look from another angle, the power of pure consciousness settles in its own pure nature (sutra 4.34)

According to Gurunath, transcending these Gunas is the first degree of liberation from suffering.

Theory of evolution

We will first examine the theory of evolution and liberation in the Samkhya system because it is easier to understand and Gurunath will simplify his philosohpy for beginners by alluding to this proccess.

As stated previously, evolution began when the perfect balance of the three gunas in the Mula Prakriti was disturbed, resulting in the evolution of the 23 elements (tattvas) . The first evolute that appears as a result of this "vikriti" (mutation) is mahat or buddhi (intellect). From buddhi evolves "ahamkara" (ego), the individual principle. From ahamkara, the dominance of sattva guna results in the evolution of 11 indriyas or sense perceptions. These are:

- Five jnanendriyas (organs of knowledge or perception) – the eye, the ear, the nose, the skin and the tongue

- Five karmendriyas (organs of action) – hands and arms, feet and legs, tongue for speech, organs of elimination and organs of procreation

- Manas (mind) that supports both the organs of action as well as the organs of perception

From ahamkara, the dominance of tamas guna results in the evolution of the five tanmatras (the subtle sense perceptions) – the senses of touch, smell, taste, vision and hearing. From these five tanmatras evolve the corresponding five "mahabhutas" (the great elements) – earth (smell), water (taste), fire (vision), air (touch) with Prakriti and the intellect (buddhi) has become fully aware of this separation. This is termed as liberation or self-realization.

The process of involution – going from the gross back to the subtle-most element, finally merging with Mula Prakriti or the unmanifest Prakriti. This process has been termed as "prati-prasava" (going back to the womb) in both Samkhya and the yoga sutras. It is stated in the Karika, "Through the practice of the 25 tattvas (elements) and realizing the truth, one attains the wisdom of "I am not", "nothing belongs to me" and "not-I". This wisdom is free of any misconception, is pure and leads to the knowledge of absolute truth."

In essence, to attain liberation, we need to reverse the path described above for the process of evolution. As described there, evolution begins at the Mula Prakriti level, and goes through buddhi (intellect), ahamkara (ego), mind, the five tanmatras (sense perceptions) and finally all the indriyas (11 senses) and the 5 great elements. The involution process is just the reverse – one starts by contemplating on the gross elements. Then, moving up the chain, one goes through contemplation on the five tanmatras, ego and the intellect. When the intellect is purified and the ego has been completely subdued, the final state of self-realization is reached.

Gurunath talks about the attributes and characteristics of both Purusha and Prakriti, as well as the roles they play. Prakriti (He uses the term Shakti also) has two roles to perform – bhoga (experiencing life) and apavarga (liberation).

The seen (Prakriti) is of the nature of the three gunas: illumination (sattva), activity (rajas) and inertia (tamas); and consists of the elements and sense organs, whose purpose is to provide both experiences and liberation to the Purusha.

and ether (hearing).

When we add the Mula Prakriti and the Purusha (pure consciousness) to these 23 elements, we get a total of 25 elements (tattvas). In essence, then, we as individuals are a composite of these 25 elements.

In sutra 2.19, Patanjali reference these tattvas. He defines the stages of the gunas as:

- specific (vishesha) –Five gross elements – earth, water, fire, air, ether–Five sense organs – ears, skin, eyes, nose, tongue –Five organs of action – hands, legs, speech, excretion, procreation –Mind

- non-specific (avishesha) –Ahamkara (ego) –Five tanmatras (subtle elements) – smell, taste, for m, touch, sound

- with indicator only (linga-matra) – intellect

- without any indicator (alinga) – unmanifest Prakriti

Concept of liberation (Moksha)

In our human condition, we must all recognize that we are always dealing with three types of suffering. Even what may seem pleasurable for the time being will ultimately result in disappointment and suffering. The reason for this suffering is our ignorance – we are not aware of our true nature. We are constantly identifying ourselves with the mind-body complex which results in the perpetual cycle of birth, death and re-birth.

The way to overcome this suffering is to develop a pure discriminatory wisdom (viveka) which will lead to the state of complete freedom (kaivalya). In this state Purusha, who is free from any limitations of space, time and causation, is no more entangled

Prakriti presents all life experiences to the Purusha either as a result of perception through the five senses, or by bringing up thoughts, feelings and emotions based on memory. Through practice of yoga, buddhi (intellect) begins to realize that to eliminate suffering, it needs to allow Purusha to let go of the bondage with prakriti. The realization that Purusha and Prakriti are independent entities, is termed as Kaivalya (liberation).

Gurunath often refers to Kaivalya and considers that this is a higher state than that of 'Aham Brahm Asmi' because there is not even a subtle concept of "I-ness".

Theory of knowledge

Samkhya acknowledges three sources of valid knowledge:

- direct perception (drishtam)
- inference (anumana)
- valid testimony (apta-vachana)

Sutra SK-4 states, "Perception, inference, and valid testimony are the sources for establishing all correct knowledge. Through these three, any knowable object is completely known."

Direct perception is attributed to the five sense perceptions – touch, taste, smell, sight and hearing. Of course, the mind (manas) and the intellect (buddhi), being a part of Prakriti, do not have consciousness of their own. They need the reflected consciousness from the Purusha to perform any of their functions, including processing of perception through the five senses.

Inference (anumana) is dependent on something that has been experienced in the past based on direct perception. There are three categories of inference:

- Purvavat – when an inference is made from a perceived cause about an effect that is yet to come. For example, future rain is inferred by seeing thick, dark clouds.

- Sheshavat – when an inference is made about the cause of something perceived at the present moment as the effect. For example, recent rain is inferred by the sight of fast flowing, muddy river water.

- Samanyato-drishtam – when inference is made from something that is commonly known. Inference of fire by seeing smoke on a distant hill is a common example of this category.

Patanjali, in the Yoga Sutras, also defines the same three categories of valid knowledge. The sources of right knowledge are direct perception, inference and scriptural testimony (sutra 1.7). However, he uses different Sanskrit terms than used in the Karika for direct perception (pratyaksha) and valid testimony (agama).

Gurunath uses these basic concepts from the Samkhya philosophy. The objective of Samkhya is to eliminate the three-fold suffering as given above. This suffering is caused by our ignorance (avidya) which makes the Purusha identify itself with the mind-body complex (Prakriti). Elimination of this suffering is achieved through a realization of the separation between Purusha and Prakriti.

As mentioned earlier, Patanjali, in his yoga sutras, has used many of the Samkhya concepts as a foundation for his yoga philosophy which he develops as a practical guide for the attainment of the goals of yoga. Patanjali also introduces the principle of Ishwara (God) which he defines as a "special Purusha" which undergoes no change caused by afflictions or karma etc. He recommends "Ishwara pranidhana" (surrender to Ishwara) as a means to achieve the state of "samadhi" which will lead to final liberation. As a practical approach to yoga, he presents the eight limbs of yoga (Ashtanga Yoga) as the means to attain a pure, discriminatory wisdom which will ultimately lead to final liberation (kaivalya).

Although Gurunath uses the Samkhya framework and concepts, he rejects the dualism inherent in their path. He further incooporates the expanded tattvas and non-dual path brought in by Kashmir Shaivism, which uses the 36 Tattvas that represent the fundamental elements of reality making up both the inner and outer universe. These tattvas offer a structured map of spiritual evolution, leading toward liberation (moksha) from suffering (dukkha). The journey of understanding these tattvas mirrors the soul's journey from ignorance to self-realization, culminating in union with the universal consciousness, Shiva.

Expanding the Categories of Tattvas

In the Himalayan, Nath and Kashmir Shaivism traditions, the cyle of manifestation is further expanded into 36 Tattvas, which are divided into three main categories that map out different levels of existence:

1. Shuddha Tattvas (Pure Tattvas) – These relate to the domain of pure consciousness (Parashakti) and correspond to higher levels of spiritual awareness.

2. Shuddhashuddha Tattvas (Mixed Tattvas) – These represent the boundary between pure and impure reality, acting as a bridge between the material world and the spiritual essence.

3. Ashuddha Tattvas (Impure Tattvas) – These are the building blocks of the material and mental universe, representing the domain of limitation and ignorance.

Description of the 36 Tattvas

I. Shuddha Tattvas (1–5) – Domain of Pure Consciousness

1. Shiva Tattva: The first and highest principle, representing the state of pure consciousness. It is the transcendental, unmanifested reality, the formless state where no differentiation or duality exists. It symbolizes ultimate oneness. Realizing Shiva tattva means merging into the undifferentiated absolute, where individual identity dissolves into universal consciousness.

2. Shakti Tattva: The dynamic aspect of Shiva, Shakti is the creative energy that brings the universe into being. Shiva and Shakti are inseparable, representing the dual aspect of reality—consciousness and energy. In spiritual evolution, the realization of Shakti is recognizing the creative potential within oneself, leading to the awareness that the universe is a manifestation of divine energy.

3. Sadashiva Tattva: In this level, the first hint of individuality appears, though it is still deeply connected to the universal. There is awareness of "I am this" (Aham idam). This is the beginning of awareness of the universe as a reflection of the Self. A spiritual aspirant sees everything as a manifestation of the divine "I."

4. Ishvara Tattva: This is the state of cosmic lordship, where the awareness is focused outward, toward "This is I" (Idam aham). Ishvara is the power of cosmic oversight. At this stage, there is still unity, but the focus has shifted toward awareness of the divine in the cosmos.

5. Shudhashivaya Tattva: This level marks the beginning of duality—knowledge of both the Self and the world as interconnected. It is the realization of the divine play of Shiva and Shakti in the multiplicity of forms. Liberation begins here with the un-

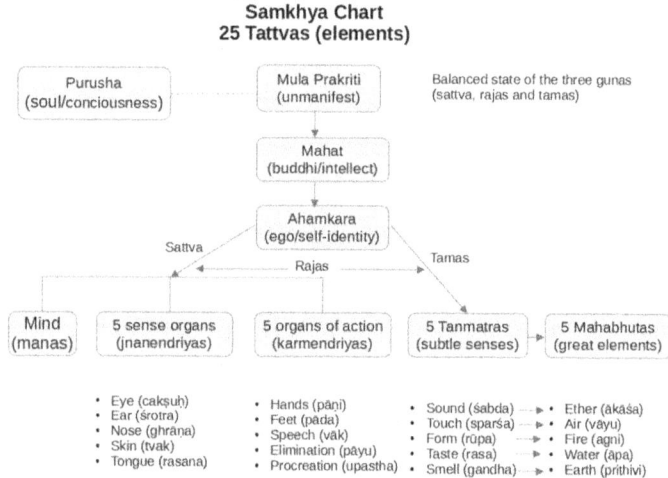

The Samkhya Tattva Model

This is the core model that is used by all spiritual practice oriented yogic traditions

derstanding that while the world appears dual, everything is fundamentally an expression of the same divine consciousness.

II. Shuddhshuddha Tattvas (6–12) – The Mixed Realm of Maya and Limitation

6. Maya Tattva: Maya creates the illusion of separation and multiplicity. Through this tattva, the one reality appears as many, giving rise to limited individuality. Spiritual evolution involves piercing the veil of Maya and recognizing the underlying unity of all existence.

7. Kalaa Tattva: This is the principle of limitation, where the infinite Shiva is limited in power, knowledge, and creativity. Kalaa represents a partial manifestation of Shiva's powers. Awareness of one's limitations in this world is the beginning of spiritual inquiry.

8. Vidya Tattva: Vidya means knowledge, but at this level, it is limited knowledge. This tattva gives limited awareness, allowing individuals to know only in a partial way. Understanding that one's knowledge is incomplete drives the seeker toward higher wisdom.

9. Raga Tattva: This is the principle of attachment and desire. Through Raga, individual souls become attached to specific experiences, objects, and relationships. Spiritual evolution involves recognizing how desire binds the soul to the world of duality and suffering.

10. Kaala Tattva: Kaala refers to time, which imposes limitations on the experience of the soul. Time is the measure by which change and impermanence are experienced. Realizing the constraints of time leads to understanding the eternal, unchanging reality beyond it.

11. Niyati Tattva: Niyati is the principle of cosmic law or order, which governs the limitations imposed by space and time. It is the concept of fate or the inevitability of certain events. Awareness of Niyati inspires the seeker to transcend the limitations of fate through spiritual awakening.

12. Purusha Tattva: Purusha is the individual soul, the limited self, experiencing individuality while still being connected to the whole. The realization that the individual soul (jivatman) is ultimately not separate from the universal soul (paramatman) is key to liberation.

III. Ashuddha Tattvas (13–36) – The Material and Mental Universe

13. Prakrti Tattva: Prakrti is the primordial matter, the substance from which the entire material universe is created. It consists of the three gunas (Sattva, Rajas, and Tamas). Realizing the impermanence of material creation and the interplay of the gunas leads to detachment and spiritual growth.

14–16. Buddhi, Ahamkara, and Manas Tattvas: These represent different aspects of the mind:

- Buddhi (intellect) is responsible for discernment and decision-making.

- Ahamkara (ego) gives the sense of individuality and separateness.

- Manas (mind) is responsible for processing sensory information. Liberation from suffering involves transcending the limitations of the mind and ego to realize higher consciousness.

17–21. The Five Tanmatras: These are the subtle elements (sound, touch, form, taste, and smell) that give rise to sensory experiences. Attachment to sensory pleasures creates bondage; liberation comes from detaching from the Tanmatras.

22–36. The Five Mahabhutas and Five Karmendriyas and Five Jñanendriyas:

- Mahabhutas: The five great elements (earth, water, fire, air, ether) make up the physical world.

- Karmendriyas: The five organs of action (speech, hands, feet, reproduction, elimination) allow engagement with the world.

- Jñanendriyas: The five senses (hearing, touch, sight, taste, smell) facilitate perception. These are the tools through which we interact with the world. Spiritual evolution involves transcending attachment to material existence, recognizing these as temporary forms, and reorienting oneself toward the eternal.

On Spiritual Evolution and Liberation

The 36 Tattvas map out the soul's descent into material existence and its journey back to divine consciousness. Liberation from suffering occurs as one ascends through these tattvas by shedding layers of ignorance, attachment, and limitation. Starting from the grossest material level (Aśuddha Tattvas), spiritual evolution involves realizing the illusory nature of separateness created by Māyā and gradually recognizing one's true nature as pure consciousness (Śuddha Tattvas).

Understanding the tattvas helps to dissolve the false identification with the body, mind, and ego, which are the sources of suffering. Liberation (moksha) is achieved when the soul realizes its inherent oneness with Paramshiva, transcending the illusion of duality and merging with the pure, infinite consciousness that pervades all existence.

This system provides a powerful framework for understanding spiritual growth and the path toward freedom from suffering in the philosophy of Gurunath.

The Philosophy of Practical Spirituality

Gurunath philosophy can be applied in everyday life to overcome challenges and cultivate ethical, moral, and spiritual growth. His approach emphasizes the integration of spiritual principles into daily actions and decisions, promoting a life of harmony and inner peace.

Applying Spiritual Lessons in Daily Life

Gurunath teaches that spirituality is not just about meditative practices and esoteric knowledge; it's about how we live our lives every moment. "Spirituality is not for the mountains and caves; it's for the marketplaces and homes," he often says. This means applying principles such as patience, compassion, and mindfulness in our daily interactions and tasks.

Mindful Eating: Gurunath teaches his students to consider every meal as a spiritual activity - a food mantra is necessary to sanctify this activity. He also discusses the importance of mindfulness in eating, treating it as a meditative practice. He advises being fully present while eating, appreciating the flavors, and being grateful for the nourishment, which transforms a simple meal into a spiritual experience that respects life and the environment.

Overcoming Challenges with Yogic Principles

Life's inevitable challenges, according to Gurunath, are opportunities for spiritual growth. He advocates using these situations to practice yogic principles such as detachment, acceptance, and resilience. "Challenges are the Universe's way of strengthening your spiritual muscles," he suggests.

Dealing with Loss: A follower of Gurunath once shared a story of coping with the loss of a loved one through the teachings of Gurunath. By embracing the impermanence of life and viewing death as a transition rather than an end, the follower found peace and acceptance amidst grief.

The Role of Ethics and Morality in Yoga

Gurunath stresses that ethical living and moral values are the foundations of a yogic lifestyle. He teaches that true spiritual progress cannot be separated from ethical conduct. "Ethics are the very essence of Yoga. Without them, it's like planting seeds in barren soil," he asserts.

Honesty in Business: He encourages his followers to apply truthfulness and integrity in their business dealings. By prioritizing honesty over profit, a businessperson can foster trust and long-term relationships, which Gurunath considers a reflection of one's spiritual values in the marketplace.

Integrating Yoga into Family and Community Life

Gurunath believes that the principles of Yoga can greatly enhance family and community relationships. He advocates for the practice of ahimsa (non-violence) and karuna (compassion) in dealing with family members and community interactions.

Family Yoga Sessions: Gurunath recommends families practice yoga together to strengthen bonds and improve collective wellbeing. He shares stories of families who have transformed their relationships by setting aside time for shared yoga and meditation sessions, fostering a peaceful and supportive home environment.

Spiritual Guidance in Modern Society

Gurunath often addresses how spirituality can offer guidance in navigating the complexities of modern society. He discusses the importance of adapting ancient wisdom to contemporary life, ensuring that spiritual practices remain relevant.

Technology and Spirituality: He talks about using technology mindfully to enhance spiritual growth rather than distract from it. For instance, using apps for guided meditations or participating in online spiritual forums can be ways to integrate spirituality with modern technological advancements.

Gurunath encourages his students to participate in everyday life, illustrating that spirituality is not confined to retreats and meditation sessions but is woven through every aspect of living. By adopting these principles, individuals can lead lives that are not only personally fulfilling but also beneficial to society at large.

He goes so far as to playfully joke with young students tha the first technique of Kriya Yoga is to "find a job".

On Healing and Transformation

Gurunath's approach to healing and personal transformation is always through yogic practices. Gurunath emphasizes that true healing encompasses the body, mind, and spirit, and he offers guidance on harnessing spiritual energy to facilitate profound changes.

Yogic Approaches to Healing

Gurunath believes that the body has an inherent ability to heal itself, which can be enhanced through yogic practices like Kriya Yoga. He teaches that aligning with one's spiritual energy facilitates a deeper healing process. "Healing begins when you harmonize with your inner spirit," Gurunath explains, advocating for a holistic approach to health.

Healing Breath Techniques: Gurunath teaches specific breathing techniques that increase pranic energy, which is vital for healing the body and calming the mind. One such technique involves visualizing a healing light enveloping the body with each breath, cleansing and rejuvenating each cell.

Individuals have experienced significant transformations through their practice under Gurunath's guidance. These stories illustrate the potential of his teachings to change lives.

Overcoming Anxiety: A long-time follower of Gurunath shares how Kriya Yoga practices helped her overcome severe anxiety. Through regular meditation and breathing exercises, she managed to find inner peace and stability, significantly improving her quality of life.

Guided Practices for Self-healing

Gurunath provides detailed guided practices that even novice practitioners can follow to embark on their healing journey. These include meditation, pranayama (breath control), and asana (physical postures) sequences designed to promote healing and balance within the body.

Meditation for Emotional Healing: Gurunath offers a guided meditation that focuses on healing emotional wounds. The practice involves sitting quietly, focusing on the heart center, and visualizing a golden light filling the heart with warmth and healing energy, dissipating any emotional pain. He calls this the Golden Lotus Meditation and it is offered freely and at no charge to everyone who are looking to improve their quality of life.

The Role of Diet and Lifestyle in Healing

Understanding that healing is not only a spiritual or physical journey, Gurunath also touches upon the importance of diet and lifestyle. He advocates for a sattvic (pure, balanced) diet that supports both physical health and spiritual clarity.

Sattvic Diet Plan: Gurunath recommends a diet rich in fruits, vegetables, whole grains, and legumes, which are energetically cleansing and conducive to higher states of consciousness. He explains how incorporating these foods can lead to improved physical health and deeper meditative experiences.

The Impact of Healing on Spiritual Growth

Gurunath strongly advocates that healing can serve as a catalyst for spiritual growth. He teaches that as individuals heal, they become more in tune with their higher selves, which facilitates a deeper understanding and connection with the universal consciousness.

Transformation Through Physical Illness: A disciple of Gurunath describes how a serious illness became a turning point in his spiritual journey. Through the illness, he engaged deeply with Gurunath's teachings, which not only helped him recover but also brought profound spiritual insights and growth.

Gurunath's holistic approach to healing and transformation underscores the idea that true healing is interconnected with spiritual development and offers a pathway to a more fulfilled and purposeful life.

Gurunath emphasizes the importance of maintaining a healthy physical body as it serves as the essential vehicle for spiritual growth and evolution. He often uses the metaphor of the body as a temple or a vessel that houses the soul, underscoring the need for its care to facilitate higher spiritual practices.

The Body as a Temple

Gurunath teaches that the body is the temple where the soul resides and the site where all spiritual practices are performed. He stresses the sanctity of this temple by saying, "The body is your temple, and your breaths are your prayers." This analogy encourages a respectful and reverent attitude towards one's physical existence, treating it with the same care one would a sacred place of worship.

Daily Routine: Gurunath recommends starting the day with practices that honor the body, such as yoga asanas and pranayama. These practices are not just physical exercises but are meant to align the body, mind, and spirit, enhancing the flow of prana (life energy) and preparing the body for meditation and other spiritual activities.

Holistic Health and Spirituality

Gurunath often discusses the interconnection between physical health and spiritual well-being. He believes that a healthy body supports a clear mind and a vibrant spirit, making it easier to engage in deeper spiritual practices. "A diseased body often clouds the mind. Keep the body fit, and the mind and spirit will flourish," he advises.

To support physical and spiritual health, Gurunath advocates for a sattvic diet, which consists of foods that are pure, essential, and nourishing. These foods help calm the mind and are easily digested, which enhances meditative practices. He often provides guidelines on how to incorporate more fruits, vegetables, nuts, and whole grains into one's diet to improve health and aid spiritual practice.

Physical Ailments as Spiritual Lessons

In Gurunath's view, physical ailments can also serve as important spiritual lessons. He teaches that illness can be an opportunity for spiritual growth, prompting introspection and realignment with one's higher purpose. "Illness can be a wake-up call from your soul, asking you to notice and rectify imbalances in your life," he might say.

Healing Through Yoga: Gurunath shares stories of individuals who turned to yoga and meditation as a way to address chronic illnesses. These individuals not only experienced relief from their symptoms but also discovered a deeper spiritual path through their healing journey. This transformation often led them to adopt a more spiritually aligned lifestyle.

Fitness and Energy Levels

Gurunath also links physical fitness to energetic capacity. He teaches that a fit body can sustain higher levels of energy, which is crucial for engaging in prolonged spiritual practices like meditation and kriya yoga. "Physical fitness enhances your capacity to hold and channelize spiritual energy," he explains.

Regular Exercise: Beyond yoga, Gurunath encourages regular physical activities such as walking, swimming, or other forms of exercise that keep the body vigorous and capable of enduring longer meditation sessions without discomfort.

Through these teachings, Gurunath conveys a message that caring for the physical body is not just about health; it's a fundamental aspect of spiritual practice. By maintaining physical health, practitioners are better prepared to undertake spiritual endeavors and advance on their path toward enlightenment.

Gurunath's teachings often emphasize the profound impact that a true spiritual master can have on a disciple, particularly through the transformative power of their presence. According to Gurunath, this transformation stems from the master's ability to influence and elevate the consciousness of those around them, primarily through the states of Samadhi (a state of intense concentration achieved through meditation) that they can impart.

The Transformative Power of a Master's Presence

Gurunath teaches that a true master carries an aura of high spiritual energy, cultivated through deep and prolonged states of Samadhi. This energy is not confined to the master's body but permeates the environment, affecting those who come into their presence. "The air around a true master is charged with the vibrations of enlightenment, which can awaken dormant spiritual energies in the disciple,"

Gurunath often explains. This concept is rooted in the idea that the physical proximity to a master can initiate a subtle, yet profound, energetic transfer.

Immediate Impact of Presence: Disciples often report feeling a sense of profound peace and heightened awareness when in the presence of Gurunath. Even those new to meditation have experienced moments of clarity and deep serenity during satsangs (a gathering of truth where spiritual discussions are held), suggesting that the master's energy field can help quiet the mind and align one's inner vibrations with higher frequencies.

Samadhi States and Their Influence

Gurunath believes that the master's attainment of various Samadhi states allows them to operate from a level of consciousness that is deeply connected with the universal consciousness. By merely being in such a state, a master can project this elevated consciousness onto others. "When a master is in

Samadhi, the space around him becomes a field of higher consciousness, pulling those nearby into a similar state."

Group Meditations: During group meditations led by Gurunath, participants often report experiencing a deeper meditative state than when practicing alone. Gurunath attributes this to the collective energy field enhanced by his Samadhi state, which facilitates a more profound experience for everyone present.

Spiritual Transmission (Shaktipat)

A significant aspect of Gurunath's teachings is the concept of Shaktipat, or spiritual transmission, where the master intentionally directs their spiritual energy towards a disciple. This energy can initiate or deepen the disciple's spiritual awakening, effectively speeding up their evolutionary journey. "Through Shaktipat, the master lights the lamp of enlightenment in the disciple, sometimes with a mere glance or gesture," Gurunath claims.

Direct Transmission: There are accounts of Gurunath placing his hand on a disciple's head or simply looking into their eyes, leading to immediate experiences of bliss and spiritual visions. These experiences often mark a turning point in the disciple's spiritual path, leading to accelerated personal growth and understanding.

The Role of the Disciple's Openness

While the master's presence is powerful, Gurunath also emphasizes the disciple's role in this transformative process. The openness and receptivity of the disciple determine how much they can benefit from the master's presence. "Like the sun, the master shines for all, but only those with open eyes will see the light," he metaphorically states.

Readiness and Reception: Gurunath often speaks of disciples who, after years of practice, suddenly experience profound transformations during a retreat or seminar. Their readiness and openness to receive what the master offers turn these moments into pivotal spiritual experiences.

Gurunath's teachings highlight that the presence of a spiritual master, imbued with deep Samadhi states, can have a significant transformative effect on disciples. This influence is not merely psychological but is a direct energetic impact that accelerates the disciple's spiritual evolution, helping them advance toward enlightenment. The master-disciple relationship is thus central to the path of Kriya Yoga and spiritual development, according to Gurunath's teachings.

The following topics are explored in greater detail in the the follow-up volume called 'Teachings of the Himalayan Master Yogiraj Gurunath Siddhanath' coming in early 2025.

Karma and Chakras

Gurunath's teachings on Karma, the chakras, and the transformative potential of Kriya Yoga provide a profound framework for understanding spiritual evolution. He teaches that Karma — which includes both the actions of past lives and the present — is energetically stored in the chakras along the sushumna nadi, the central energy channel within the astral spine. According to Gurunath, the practice of Kriya Yoga, particularly the Kriya breath techniques, plays a crucial role in purifying these karmic imprints, leading to spiritual liberation and Self-realization

In Gurunath's view, each chakra represents different aspects of our consciousness and related karmic residues. For instance, basic survival instincts are linked to the root chakra, while higher spiritual aspirations correlate with the third-eye chakra. "Karmic residues are like sediments settled in the chakras, and each breath of Kriya Yoga stirs these sediments, allowing them to be flushed out," Gurunath explains. This metaphor illustrates how Kriya practices directly influence the energy centers by cleansing them of karmic blockages.

A disciple of Gurunath shared how regular practice of Kriya Yoga led to significant changes in his behavioral patterns and emotional responses. Over time, practices that specifically targeted the heart chakra resulted in him overcoming deep-seated anger and resentment, evidencing a cleansing of karmic residues.

Kriya Breath and Sushumna Nadi

In non-practitioners, the life force prana flows in the right and left energy channels, while for Kriya practitioners, it flows in the central channel (sushumna nadi). According to Gurunath, this is the main conduit we should direct prana to flow, connecting all chakras from the base of the spine to the crown of the head. Kriya Yoga involves a series of integrated techniques designed to awaken and channelize this energy through the sushumna nadi, effectively awakening the kundalini and purifying the karmic imprints stored in the chakras.

"The breath is the vehicle of consciousness and hence of the soul: it is the mechanism of cleansing the channels, allowing the soul to ascend," Gurunath teaches. By using the breath to move energy up and down the sushumna nadi, practitioners can consciously influence their karmic disposition, accelerating their spiritual progress.

Kriya Yoga Practice: Practitioners describe feeling a rush of energy or warmth moving up their spine during Kriya breathing practices, often accompanied by a sense of peace and clarity. These experiences indicate the activation of sushumna nadi and the beginning of the purification process.

Self-Realization through Kriya Yoga

The ultimate goal of Kriya Yoga, as taught by Gurunath, is Self-realization — the direct experience of one's true nature beyond the egoic self. By cleansing the karmic residues through Kriya breath techniques, practitioners clear the path for the Kundalini energy to rise from the base of the spine to the crown chakra, culminating in enlightenment.

"Self-realization is the knowing in all parts of body, mind, and soul that you are now in possession of the kingdom of God; that you do not have to pray that it come to you; that God's omnipresence is your omnipresence; and that all that you need to do is improve your knowing," Gurunath asserts.

He explains this state as one of a travelller who has come home and also one of desirelessness - total satisfaction.

Spiritual Awakening: Gurunath often recounts his own experiences with Kriya Yoga leading to moments of profound insight and unity with the divine. His narrative includes visualizations of light and expansions of consciousness, typical markers of Kundalini rising, which he attributes to his diligent practice of Kriya techniques.

It can be asserted that Gurunath's teachings on Kriya Yoga offer a compelling pathway to spiritual liberation. By understanding and applying these techniques to cleanse the sushumna nadi and chakras of karmic debris, individuals can embark on a transformative journey that leads to the ultimate realization of their divine nature

Alchemy of Total Transformation

Gurunath's teachings on the internal alchemy of total transformation delve into the profound process of converting basic life energies, including mental energy, prana (life force), and sexual energy, into a refined spiritual force known as Kundalini. This transformation is aimed at removing all obstacles to higher consciousness and achieving Self-realization. Gurunath's approach is holistic, viewing the spiritual journey as one of converting all aspects of human experience into fuel for spiritual enlightenment.

Understanding the Three Energies

Mind Energy: Gurunath teaches that the energy of the mind, often dispersed and distracted, can be harnessed through meditation and focused awareness. "The mind is like wild horses. Once tamed, it can carry you to the heights of spiritual consciousness," Gurunath often explains. Meditation techniques, particularly those in Kriya Yoga, are designed to calm the mind and focus its energy upward toward spiritual pursuits.

Prana: This is the vital life force that animates all living beings. Gurunath emphasizes the importance of controlling and directing this energy through practices like Pranayama (breathing exercises) to awaken the dormant Kundalini energy at the base of the spine. "Prana is the key that unlocks the door to the divine," he states, suggesting that mastery over prana leads to control over the body and mind.

Sexual Energy: Gurunath speaks of sexual energy as a powerful force that, when conserved and transformed, can be directed upwards to fuel spiritual growth. This concept is rooted in traditional yogic teachings on brahmacharya (celibacy or right use of energy), where sexual energy is viewed as a potent source of vitality and creativity. "Sexual energy, when transformed, becomes a rocket fuel for spiritual ascension," he teaches, advocating for its sublimation through yogic practices.

The Process of Kundalini Awakening

Kundalini, according to Gurunath, is the ultimate power of consciousness coiled at the base of the spine. Through the practices of Kriya Yoga, the energies of the mind, prana, and transformed sexual energy are unified and directed to awaken this sleeping serpent power. The awakening of Kundalini is described as an explosive and transformative experience that propels the practitioner towards spiritual enlightenment.

Gurunath shares that there are seven levels of Kundalini awakening, the last two of which are beyond the capacity of our physical world. His descriptions of the various stages are both illuminating and awe-inspiring.

A Master's guidance and grace are critical factors for the safe and transformative effects of kundalini awakening.

Achieving Self-realization

The ultimate goal of this internal alchemy, as taught by Gurunath, is Self-realization — the recognition of one's true self beyond the egoic mind and physical body. This state is characterized by a permanent shift in consciousness where one experiences continuous union with the divine. "When Kundalini reaches the Sahasrara (crown chakra), it is not the end but the beginning of true life in God-consciousness," Gurunath articulates.

Transformation of a Disciple: A disciple of Gurunath recounted how, through diligent practice under Gurunath's guidance, he experienced the awakening of his Kundalini, which led to a profound transformation in his perception of self and the world. This disciple described an ongoing sense of peace and detachment from worldly concerns, indicative of the state of Self-realization.

Gurunath's teachings on the internal alchemy of total transformation emphasize that true spiritual ascent involves converting all aspects of human energy into a unified spiritual force. This transformation is both a science and an art, requiring disciplined practice, guided by a knowledgeable master, and leading to the ultimate realization of one's divine nature.

The Three Gunas

In Yogiraj Gurunath Siddhanath's cosmology, the theory of the three gunas is foundational. The three gunas—Sattva (purity, balance, harmony), Rajas (activity, passion, restlessness), and Tamas (inertia, darkness, ignorance)—represent the fundamental qualities that permeate all of creation. According to Yogiraj's teachings, these gunas govern the material world and the mind's states, playing a crucial role in shaping an individual's spiritual evolution.

The Role of the Gunas in Creation

1. Sattva reflects the state of clarity and wisdom. It is responsible for the natural order, spiritual light, and upward tendencies towards unity with the divine. A Sattvic mind is calm, balanced, and inclined toward higher spiritual knowledge and realization.

2. Rajas is characterized by movement and energy. It is the force of change, activity, and dynamism that drives creation and transformation in the universe. Rajas often leads to desires, attachment, and worldly pursuits, resulting in action-oriented but sometimes restless behavior.

3. Tamas represents inertia and ignorance. It is the quality of resistance, obscuration, and dissolution. Tamas can lead to confusion, delusion, and stagnation, keeping beings trapped in lower forms of consciousness and material attachment.

Spiritual Progress and the Gunas

Yogiraj emphasizes that to attain higher states of consciousness—such as No-Mind and eventually Nirbija Samadhi—one must transcend the dominance of Tamas and Rajas, allowing Sattva to prevail. However, even Sattva, while pure, is ultimately still part of Prakriti (Nature). The highest spiritual states are those beyond the influence of the three gunas altogether, where one realizes the undifferentiated consciousness, or Purusha.

Kriya Yoga and the Gunas

Kriya Yoga, as taught by Yogiraj, works directly on the energies and mind, helping individuals harmonize the gunas. Through the practice of Kriya, one purifies the mind and body, reducing the influence of Tamas and Rajas, and enhancing Sattva. As one progresses, the practitioner moves beyond the play of the gunas, entering deeper states of soulfulness, ultimately leading to liberation (moksha).

This teaching illustrates how Yogiraj integrates this ancient yogic framework into his broader cosmology, emphasizing the need to transcend the influences of material nature (Prakriti) to achieve union with the divine (Purusha).

The journey of life, complex and woven with countless threads, holds within it both the potential to bind the soul in its illusions and to liberate it into the light of truth. To navigate this intricate web, the ancient wisdom of Samkhya philosophy, which sums up the essence of reality, offers a profound teaching. It reveals the duality between Purusha, the eternal knower, and Prakriti, the ever-changing known.

Purusha, the Self, is the silent witness, ever-present but never an object of experience. It is the seer behind all perceptions, the eternal consciousness that illuminates all. Prakriti, in contrast, is the world of forms, of all that is perceived—both within the mind and without in the material universe. It is the stage upon which the play of existence unfolds, with all its beauty and turmoil.

In its unmanifest state, Prakriti holds infinite potential, a cosmic reservoir of boundless energy. This primordial source is composed of three fundamental forces—the gunas—Sattva, Rajas, and Tamas. In perfect equilibrium, they are the forces through which the universe manifests, bringing forth the seen and unseen into the realm of experience.

As the soul embarks on its journey through the veils of existence, an awareness of the gunas becomes a key to freedom. By attuning oneself to the subtle dance of these forces, one can discern the pathways that lead back to the knower—the Purusha—hidden within.

The Weaving of the Gunas

The gunas, like delicate strands in the cosmic tapestry, are woven together to form the universe as we know it. Each strand pulls and shifts, setting the tone of creation. Sattva is the luminous strand, clear as crystal, allowing the light of consciousness to shine through and reveal the truth. It brings forth beauty, balance, and harmony, guiding the soul towards higher awareness and the serene contentment of life in alignment with the Self. Sattva is the gentle breeze of purity, lifting the soul closer to the divine.

Rajas, the force of energy and change, propels the wheel of life with its restless motion. It is the fire of desire, the storm of passions, the drive to transform. It moves the soul through the trials of action and attachment, stirring both joy and pain, pulling the mind towards the material and the sensual. Like a flame that flickers wildly, Rajas may lead upward toward clarity or downward into the shadows, its direction swayed by the intent of the soul.

Tamas, the dark strand of inertia, shrouds consciousness in a heavy veil of ignorance. It binds the soul in the weight of delusion, dulling the light of awareness with lethargy and confusion. It is the force that anchors the soul in the material, making the unreal seem real. And yet, even in Tamas there is a stillness that, when purified, can bring stability and rest. But unchecked, it leads only to stagnation and the forgetfulness of the spirit.

The Dance of the Gunas in Life

The interplay of the gunas is ever-present, a subtle but powerful force guiding our actions, thoughts, and experiences. Imagine standing on the mat in a yoga class, folding into an asana. On a day where lethargy clouds your mind, and you slump thoughtlessly into the pose, rounding your back, collapsing into the posture, you feel the heaviness of Tamas weighing down your spirit. The body is there, but the soul is asleep.

On another day, filled with ambition, you push yourself with fierce determination, driven by an inner competition. Your mind races, your body strains, and discomfort sets in, yet you persist, caught in the fire of Rajas. Passionate but distracted, your attention wavers between the pose and fleeting desires, chasing after fleeting satisfactions.

But then, there are moments when the mind quiets, the breath deepens, and you settle into the pose with calm precision. The body aligns naturally, the mind focuses inward, and in that stillness, Sattva reveals itself. The light of awareness floods in, bringing clarity and contentment. In that moment, the posture becomes a vehicle for spiritual unfolding, revealing a glimpse of the divine harmony that lies within.

Mastering the Gunas

The soul's path is to discern the qualities of each guna and, through this awareness, to cultivate the balance that leads to liberation. By nurturing Sattva, softening the restless urges of Rajas, and using Tamas wisely to ground oneself when needed, the seeker begins to harmonize the forces of nature, aligning them with the light of the Self.

In life, the gunas reveal themselves in every moment. The food we eat, the thoughts we think, and the choices we make—all are expressions of the gunas at work. Sattvic foods nourish and uplift the spirit, while rajasic cravings stir the senses, and tamasic indulgence pulls the soul into dullness. The soul must learn to discern the subtle qualities in all aspects of life, moving ever closer to the light of truth.

Transcending the Gunas

As the Bhagavad Gita teaches, these three gunas, born of Prakriti, bind the soul to the wheel of birth and death. Yet, the soul's destiny is not to remain bound. By becoming a witness to the play of the gunas, and recognizing that they are the doers—not the Self—the soul begins to transcend. The knower, Purusha, is free from these forces, untouched by the fluctuations of the mind and matter. It is through the realization of this eternal witness that the soul finds liberation, freed from the cycles of sorrow and delusion.

Thus, life's journey is not merely to navigate the gunas but to rise above them, to see the play of nature for what it is—a divine dance leading the soul back to its source. When the soul ceases to identify with the play of the gunas, it rests in the boundless peace of the knower, where the light of consciousness shines eternally.

Yogiraj Gurunath Siddhanath presents a unique interpretation of the gunas by connecting their cosmic forces to the building blocks of the material universe, particularly in how they give rise to subatomic particles. He extends the classical understanding of the gunas—Sattva, Rajas, and Tamas—by identifying their roles in the creation of electrons, protons, and neutrons, thus linking metaphysical principles to the realm of modern physics.

The Gunas and Subatomic Particles

1. Rajas and the Proton: Rajas, the force of activity, energy, and passion, is the dynamic principle that drives movement and change. In Yogiraj's teaching, this quality is directly related to the proton, which is positively charged and plays a central role in determining the identity of an atom. The proton, as a manifestation of Rajas, embodies the qualities of force and action, exerting an energetic influence that defines the structure of matter. Rajas, like the proton, drives the processes of creation and transformation, fueling the ongoing movement and evolution of the cosmos.

2. Sattva and the Electron: Sattva, the guna of purity, clarity, and balance, is the force that illuminates and harmonizes. According to Yogiraj, this corresponds to the electron, which carries a negative charge and orbits the nucleus. The electron's movement around the nucleus can be seen as a stabilizing force, much like how Sattva provides balance and harmony in the cosmos. Its lightness and quickness echo the clarity and transparency of Sattva, allowing for the flow of energy (such as electricity) without obstruction. The electron, in this sense, becomes a carrier of Sattvic energy, contributing to the equilibrium in the atomic structure.

3. Tamas and the Neutron: Tamas, the principle of inertia, darkness, and resistance, is linked to the neutron, which has no charge and provides mass and stability to the atom. The neutron's neutral quality mirrors the inert, grounding nature of Tamas. Though Tamas can obscure consciousness and create inertia in spiritual evolution, it also provides the necessary grounding for material existence, as the neutron helps hold the nucleus together, stabilizing the atom. Without Tamas, there would be no foundation for form; matter would dissolve into pure energy. Thus, Tamas, through the neutron, becomes the steadying force that allows the material universe to take shape and persist.

The Gunas as Cosmic Forces in Material Formation

Gurunath's insight into the gunas' role in atomic structure illustrates his broader teaching that the material world is a reflection of deeper, spiritual energies. The interaction of protons (Rajas), electrons (Sattva), and neutrons (Tamas) at the subatomic level represents the ongoing dance of creation, maintenance, and transformation that is present in the entire cosmos.

This idea offers a mystical yet scientific explanation of how the universe transitions from the subtle realm of potential (unmanifest prakriti) to the tangible realm of form and matter. The three gunas, as the fundamental forces within prakriti, give rise to the very particles that compose all matter, each guna influencing the behavior of the particles in accordance with its essential nature.

Through this lens, the atom becomes a microcosm of the larger cosmic forces at play, reflecting the balance between energy, form, and consciousness that drives the entire universe.

Yogiraj Gurunath Siddhanath's profound teaching on the gunas reveals that the balance and interplay of Sattva, Rajas, and Tamas in a person's life are not arbitrary but are deeply influenced by the individual's karma. Karma, as the accumulation of actions from past lives and the current one, shapes how these fundamental forces express themselves in a person's physical, emotional, and mental states. Furthermore, an individual's dharma—or soul purpose—is also conditioned by the gunas, which are shaped by this very karma.

Karma and Its Role in Shaping the Gunas

In Yogic philosophy, karma refers to the law of cause and effect, where every action, thought, and intention creates consequences that ripple across lifetimes. Karma is not just about physical actions but also includes emotional responses, desires, and mental tendencies. These karmic imprints (or samskaras) are stored in the subtle body, and they create patterns that determine how the gunas express themselves in an individual's current life.

1. Tamas and Karma: If an individual's past actions have been rooted in ignorance, lethargy, or harmful tendencies, these will strengthen the guna of Tamas in their present life. This could manifest in the form of physical sluggishness, emotional dullness, or mental confusion. Tamas, in its unrefined state, leads to inertia and stagnation, preventing spiritual progress. A person with tamasic karma may find themselves trapped in repetitive cycles of negative habits, procrastination, and avoidance, weighed down by the denser, material aspects of existence. Overcoming tamasic influences requires consciously working through these karmic debts, bringing in more light and awareness (Sattva) to rise above ignorance.

2. Rajas and Karma: Rajas is the force of activity, desire, and passion, and its presence in an individual's life is shaped

by karma that is rooted in excessive attachment to material success, restlessness, and unchecked desires. Rajasic karma often results in a life filled with constant movement, driven by cravings for pleasure, recognition, and worldly achievements. While Rajas can be a catalyst for positive action and transformation, it often binds individuals to the outcomes of their actions, causing attachment and dissatisfaction. Karma linked to Rajas creates emotional turbulence and mental agitation, keeping a person caught in the cycle of action and reaction. It is through conscious redirection of this energy towards higher spiritual goals that one can move toward Sattva.

3. Sattva and Karma: Sattvic karma is the result of past actions aligned with truth, harmony, and selflessness. When Sattva predominates, the individual experiences clarity, purity, and balance across the physical, emotional, and mental realms. Sattva opens the door to spiritual insight and brings a sense of peace and fulfillment. A person with sattvic karma will find themselves naturally drawn to practices and lifestyles that nurture health, harmony, and spiritual growth. They are more inclined toward acts of compassion, meditation, and service. However, even Sattva, though it is a force of light, must ultimately be transcended, as it too is part of the phenomenal world (Prakriti).

Dharma and Its Connection to the Gunas and Karma

Dharma, in the context of Gurunath's teachings, is the individual's soul purpose or cosmic duty. It is the unique path that each soul must walk, guided by their inner nature and the cosmic law. While dharma is often seen as a divine calling or spiritual responsibility, it is influenced by the gunas, which, in turn, are shaped by the individual's past karma.

1. Karma Conditioning Dharma: The karmic patterns (samskaras) that a soul carries into its current life lay the foundation for its dharma. For example, if one's past lives have been filled with rajasic activity—ambition, leadership, and material success—this karmic inheritance might shape a dharma that involves dynamic action in this lifetime, perhaps as a leader, entrepreneur, or innovator. On the other hand, an individual with a predominance of sattvic karma may be drawn to a dharma of teaching, healing, or spiritual guidance.

2. The Role of the Gunas in Dharma: The proportions of Sattva, Rajas, and Tamas within an individual not only reflect their past karma but also provide the framework through which their dharma unfolds. An individual dominated by Sattva may have a dharma centered on selfless service, spiritual teaching, or artistic expression that uplifts others. Those with a predominance of Rajas may find their dharma in creative or action-driven roles where energy and passion are required to bring about change. Those with a tamasic influence may have to overcome inertia and lethargy before stepping into their dharma fully, using that same steadying force of Tamas to ground themselves in practical work once the ignorance is lifted.

3. Transcending the Gunas and Fulfilling Dharma: The ultimate goal of life, according to Yogiraj Gurunath Siddhanath's teachings, is not merely to function within the framework of the gunas but to transcend them entirely. While one's dharma is influenced by the interplay of the gunas, the spiritual aspirant's higher dharma is to rise above these forces and realize the Purusha, the undying Self. The path to transcendence involves recognizing the influence

of the gunas, understanding how they condition our karma and dharma, and gradually moving beyond them.

By cultivating awareness of how the gunas shape one's thoughts, emotions, and actions, and by working consciously to elevate one's predominant guna toward Sattva, the individual aligns more closely with their higher dharma. Through meditation, selfless action, and spiritual practices such as Kriya Yoga, the aspirant begins to dissolve the karmic imprints that bind them to the lower gunas and open themselves to the direct experience of the soul's eternal purpose.

The Interplay of Gunas, Karma, and Dharma

In Gurunath's cosmology, the gunas act as the agents through which karma is expressed, and they directly influence how a person's dharma unfolds. Tamas binds one to ignorance and darkness, Rajas to endless striving and attachment, and Sattva to clarity and balance. However, the journey of the soul is to go beyond all three, transcending the karmic influences and realizing the divine truth of Purusha.

Thus, while the gunas condition the physical, mental, and emotional spheres of a person's existence, their purpose is to guide the individual through the lessons of karma, ultimately leading to the fulfillment of dharma and the realization of liberation (moksha).

Conclusion

True philosophy is not some idle game of the mind, nor the hollow echo of academic words. It is the fire that burns away the illusion of mediocrity, elevating life into the highest sphere of wisdom! To philosophize is not to retreat into abstraction but to engage with the raw reality of existence, to peer into the essence of life and emerge with a sword of clarity! Real philosophy cuts through the imperfections of the common, unphilosophical life and stands as a guide to living a life untethered by delusion, grounded in the Supreme Truth. This is not a game for the faint-hearted, nor a pastime for those content with half-truths. Philosophy is the hammer and anvil upon which the soul is forged into something greater, a tool of the highest order that reveals the Supreme Being, the very essence of existence.

And behold, in Gurunath, we find such a force—a seer, a titan of wisdom, who embodies the very truths of non-dualism. He is not merely an expositor of theory but a living, breathing testament to the integration of all life's forces. His philosophy is no distant doctrine, no mere intellectual fancy—it is life itself, pulsating with the divinity of the universe and the immortality of the soul! His teaching obliterates the false dichotomy between the world of senses and the realm of spirit, merging them into one grand Reality. He shows us the unity of all things in Brahman, the eternal oneness that transcends the trivialities of human existence.

Gurunath's philosophy is not a retreat into illusion, nor does it bow to the crude materialism of the world. It stands as a pillar of Truth, illuminating the divine nature of the cosmos. His philosophy thunders with the realization that the universe is but an expression of the Supreme Self, and every soul is destined to merge with this Absolute. His is a philosophy that takes into account every degree of Reality—no corner of existence is ignored, no experience dismissed as unworthy. From the highest heights of spiritual realization to the daily grind of earthly life, Gurunath leaves no stone unturned.

He exhorts the aspirants, those brave enough to seek the highest truth, not to shy away from the world's harsh realities, nor to flee from the challenges that life presents. Every aspect of life demands respect; every degree of existence must be reckoned with! Those who trample over the lower realms in their quest for the divine will find themselves cast down, for every level of reality has its place in the grand cosmic order. Gurunath stands at the crossroad where the ancient wisdom of the Upanishads meets the relentless demands of daily life, embracing both with equal fervor.

This is no weak philosophy of escapism or renunciation—it is an all-encompassing, all-powerful vision of existence. Gurunath does not reject the world but transforms it! The earth is not something to be fled from in disgust, but a brother to be transfigured by divine light. The universe, when stripped of its limitations, is nothing but Consciousness itself, and it is the duty of the seeker to pay homage to each manifestation of this great truth before ascending to the highest.

Gurunath, with his vast experience, reveals that the one Brahman appears in all forms, from the lowest to the highest. To realize this truth, one must develop in all dimensions—physically, mentally, morally, and spiritually. Health, wisdom, willpower, and purity are not optional in this great journey—they are the pillars of the path! His teachings embraces the disciplines of Yoga, Bhakti, and Karma, weaving them into one indomitable whole. "Adjust, adapt, and but have a fixity of purpose," he declares, urging his followers to see the good in all things and to harness the forces of nature in their quest for self-realization.

Here stands Gurunath—both idealist and realist, philosopher and humanitarian—a paradox of opposites united in divine harmony. His call is simple yet profound: Love all, serve all, for God is in all. The universe is nothing but the outflow of the Divine, and to realize this is to embrace the entire cosmos in one sublime act of recognition. To know oneself is to know God, and in that realization, the individual becomes the savior of all beings.

His philosophy is no intellectual abstraction, no mere hypothesis of the mind—it is born of direct, living experience (Anubhuti), realized through union with the infinite Ishvara, the cosmic force known as Shiva-Goraksha-Babaji. This is not a path for the faint of heart, for it demands the complete mastery of the self, the purification of body, mind, and soul through selfless action. Gurunath's Vision for Earth Peace is the pinnacle of all philosophical systems, accepting the truths of each as steppingstones to the ultimate realization of the non-dual Absolute.

This philosophy is a complete, harmonious fusion of reality's many layers. The physical universe, though seemingly material, is nothing but a mode of spiritual reality when viewed from the highest perspective. Every aspect of human life—whether material, mental, or spiritual—finds its place in this grand vision, for the universe is the playground of the Divine Mind. It is both free and determined, subject to the universal laws yet ultimately transcending them. In this dance of evolution and involution, the universe and all within it moves toward its inevitable return to the Absolute.

Nothing exists that is not rooted in Pure Consciousness! Every form, every phenomenon, bows before this eternal truth. God, the dynamic force of the universe, is the cause and substance of all creation, and the universe itself is but a play of appearances within this infinite reality. It is not separate from God, but an expression of the divine. And though human knowledge is limited by the senses, the soul can ascend to a higher realization through mystical intuition and direct experience of the Absolute.

In Gurunath's vision, all philosophies have their place as partial expressions of truth, but they must ultimately bow before the facticity of no-thought, the transcendence of all limitations. His philosophy is one of the non-dual Consciousness, the supreme essence that encompasses all things and transcends them. True religion, in Gurunath's eyes, is the practice of this philosophy, the living realization of the universe's divine nature. His religion is one of unity, of humanity, of the entire cosmos—each soul is but a step in the grand evolution of Consciousness, moving toward the final realization of oneness with the Self.

Gurunath's philosophy is not a theory—it is a living, breathing reality. His teachings are a beacon of practical wisdom, much like those of Sri Krishna in the Bhagavad Gita, revealing the path to live a life of glory, to rise from the limitations of the body into the boundless expanse of the Absolute. In his life, Gurunath embodies the highest ideal—a sage, a monarch of wisdom, who guides others toward the realization of the Supreme, toward a life where nothing but the Self remains.

This is no ordinary philosophy—it is the science of life itself, the art of being, the path to the infinite! In the blaze of this realization, the sage becomes not just a master of himself but a savior of all beings, a light in the darkness of the world, a force of divine transformation.

Appendix

Glossary of Western Philosophers and Schools of Philosophy

Socrates (469–399 BCE) was a classical Greek philosopher from Athens, widely regarded as one of the founders of Western philosophy. He did not leave any written works himself; most of what we know about him comes from the writings of his students, especially Plato and Xenophon. Socrates is often remembered for his role in shaping the development of ethical thought and his distinctive method of inquiry, which is known as the Socratic Method.

He spent much of his life engaging people in philosophical discussions in the public spaces of Athens, questioning their beliefs and stimulating critical thinking. Socrates was known for his modest lifestyle and emphasis on self-knowledge. He famously stated, "The unexamined life is not worth living."

His relentless questioning often made him unpopular among the Athenian elite, as it challenged traditional beliefs and the status quo. In 399 BCE, Socrates was put on trial for corrupting the youth and impiety (not believing in the gods of Athens). He was sentenced to death and willingly drank hemlock, accepting his punishment rather than fleeing or renouncing his beliefs.

Philosophy of Socrates

Socrates' philosophy centers around ethics, virtue, and knowledge. He believed that moral virtues were paramount and that knowledge is intimately tied to living a good life. According to Socrates, true wisdom was in knowing one's own ignorance, and the pursuit of truth was the highest good. His approach to knowledge was not based on teaching specific doctrines but on encouraging critical thinking and dialogue.

The Socratic Method

The Socratic Method is a form of cooperative dialogue in which Socrates would ask probing questions to help someone clarify their beliefs or reveal inconsistencies in their thoughts. This method is a key component of his philosophical approach. The steps generally include:

1. Questioning: Socrates would begin with a question about a commonly held belief.

2. Critical Examination: He would then follow with more questions, prompting the person to think more deeply and identify any contradictions in their answers.

3. Elimination of Contradictions: By pointing out inconsistencies, Socrates would lead the person to reconsider their assumptions.

4. Refinement of Ideas: Through this process, the person would ideally arrive at a clearer, more refined understanding of the issue.

The purpose of the Socratic Method was not necessarily to reach a definitive answer, but to stimulate deeper thinking and self-reflection. Socrates believed that this kind of critical examination could help people move closer to truth and wisdom. It's a method still widely used in modern education, particularly in law and philosophy.

This approach reflects Socrates' belief that knowledge comes from questioning and that wisdom begins with the recognition of one's ignorance.

Plato (c. 427–347 BCE) was an ancient Greek philosopher, a student of Socrates, and the teacher of Aristotle. He founded the Academy in Athens, one of the earliest institutions of higher learning in the Western world. Plato's writings, which are mostly in the form of dialogues, cover a range of topics including ethics, politics, metaphysics, and epistemology. His philosophy has had a profound influence on Western thought and continues to be studied widely today.

Key Aspects of Plato's Philosophy:

1. Theory of Forms (Ideas): Plato proposed that beyond the physical world, there exists a higher realm of unchanging, perfect "Forms" or "Ideas." Everything in the material world is an imperfect reflection of these Forms. For instance, a beautiful object participates in the Form of Beauty, but the Form itself is eternal and unchanging.

2. Dualism: Plato believed in the separation of the physical body and the immaterial soul. The soul, he argued, is immortal and existed before inhabiting the body. True knowledge, according to Plato, is the soul's recollection of the Forms, which it knew before being incarnated in the physical realm.

3. Theory of Knowledge (Epistemology): For Plato, knowledge is not based on sensory experience, which he considered unreliable and subject to change. Instead, real knowledge is intellectual and arises from understanding the eternal Forms. This process involves moving from opinion (based on sensory experience) to true knowledge (based on reason and intellect).

4. Philosopher-King: In his most famous work, The Republic, Plato outlines his vision of an ideal society ruled by philosopher-kings. He believed that only those who have attained knowledge of the Forms, particularly the Form of the Good,

are fit to rule, as they can make decisions based on reason and justice rather than personal interest.

5. The Allegory of the Cave: In this famous metaphor from The Republic, Plato describes prisoners in a cave who only see shadows cast on a wall. These shadows represent the illusory perceptions of the physical world. The philosopher is like a prisoner who escapes the cave and discovers the reality of the Forms, symbolizing the journey from ignorance to knowledge and enlightenment.

6. Ethics and Justice: Plato believed that the soul has three parts: reason, spirit, and appetite, which correspond to the classes in an ideal society: rulers, warriors, and producers. Justice, both in the individual and the state, is achieved when these parts are in harmony, with reason guiding the other two. For Plato, a just life is one that leads to the well-being of the soul and the pursuit of the Good.

Plato's ideas laid the foundation for much of Western philosophy, influencing not only his immediate successors but also entire intellectual traditions such as Neoplatonism, Christian theology, and modern philosophical thought.

Socrates focused on ethical inquiry and self-examination through dialogue, without constructing a formal system of metaphysics or political theory.

Plato expanded Socratic methods into a comprehensive philosophical system, introducing the Theory of Forms, a more structured political philosophy, and metaphysical views about the nature of reality and knowledge.

In essence, while Plato built upon Socrates' foundations, he extended them into more formalized, abstract, and systematic philosophies, whereas Socrates remained primarily focused on practical ethics and questioning assumptions.

Aristotle (384–322 BCE) was an ancient Greek philosopher and polymath, a student of Plato, and tutor to Alexander the Great. He was born in Stagira, a small town in northern Greece. After studying at Plato's Academy for about 20 years, Aristotle left Athens and later founded his own school, the Lyceum. His works span various subjects, including metaphysics, ethics, politics, biology, logic, and rhetoric. Aristotle is regarded as one of the most influential figures in Western philosophy and science.

Key Aspects of Aristotle's Philosophy:

1. Empiricism and Scientific Method: Unlike Plato, who emphasized the realm of ideal Forms, Aristotle focused on empirical observation and believed knowledge is derived from sensory experience. He is often considered the father of empirical science and formal logic, as he relied on systematic observation and classification of the natural world.

2. Theory of Substance: Aristotle rejected Plato's Theory of Forms. Instead, he argued that Forms exist within things rather than in a separate, transcendent realm. In his view, substances are a combination of form (the essence of a thing) and matter (the material aspect). For example, the form of a tree is what makes it a tree, while its matter is what it's made of (wood, leaves, etc.).

3. Four Causes: Aristotle introduced the concept of four causes to explain why things exist or happen:

• Material cause: What something is made of.

• Formal cause: The form or essence of a thing.

• Efficient cause: The agent or process that brings something into being.

• Final cause: The purpose or end for which something exists.

4. Ethics and Virtue (Nicomachean Ethics): Aristotle's ethics are based on the concept of eudaimonia (flourishing or happiness), which he considered the highest good. He believed that achieving eudaimonia comes from living a virtuous life, which is attained through balance or moderation—known as the "Golden Mean." Virtue, for Aristotle, is a habit of choosing the mean between extremes of excess and deficiency, such as courage (between rashness and cowardice) or generosity (between prodigality and stinginess).

5. Politics: In his work Politics, Aristotle examined different forms of government and emphasized the importance of the polis (city-state) as the best environment for achieving human flourishing. He believed in a mixed form of government that balances democracy, oligarchy, and monarchy. The best society, according to Aristotle, is one that encourages its citizens to live virtuously.

6. Logic and Syllogism: Aristotle is known for developing formal logic, particularly the concept of the syllogism, a form of deductive reasoning where a conclusion follows necessarily from two premises (e.g., "All men are mortal; Socrates is a man; therefore, Socrates is mortal").

7. Teleology: Aristotle's philosophy is deeply teleological, meaning he believed that everything in nature has a purpose or goal (telos). For example, an acorn's goal is to become an oak tree. This teleological view of nature permeates his biology and metaphysics.

Overall, Aristotle's philosophy is more empirical, practical, and grounded in observation, while Plato's is more abstract and metaphysical, focusing on ideal Forms beyond the material world.

Plotinus (c. 204–270 CE) was a major philosopher in the late Roman Empire and the founder of Neoplatonism, a philosophical system that developed the ideas of Plato. Born in Lycopolis, Egypt (modern-day Asyut), Plotinus was deeply influenced by Plato and sought to refine and expand on his ideas. He studied in Alexandria under the philosopher Ammonius Saccas and later moved to Rome, where he established a school of philosophy. His teachings were compiled by his student Porphyry into six groups of nine treatises, called the Enneads.

Influence on Christianity:

Plotinus' philosophy, particularly through the work of his followers like Porphyry, had a profound influence on early Christian thought, especially in the development of Christian mysticism and theology. Though Plotinus himself did not identify with Christianity and sometimes expressed criticism of certain religious beliefs, many of his ideas were adapted by Christian thinkers, particularly in the following ways:

1. The Concept of God: Plotinus' idea of The One as an ineffable, transcendent source influenced the Christian conception of God, particularly in the development of negative theology (apophatic theology), which emphasizes that God is beyond human comprehension and can only be described in terms of what He is not.

2. Emanation and Creation: The Neoplatonic notion of emanation influenced the way Christian theologians understood creation ex nihilo (creation out of nothing). While Plotinus taught that everything flows from The One by necessity, Christians adapted this to the idea that God freely created the world, but they still retained a hierarchical view of reality similar to Plotinus' system.

3. The Soul's Ascent and Mysticism: Plotinus' teaching about the soul's ascent to mystical union with The One influenced Christian mysticism, particularly in the works of early Church Fathers like Origen and Augustine. The idea that the soul can rise to direct experience of the divine became a cornerstone of Christian contemplative practice. In particular, the concept of the Beatific Vision (the direct experience of God in heaven) resonates with Plotinus' idea of mystical union with The One.

4. Influence on Augustine: Saint Augustine (354–430 CE), one of the most influential Christian theologians, was deeply influenced by Neoplatonism, particularly Plotinus. Before his conversion to Christianity, Augustine was a follower of Manichaeism, but after encountering the works of Plotinus and other Neoplatonists, he integrated many of their ideas into his theology. Augustine adopted Plotinus' hierarchical cosmology and adapted the idea of the soul's journey back to God. Augustine's understanding of God's nature, evil as privation of good, and the inner ascent of the soul toward divine union bear clear traces of Plotinus' influence.

5. Christian Mysticism: Plotinus' influence extended into the Christian mystical tradition, particularly in the writings of Pseudo-Dionysius the Areopagite and the Cappadocian Fathers (Basil the Great, Gregory of Nyssa, and Gregory of Nazianzus). The themes of divine unity, the soul's ascent, and apophatic theology became central to Christian mystical practices throughout the Middle Ages, inspiring figures like Meister Eckhart and John of the Cross.

Stoicism is an ancient Greek school of philosophy founded in Athens by Zeno of Citium in the early 3rd century BCE. Stoicism emphasizes ethics as the central focus of human life and teaches that virtue, understood as living in harmony with nature and reason, is the highest good. The philosophy is based on understanding the workings of the world and aligning oneself with the natural order to achieve tranquility, resilience, and fulfillment. Stoicism has had a profound influence not only on ancient philosophical thought but also on later Western intellectual traditions, particularly in ethics and personal development.

Key Principles of Stoicism:

1. Living According to Nature: The core idea of Stoicism is that we should live in accordance with nature. This means understanding the world as a rational, ordered system (the cosmos) and aligning our actions and desires with the natural laws of the universe. According to Stoics, nature is governed by reason (logos), and humans, as rational beings, should live in harmony with this natural order.

2. Virtue as the Highest Good: For Stoics, virtue is the only true good and the ultimate aim of life. Virtue is defined as excellence of character and wisdom, and it involves living in accordance with reason. External things like wealth, health, and fame are considered "indifferents"—neither good nor bad in themselves. The Stoics taught that we should not base our happiness on things outside of our control but rather on our own virtuous actions.

3. Four Cardinal Virtues: Stoicism identifies four cardinal virtues, which are essential for living a virtuous and good life:

   • Wisdom (Sophia): The ability to judge correctly and to know what is good, bad, or indifferent.

- Courage (Andreia): The strength to act in accordance with reason despite fear, adversity, or suffering.

- Justice (Dikaiosyne): Treating others fairly and recognizing the common good.

- Temperance (Sophrosyne): The ability to control one's desires and impulses, exhibiting moderation and self-discipline.

4. Dichotomy of Control: A central tenet of Stoicism is the dichotomy of control, which teaches that some things are within our control (our thoughts, actions, and attitudes), while others are not (external events, other people's actions, and outcomes). Stoics emphasize focusing on what is within our control and accepting whatever happens beyond that. This idea is captured in the Stoic maxim: "Focus on what you can control and let go of what you cannot."

5. Emotions and Rationality: Stoicism teaches that destructive emotions like anger, fear, and grief arise from errors in judgment, particularly from placing too much value on external things. Stoics do not advocate for suppressing emotions but for understanding and transforming them through reason. They distinguish between pathē (passions), which are irrational and harmful emotions, and eupatheiai (good emotions), such as joy and love, which are in harmony with reason.

6. Amor Fati (Love of Fate): Stoicism advocates embracing amor fati, the love of fate. Stoics believe that everything that happens is part of a greater rational plan, and we should accept whatever comes with equanimity, understanding that it is part of nature's design. This attitude cultivates resilience and prevents unnecessary suffering over things that cannot be changed.

7. Cosmopolitanism: Stoics view all human beings as part of a

larger community or cosmos. They taught that we are all citizens of the world, bound by shared rationality and a common humanity. This belief led to a deep commitment to justice and ethical treatment of others, regardless of nationality, social status, or race.

Influence and Legacy of Stoicism:

1. Modern Philosophy and Psychology: Stoicism has influenced many modern philosophical movements, especially existentialism and pragmatism. In recent years, Stoic ideas have been revived in modern contexts like Cognitive Behavioral Therapy (CBT), which shares Stoicism's focus on controlling thoughts and emotions by changing one's perspective. Stoicism has also seen a resurgence in the self-help movement, where its emphasis on personal responsibility, resilience, and focusing on what is within one's control resonates with contemporary values.

2. Popular Stoicism: Stoicism has seen a revival in modern popular culture, particularly in the context of personal development and leadership. Figures like Ryan Holiday have helped bring Stoic principles to a wide audience, emphasizing the practical application of Stoic wisdom for success and mental fortitude in modern life.

Stoicism is a philosophy focused on living virtuously in harmony with nature and reason, recognizing what is within our control and accepting what is not. Its teachings on virtue, emotional resilience, and the importance of rational action have had a lasting influence on both ancient and modern thought. The major Stoic philosophers—Zeno, Chrysippus, Seneca, Epictetus, and Marcus Aurelius—each contributed to the development and practical application of this influential philosophical tradition.

Meister Eckhart (c. 1260–1328) was a German Dominican friar, theologian, philosopher, and mystic, widely regarded as one of the most profound Christian mystics of the Middle Ages. Born near Gotha in modern-day Germany, Eckhart joined the Dominican Order at a young age and studied in Cologne and Paris. He became a renowned teacher and preacher, holding positions such as prior of the Dominican monastery in Erfurt and vicar general of Bohemia. Later in life, he faced charges of heresy due to the radical nature of some of his mystical teachings, but he died before the final verdict of the inquisition was delivered.

Influence and Legacy:

1. Mystical Theology: Eckhart's thought profoundly influenced Christian mysticism, particularly the Rhineland mystics, such as Johannes Tauler and Henry Suso, who were also part of the Dominican tradition. His emphasis on inner experience, detachment, and union with God helped shape the spiritual practices of many later Christian mystics.

2. Charges of Heresy: Some of Eckhart's teachings were controversial in their time, especially his statements about the identity of the soul with God and his ideas of detachment. In 1326, he was brought before the Inquisition, and after defending himself, several of his propositions were condemned as heretical in 1329, after his death. However, modern scholars often interpret Eckhart's ideas as attempts to express the ineffable nature of mystical experience, and he has since been recognized as an important figure in Christian theology.

3. Modern Influence: In the modern era, Eckhart's teachings have influenced a wide range of religious thinkers and philosophers, including those outside the Christian tradition. He has been appreciated by existentialists, Buddhists, and ad-

herents of Eastern philosophies for his emphasis on detachment, inner stillness, and direct experience of the divine.

René Descartes (1596–1650) was a French philosopher, mathematician, and scientist, often regarded as the father of modern Western philosophy. Born in La Haye en Touraine, France, he was educated at the Jesuit college of La Flèche and later earned a law degree. Descartes sought a new approach to knowledge, one that emphasized reason and certainty. He is known for his groundbreaking contributions to philosophy and mathematics, particularly his formulation of Cartesian dualism and the development of analytical geometry. Descartes spent much of his life traveling across Europe and living in the Netherlands before moving to Sweden, where he died while serving as a tutor to Queen Christina.

Key Aspects of Descartes' Philosophy:

1. Cogito, Ergo Sum (I Think, Therefore I Am): Descartes is perhaps most famous for his declaration, "Cogito, ergo sum" ("I think, therefore I am"). This statement is the foundational element of his epistemological project. Descartes sought to establish a certain and indubitable foundation for knowledge. By systematically doubting everything, including his own senses and the external world, he arrived at the conclusion that the very act of doubting proves the existence of the doubter. Thinking, in any form (doubt, questioning, affirming), confirms the reality of the self as a thinking being. This became the cornerstone of his philosophy.

2. Method of Doubt: Descartes employed a radical skepticism, often referred to as methodical doubt, in his quest for certainty. He proposed that all beliefs and knowledge should be subjected to doubt until something indubitable could be

found. This led him to doubt everything that could potentially be false, including the evidence of the senses, memories, and even the existence of the physical world. His method of doubt culminated in the certainty of the Cogito, which he considered the first principle of philosophy.

3. Dualism (Mind-Body Distinction): Descartes is famous for his theory of substance dualism, also known as Cartesian dualism. He argued that reality consists of two fundamentally distinct substances:

- Res cogitans (the thinking substance, or mind): The immaterial mind or soul, characterized by thought, reason, and consciousness.

- Res extensa (the extended substance, or body): The material, physical world that occupies space and is subject to the laws of physics.

4. Descartes maintained that the mind and body are separate and distinct, but they interact with each other. He famously proposed that the pineal gland in the brain might be the point of interaction between the immaterial mind and the physical body, though this view was speculative. Descartes' dualism had significant implications for the development of modern philosophy, particularly in discussions about the nature of consciousness and the relationship between mind and body.

5. Mechanistic View of the Physical World: Descartes viewed the physical world, including the human body, as a machine that operated according to deterministic laws. He applied a mechanistic approach to biology and physics, seeing the body as a complex machine composed of parts interacting in a predictable manner, much like a clock or other mechanical devices. This approach laid the groundwork for the scientific revolution and the development of modern physics.

6. Clear and Distinct Ideas: Descartes believed that clear and distinct ideas were the foundation of true knowledge. He argued that if an idea could be grasped clearly and distinctly by the mind, then it must be true. This criterion of clarity and distinctness became the standard by which Descartes evaluated knowledge, including the existence of God and the external world.

7. Proof of God's Existence: Descartes offered several arguments for the existence of God, most famously his version of the ontological argument. He reasoned that the idea of a perfect, infinite being (God) must have come from a perfect, infinite source, as finite beings like humans cannot conceive of infinity on their own. Therefore, the very idea of God implies His existence. Descartes also argued that the existence of a benevolent God guarantees the reliability of human reasoning and the existence of the external world, as a good God would not deceive us about the basic nature of reality.

8. Mathematical and Scientific Contributions: In addition to his philosophical contributions, Descartes made important advances in mathematics, particularly in the development of analytical geometry. He introduced the idea of using algebraic equations to describe geometric shapes, which led to the Cartesian coordinate system (named after him). This innovation helped bridge the gap between algebra and geometry and became fundamental to modern mathematics.

9. The "Cartesian Circle": One critique of Descartes' philosophy is the so-called Cartesian Circle, a potential circular reasoning in his argument. Descartes claimed that clear and distinct ideas are true because God guarantees their truth, but he also used the clarity and distinctness of his idea of God to prove God's existence. Critics argue that this creates a circular dependency between the proof of God and the reliability

of clear and distinct ideas.

Influence and Legacy:

• Rationalism: Descartes is often seen as the father of rationalism, a philosophical approach that emphasizes reason as the primary source of knowledge. He, along with philosophers like Spinoza and Leibniz, formed the core of the rationalist tradition, which contrasts with empiricism (which emphasizes sensory experience) as represented by figures like John Locke and David Hume.

• Modern Philosophy: Descartes' emphasis on skepticism, the individual thinker, and the primacy of reason influenced the development of modern philosophy, including both continental philosophy and analytic philosophy. His work laid the groundwork for later philosophical discussions about the nature of mind, knowledge, and reality.

• Mind-Body Problem: Descartes' mind-body dualism sparked centuries of debate about the relationship between consciousness and the physical world, a discussion that continues to be central to philosophy of mind and cognitive science.

• Scientific Method: Descartes' mechanistic worldview contributed to the development of the scientific method and the modern scientific approach to understanding the natural world. His idea that the physical universe could be understood in terms of mathematical laws helped advance the study of physics and other sciences.

John Locke (1632–1704) was an English philosopher and physician, widely regarded as one of the most influential thinkers of the Enlightenment and a founding figure of modern empiricism.

Born in Wrington, Somerset, Locke studied at the University of Oxford, where he became interested in medicine and natural philosophy. He later worked as a tutor and physician, forming close relationships with political figures, which led him to become involved in government and political thought. His major works, particularly An Essay Concerning Human Understanding (1689) and Two Treatises of Government (1689), had a profound impact on both epistemology and political theory.

Key Aspects of John Locke's Philosophy:

1. Empiricism: Locke is often seen as the father of empiricism, a theory of knowledge that asserts that all knowledge comes from sensory experience. He rejected the notion of innate ideas—the idea that certain concepts or knowledge are present in the mind at birth (as was proposed by thinkers like Descartes and Plato). Instead, Locke argued that the mind at birth is a tabula rasa (a blank slate), and that all knowledge is built up through experience—both sensation (external sensory experiences) and reflection (internal operations of the mind).

2. Theory of Knowledge: In An Essay Concerning Human Understanding, Locke sought to explore the nature of human knowledge and how we come to know the world. He divided knowledge into three types:

   • Intuitive knowledge: Immediate and self-evident truths, such as "I exist."

   • Demonstrative knowledge: Knowledge that is logically deduced, such as mathematical proofs.

   • Sensitive knowledge: Knowledge gained from the senses, which Locke believed was less certain than the other two but still reliable for navigating the world.

3. Locke emphasized that our understanding is limited, and we can never achieve absolute certainty about the external world, but we can have a reasonable degree of confidence based on experience.

4. Primary and Secondary Qualities: Locke distinguished between primary qualities and secondary qualities in objects.

    • Primary qualities are inherent in the object and exist independently of the observer (e.g., solidity, extension, motion, number).

    • Secondary qualities depend on the perception of the observer and do not exist in the object itself (e.g., color, taste, sound, and smell). According to Locke, primary qualities are objective, while secondary qualities are subjective.

5. State of Nature and Political Theory: In his Two Treatises of Government, Locke developed a theory of politics grounded in natural rights and social contract theory. He rejected the divine right of kings, a dominant idea in his time, and argued that legitimate government is based on the consent of the governed.

    • State of Nature: Locke described the state of nature as a state of equality and freedom, where individuals have the natural rights to life, liberty, and property. Unlike Thomas Hobbes, who saw the state of nature as chaotic and violent, Locke viewed it more positively, as a place of relative peace and equality, though not without its challenges.

    • Natural Rights: Locke argued that individuals have certain inalienable rights by virtue of being human. These include the right to life, liberty, and property, which exist prior to and independent of government.

        • Social Contract: Locke believed that individuals form

governments through a social contract to protect their natural rights. If a government fails to protect these rights or becomes tyrannical, Locke asserted that the people have the right to revolt and establish a new government. This idea of the right to revolt had a significant influence on the development of liberal democratic theory and was a key inspiration for the American and French revolutions.

6. Religious Tolerance: Locke was a strong advocate for religious tolerance, arguing that the government should not impose any specific religion on its citizens. In his Letters Concerning Toleration, he argued that the state should focus on protecting civil interests (like life, liberty, and property) rather than enforcing religious conformity. Locke, however, excluded atheists and Roman Catholics from this tolerance because he believed their beliefs undermined social order and government authority.

7. The Right to Property: One of Locke's most significant contributions to political philosophy was his theory of property. He argued that property rights are a natural extension of the right to self-preservation. According to Locke, individuals have a right to the fruits of their labor. By mixing their labor with nature (for example, farming land), they acquire property rights over it. This theory of property laid the foundation for later capitalist and liberal thought.

8. Influence on Liberalism and Constitutionalism: Locke's political philosophy is considered foundational to modern liberalism and the development of constitutional government. His ideas about the protection of individual rights, the separation of powers, and the need for government to be accountable to the people heavily influenced later political thinkers like Montesquieu, Rousseau, and the framers of the U.S. Constitution, including Thomas Jefferson and James Madi-

son. Locke's emphasis on the right to property and individual freedoms is a cornerstone of classical liberalism and democratic governance.

Differences between Locke and Descartes:

- Locke is an empiricist who believes that all knowledge comes from experience, rejecting innate ideas, and focusing on probable knowledge based on sensory input. He emphasized political philosophy and natural rights, seeing government as a social contract aimed at protecting life, liberty, and property.

- Descartes is a rationalist who believes that certain ideas are innate and that true knowledge comes from reason rather than experience. His philosophy centers on doubt, the certainty of the self's existence, and a sharp distinction between the mind and body, rooted in his dualism.

Locke's focus on experience and practical knowledge contrasts sharply with Descartes' quest for absolute certainty and his reliance on reason as the primary source of knowledge.

Immanuel Kant (1724–1804) was a German philosopher who is considered one of the most influential figures in Western philosophy. He was born in Königsberg, East Prussia (now Kaliningrad, Russia), and spent his entire academic career there, primarily as a professor at the University of Königsberg. Kant made groundbreaking contributions to metaphysics, epistemology, ethics, and aesthetics. His most famous work, Critique of Pure Reason (1781), profoundly shaped modern philosophy, especially through his theory of transcendental idealism. Kant's other major works include the Critique of Practical Reason

(1788), which deals with his moral philosophy, and the Critique of Judgment (1790), which addresses aesthetics and teleology.

Kant sought to reconcile the empirical philosophy of David Hume and the rationalist tradition of René Descartes and Gottfried Leibniz. His critical philosophy redefined the limits of human knowledge, the nature of ethics, and the relationship between reason and experience.

Key Aspects of Kant's Philosophy:

1. Transcendental Idealism: Kant's transcendental idealism is one of his most significant contributions to metaphysics and epistemology. In his Critique of Pure Reason, Kant sought to answer the question: How is knowledge possible? He argued that human beings never know things as they are in themselves (noumena), but only as they appear to us through the filter of our senses and cognitive structures (phenomena). In other words, reality is shaped by the way our mind processes it.

   • Phenomena: These are the objects and experiences as they appear to us, shaped by our perceptions, concepts, and cognitive faculties.

   • Noumena: These refer to things as they are in themselves, independent of our perceptions and understanding. Kant argued that while noumena exist, we cannot have direct knowledge of them because we are limited to experiencing phenomena.

2. Kant called his approach "Copernican Revolution" in philosophy because, like Copernicus' discovery that the Earth revolves around the Sun, Kant claimed that it is not the world that shapes knowledge, but rather the mind that shapes the way we experience the world.

3. Synthetic A Priori Judgments: One of Kant's crucial contributions to epistemology was his distinction between different kinds of judgments:

   • Analytic a priori judgments: These are statements that are true by definition and do not require experience to verify (e.g., "All bachelors are unmarried").

   • Synthetic a posteriori judgments: These are statements that require experience to be verified (e.g., "The apple is red").

4. However, Kant introduced a third category:

   • Synthetic a priori judgments: These are statements that are not true by definition but can be known independently of experience. An example is mathematics or statements like "Every event has a cause." Kant argued that these kinds of judgments are possible because the mind actively organizes experience according to certain fundamental principles, such as space, time, and causality.

5. This discovery was essential to his theory of knowledge because it showed that some truths about the world (like mathematical and causal laws) are not just derived from experience but also structured by the human mind.

6. The Categories of the Understanding: According to Kant, human experience is structured by categories of the understanding—innate concepts in the mind that organize sensory data. These categories include causality, unity, plurality, substance, necessity, and others. These are not learned through experience; rather, they are the basic framework through which all experience is interpreted. Without these categories, experience would be a chaotic collection of sensory impressions with no coherent structure.

7. Moral Philosophy and the Categorical Imperative: In

his Groundwork for the Metaphysics of Morals and Critique of Practical Reason, Kant developed his influential moral philosophy, which is based on the concept of the categorical imperative. For Kant, moral law is derived from reason, and ethical actions are those that are done out of duty, not out of desire or inclination. The categorical imperative is a universal moral law that commands us to act according to principles that could be consistently willed as universal laws. Kant proposed several formulations of the categorical imperative, the most famous of which are:

• Universalizability: "Act only according to that maxim whereby you can at the same time will that it should become a universal law."

• Humanity as an End: "Act in such a way that you treat humanity, whether in your own person or in the person of another, always at the same time as an end, and never merely as a means."

8. Kant argued that moral actions are not based on the consequences of an action but on whether they conform to these rational principles. An action is moral if it can be universally applied and respects the inherent dignity of all rational beings.

9. Autonomy and Freedom: Central to Kant's ethics is the concept of autonomy, which refers to the capacity of rational agents to legislate moral law for themselves through reason. For Kant, to be morally autonomous means to act according to principles you have rationally chosen, rather than being driven by external forces or desires. Freedom, in Kant's view, is not just the ability to do what one wants but the ability to act in accordance with reason and moral law.

10. Critique of Judgment (Aesthetics and Teleology): In his Critique of Judgment, Kant addressed questions of aesthetics (the philosophy of beauty and art) and teleology (the philosophy of purpose). He distinguished between the beautiful and the sublime in art and nature, with beauty being connected to a sense of harmony and order, and the sublime evoking awe and grandeur, often in the face of vastness or power. Kant also introduced the idea of "purposiveness without purpose" in art, suggesting that we perceive beauty when something appears to have an inherent purpose or order, even though it may not serve any practical function. In the realm of teleology, Kant examined how we perceive the natural world as having purpose, though he was careful to argue that such teleological judgments are reflective rather than constitutive. In other words, we interpret nature as though it has purpose, but this does not mean it actually does.

11. Religion and Rational Faith: In Religion within the Bounds of Mere Reason (1793), Kant explored the relationship between religion and morality. He argued that religion should be grounded in rational ethics rather than dogma or supernatural beliefs. For Kant, the ethical law within us points to the idea of God as a moral postulate—a rational necessity that helps make sense of the idea of perfect justice and the afterlife. However, he maintained that religion must be subordinate to reason and moral law.

Influence and Legacy:

1. Influence on Philosophy: Kant's work had an immense influence on nearly every branch of philosophy. His transcendental idealism directly influenced later idealist philosophers

like Johann Gottlieb Fichte, Friedrich Schelling, and Georg Wilhelm Friedrich Hegel, leading to the development of German Idealism. His ethical philosophy also laid the groundwork for deontological ethics, which remains a central theory in moral philosophy.

2. Impact on Science and Epistemology: Kant's theory that the mind actively shapes experience influenced later philosophical developments in epistemology and the philosophy of science. His ideas on the limits of human knowledge and the conditions that make knowledge possible continue to shape discussions in both analytic and continental philosophy.

3. Critique and Development by Successors: Kant's philosophy was critically developed by figures like Hegel, who argued that Kant's rigid separation between noumena and phenomena was problematic. In the 20th century, philosophers like Martin Heidegger and Jean-Paul Sartre critiqued and adapted Kant's work, especially his ideas on subjectivity and the nature of freedom.

4. Influence on Modern Ethics: Kant's moral philosophy, especially the categorical imperative, remains one of the dominant frameworks in ethical theory. His insistence on the dignity of rational beings and the universality of moral principles has had a profound impact on debates about human rights, justice, and global ethics.

John Stuart Mill (1806–1873) was an English philosopher, political economist, and one of the most influential figures in the development of liberal thought in the 19th century. Born in London, he was the son of James Mill, a Scottish philosopher and economist, and was educated rigorously from a young age. His father, a follower of Jeremy Bentham, instilled in Mill a deep commitment to utilitarianism. Mill became a prominent advocate for personal liberty, women's rights, and social reform. Throughout his life, he worked as an administrator for the British East India Company, was a member of Parliament, and produced numerous influential works, including Utilitarianism (1863), On Liberty (1859), The Subjection of Women (1869), and Principles of Political Economy (1848).

Mill's philosophical work bridges various fields, including ethics, political philosophy, economics, and epistemology, and he is particularly remembered for his defense of individual liberty, his utilitarian ethics, and his progressive views on social issues like women's rights and freedom of expressi

Mill is best known for his contribution to utilitarianism, an ethical theory developed by Jeremy Bentham, which holds that the right action is the one that maximizes overall happiness or utility. While Bentham focused on quantitative hedonism (measuring pleasure and pain solely by their amount), Mill refined utilitarianism by distinguishing between higher and lower pleasures.

The Utility of Rules: Unlike Bentham, who focused on act utilitarianism (evaluating each action by its utility), Mill leaned toward rule utilitarianism—the idea that general rules, based on their utility, should guide behavior. In this framework, following rules that generally promote the greatest happiness will, in the long term, lead to better outcomes than constantly evaluating each individual action by its immediate utility. For instance, a rule that enforces respect for property rights may promote overall happiness more than evaluating each instance of theft or charity independently.

Jeremy Bentham (1748–1832) was an English philosopher, jurist, and social reformer, best known as the founder of modern utilitarianism. Born in London to a wealthy family, Bentham was a child prodigy who began studying Latin at the age of three and entered Queen's College, Oxford, at just twelve. After completing his studies, he trained as a lawyer but became disillusioned with the English legal system and instead turned his focus to social reform and philosophy.

Bentham is renowned for his work on the principle of utility, which he summarized as "the greatest happiness of the greatest number." He applied this principle to a wide range of subjects, including law, politics, ethics, and economics, advocating for reforms in areas such as criminal justice, education, and public health. Bentham's belief in the need to maximize overall happiness led him to propose progressive ideas, including prison reform, legal codification, and animal rights.

One of Bentham's most enduring contributions was his development of the hedonic calculus, a method for calculating the balance of pleasure and pain generated by an action, which he used to determine its moral worth. He was also an outspoken advocate of individual and economic liberty, separation of church and state, equal rights for women, the abolition of slavery, and free speech. Bentham's ideas on legal positivism, which posits that laws should be based on reason and utility rather than morality or religion, were highly influential.

Though he had little direct impact during his lifetime, Bentham's works were foundational for later thinkers, particularly John Stuart Mill, who expanded upon Bentham's ideas and gave utilitarianism a more humanistic interpretation. Bentham's influence extended into law and government, particularly in the realm of legal reform, and his principles are still reflected in contemporary political and ethical theory.

John Stuart Mill and Jeremy Bentham are two of the most prominent philosophers associated with utilitarianism, a

consequentialist ethical theory that holds that actions are right if they promote the greatest happiness for the greatest number. However, despite their shared commitment to this principle, their versions of utilitarianism differ significantly in terms of how they understand pleasure, happiness, and the role of individual rights.

Aspect	Jeremy Bentham	John Stuart Mill
Pleasure and Happiness	Quantitative Hedonism: All pleasures are equal in kind, only differing in quantity.	Qualitative Hedonism: Higher intellectual pleasures are superior to lower physical pleasures.
Act vs. Rule Utilitarianism	Act Utilitarianism: Evaluate each action individually based on its consequences.	Rule Utilitarianism (leanings): General rules promote happiness over time, even if specific actions might not maximize immediate pleasure.
Individual Rights	Rights are subordinate to overall utility; can be sacrificed for greater happiness.	Individual rights are crucial to long-term happiness and should be protected to foster personal liberty.
Liberty and Freedom	No inherent belief in liberty; rights are instrumental to utility.	Strong emphasis on individual liberty and the harm principle; personal freedom is essential to happiness.
Ethical Focus	Simple calculation of pleasure and pain; focused on outcomes.	Nuanced ethical considerations; focused on human flourishing and moral development.
Social Progress	Advocated legal and social reforms based on increasing happiness.	Advocated reforms to promote human development and individual freedom for long-term societal progress.

Henri Bergson (1859–1941) was a French philosopher whose ideas significantly influenced 20th-century thought, particularly in areas such as metaphysics, psychology, and the philosophy of time and consciousness. He was born in Paris and showed early brilliance in both the sciences and the humanities. After studying at the prestigious École Normale Supérieure, he became a professor of philosophy at various institutions, including the Collège de France. His major works, such as Time and Free Will (1889), Matter and Memory (1896), Creative Evolution (1907), and The Two Sources of Morality and Religion (1932), made him one of the leading intellectual figures of his time. Bergson received the Nobel Prize for Literature in 1927 for his ability to blend philosophical thought with creative expression. His work sparked debates across philosophy, literature, and the sciences.

Key Aspects of Bergson's Philosophy:

1. Élan Vital (Vital Impulse) and Creative Evolution: One of Bergson's most famous ideas is the concept of élan vital, or vital impulse, which he described in his book Creative Evolution (1907). This idea challenges the mechanistic and deterministic views of biological evolution promoted by thinkers like Darwin. Bergson proposed that life is driven by a creative and dynamic force that cannot be fully explained by natural selection or the adaptation of organisms to their environments. The élan vital is a spontaneous, non-material, and creative force that propels life forward in unpredictable and novel ways. Evolution, according to Bergson, is not merely the result of external pressures but also of this internal creative drive.

2. Duration (La Durée): Central to Bergson's philosophy is his concept of duration (la durée), which he introduced in Time and Free Will (1889). Bergson argued that time, as experienced by human consciousness, is not the same as the quantitative, measurable time of clocks and science. Instead, real time, or duration, is qualitative and continuous, not divided into discrete units like seconds or minutes. Human ex-

perience of time is fluid and lived, involving memory and change. Bergson emphasized the difference between clock time (which he called spatialized time) and lived time, which is indivisible and experienced as an ongoing flow. Duration is critical to understanding consciousness, freedom, and creativity. He argued that human experience, particularly our sense of free will, is rooted in this lived, qualitative time rather than the mechanical, segmented time of science.

3. Intuition vs. Intellect: Bergson made a famous distinction between intuition and intellect as ways of knowing.

   Intellect is analytical, logical, and geared toward practical, scientific understanding. It tends to break things down into discrete parts and views the world in a mechanistic, deterministic way. While useful for everyday tasks and science, it fails to grasp the deeper reality of life and consciousness.

   Intuition, on the other hand, is a direct, non-analytical way of understanding reality. Bergson argued that intuition allows us to grasp the fluid and dynamic aspects of reality, particularly the nature of time and consciousness. Intuition, for Bergson, is essential to understanding duration, life, and evolution because it connects us to the continuous flow of experience, which the intellect cannot fully capture.

4. Matter and Memory: In his 1896 work Matter and Memory, Bergson explored the relationship between mind and body and developed a theory of perception and memory that challenged prevailing dualist and materialist views. He argued that memory is not merely a function of the brain but is tied to consciousness and exists independently of the material world. For Bergson, memory is a bridge between past and present, and it plays a key role in shaping our experience of duration. The body, according to Bergson, is the interface

between the mind (which stores memory and consciousness) and the external, material world.

5. Free Will: In Time and Free Will, Bergson argued against deterministic views of human action. He believed that free will exists and is rooted in duration—the lived experience of time. He argued that when we act freely, our actions are not determined by external forces but arise from the inner flow of consciousness, which integrates past experiences and present intentions. For Bergson, the deterministic view of human action is a result of confusing time with space; when we experience time as a flowing, creative process, we see that we are not bound by rigid causality.

6. The Two Sources of Morality and Religion: In this later work, Bergson explored the origins of morality and religion. He distinguished between two types of morality:

• Closed morality, which is rigid and rooted in social pressure and obligation, maintaining the cohesion of small, closed societies.

• Open morality, which is dynamic, evolving, and based on universal love and creativity, exemplified by figures like mystics and saints. Bergson also distinguished between static religion, which reinforces social cohesion and order, and dynamic religion, which is a creative force that inspires individuals to transcend narrow societal norms and aspire toward universal values.

7. Critique of Mechanism and Determinism: Bergson opposed the deterministic view of the universe advanced by classical mechanics and naturalistic science. He rejected the idea that everything in the universe, including life and consciousness, could be explained by mechanical laws. In his philosophy, life and consciousness are marked by spontaneity, creativity,

and novelty, which cannot be reduced to mechanistic causality.

Influence and Legacy of Bergson:

1. Influence on Existentialism and Phenomenology: Bergson's emphasis on lived experience and the fluid nature of time influenced later existentialist and phenomenological philosophers, such as Jean-Paul Sartre and Maurice Merleau-Ponty. His idea of duration as a continuous flow of consciousness resonated with the existentialist focus on human freedom and subjectivity, as well as the phenomenological study of human perception and experience.

2. Impact on Psychology and Literature: Bergson's ideas on memory, time, and consciousness also influenced early developments in psychology, particularly in theories about how memory shapes perception and self-identity. His work influenced writers such as Marcel Proust, who explored the idea of memory and time in In Search of Lost Time. Bergson's focus on intuition and the creative force of life resonated with many literary modernists.

3. Nobel Prize and Popular Influence: Bergson's clear, eloquent style of writing and his ability to blend philosophy with vivid metaphors made him widely popular, even beyond academic circles. In 1927, he was awarded the Nobel Prize in Literature for his work, which was praised for its philosophical and literary qualities. His lectures drew large audiences, and he was a major figure in public intellectual life in France and beyond in the early 20th century.

4. Influence on Process Philosophy: Bergson's ideas about time, evolution, and creativity had an impact on the development of process philosophy, particularly influencing thinkers like Alfred North Whitehead. Process philosophy empha-

sizes change, becoming, and the dynamic nature of reality.

Edmund Husserl (1859–1938) was a German philosopher and the founder of phenomenology, a philosophical movement that had a profound influence on 20th-century philosophy, especially existentialism, hermeneutics, and deconstruction. Born in Prossnitz, Moravia (now part of the Czech Republic), Husserl studied mathematics and philosophy at several universities, including Leipzig and Vienna, under the guidance of notable thinkers like Franz Brentano. Initially, Husserl's academic work focused on mathematics and logic, but he later shifted his attention to questions of consciousness, perception, and the nature of experience. His groundbreaking work in phenomenology laid the foundations for much of modern European philosophy.

Key Aspects of Edmund Husserl's Philosophy:

1. Phenomenology: Husserl is best known as the founder of phenomenology, a philosophical method aimed at studying structures of consciousness and the way things appear in our experience. The term "phenomenology" comes from the Greek words phainomenon (that which appears) and logos (study or reason). Husserl's phenomenology seeks to describe the essential structures of lived experience without presupposing any theories about the external world. For Husserl, phenomenology is a first-person approach to philosophy. It emphasizes the careful description of how phenomena present themselves to consciousness, aiming to uncover the underlying structures that make experience possible. The goal of phenomenology is to get to the essence of experience by "bracketing" (or suspending) assumptions about the existence of the external world—a method Husserl called epoché.

2. Intentionality: One of Husserl's key concepts is intentionality, a term he borrowed from his teacher, Franz Brentano. Intentionality refers to the idea that consciousness is always directed toward something. In other words, every mental act (whether it is perceiving, imagining, or judging) is about something external to the mind. This means that consciousness is never empty or isolated; it is always related to an object or content, even if the object is imaginary or abstract. Husserl emphasized that the relationship between consciousness and its objects is fundamental to understanding human experience. Rather than focusing on the nature of the external world in itself (which is the domain of traditional metaphysics), phenomenology focuses on how objects appear to us through the lens of consciousness.

3. Epoché (Phenomenological Reduction): A central technique in Husserl's phenomenology is the epoché, also known as the phenomenological reduction. This involves "bracketing" or setting aside all assumptions about the existence of the external world in order to focus purely on the contents of consciousness and how things appear to us. The epoché does not deny the existence of the external world; instead, it suspends judgment about it in order to explore the structures of experience without interference from preconceived notions. By employing the epoché, Husserl believed we could reach the "essence" of phenomena—the fundamental, invariant structures of experience. This method allows philosophers to describe the ways in which objects and experiences manifest themselves to consciousness, without being distracted by questions of whether the objects exist independently of the mind.

4. Noesis and Noema: Husserl introduced the distinction between noesis and noema to describe two fundamental aspects

of intentional consciousness.

• Noesis refers to the act of consciousness (e.g., perceiving, imagining, remembering).

• Noema refers to the object or content of that consciousness (what is perceived, imagined, or remembered).

5. For example, in the act of seeing a tree, the noesis is the act of seeing, while the noema is the perceived tree. Husserl's goal was to analyze how different noetic acts (perception, judgment, memory, etc.) relate to their corresponding noematic contents in experience. This analysis forms the basis of his phenomenological investigations.

6. Lifeworld (Lebenswelt): In his later work, especially in The Crisis of European Sciences and Transcendental Phenomenology (1936), Husserl introduced the concept of the lifeworld (or Lebenswelt). The lifeworld refers to the pre-reflective, everyday world of lived experience that serves as the background for all our thoughts and actions. It is the world we experience directly, before any scientific or theoretical interpretation of it. Husserl believed that modern science, with its focus on objective, quantifiable phenomena, had lost sight of this fundamental dimension of human existence. By returning to the lifeworld and exploring how we experience the world in our everyday lives, Husserl aimed to reconnect philosophy with the immediate, concrete experience of life.

7. Transcendental Phenomenology: In his mature work, Husserl developed the idea of transcendental phenomenology, a method for exploring the conditions that make experience possible. By "bracketing" the natural world, Husserl argued, we could access the transcendental ego—the pure, underlying structure of consciousness that remains when all empirical and contingent factors are set aside.

Husserl's transcendental phenomenology aimed to uncover the universal structures of experience that are shared by all human beings. By investigating the essential features of consciousness (such as time, space, intentionality, and intersubjectivity), Husserl sought to reveal the fundamental ways in which we experience the world.

8. Intersubjectivity: Although phenomenology focuses on individual experience, Husserl also explored the concept of intersubjectivity, or the ways in which different subjects share a common world of experience. He believed that we are not isolated in our own subjectivity but rather live in a world that is shared and co-constituted with others. The lifeworld is always a social world, where meanings and experiences are shaped by interaction with other people. Intersubjectivity became an important theme in later phenomenology, particularly in the work of philosophers like Maurice Merleau-Ponty and Emmanuel Levinas, who expanded on Husserl's ideas to explore the social and ethical dimensions of experience.

Martin Heidegger (1889–1976) was a German philosopher and one of the most influential figures in 20th-century philosophy. He is best known for his work in existentialism and phenomenology, particularly through his seminal work, Being and Time (1927). Heidegger was born in Messkirch, Germany, and initially trained in theology before turning to philosophy, studying under Edmund Husserl at the University of Freiburg. He later succeeded Husserl as a professor there. Though his philosophical contributions are vast, Heidegger's involvement with the Nazi party during the 1930s cast a shadow over his legacy. Despite this, his work has been crucial in shaping existentialist thought, hermeneutics, and deconstruction, influencing philosophers like

Jean-Paul Sartre, Maurice Merleau-Ponty, and Jacques Derrida.

Key Aspects of Heidegger's Philosophy:

1. Being (Sein) and Ontology: Heidegger's primary philosophical concern was with the concept of Being (what it means for something to exist). His philosophy revolves around the question of "What is Being?"—a question that had been largely overlooked since ancient philosophy. In Being and Time, Heidegger argues that philosophers have been too focused on individual beings (entities) rather than on Being itself. Heidegger's goal was to reignite the philosophical study of Being (ontology) by exploring how humans experience and understand existence.

2. Dasein: A central concept in Heidegger's philosophy is Dasein, a German term meaning "being-there." Dasein refers to human existence or being-in-the-world. For Heidegger, humans are unique because they are aware of their own existence and question what it means to be. Dasein is not a detached observer of the world; rather, it is always already embedded in the world, interacting with it and understanding itself in relation to it. This concept shifts philosophy's focus from abstract thought to lived experience.

3. Being-in-the-World: Heidegger rejected the traditional subject-object distinction found in much of Western philosophy, where the individual subject is seen as separate from the world of objects. Instead, he developed the idea of Being-in-the-World to emphasize that human beings are always already involved in their surroundings. We exist as part of the world, not as detached observers. This interaction is fundamental to understanding our own Being. Our existence is relational, meaning that we are always interacting with people, things, and situations.

4. Thrownness (Geworfenheit): Heidegger introduced the concept of thrownness to describe the condition of being "thrown" into the world without choice. We do not choose the circumstances of our birth, our culture, or the historical moment in which we live, yet these conditions shape our existence. Thrownness highlights the contingent and finite nature of human life—we are situated in a world we did not create, and this fact fundamentally shapes our experience of Being.

5. Authenticity and Inauthenticity: Heidegger made a distinction between authentic and inauthentic ways of being.

• Inauthenticity arises when individuals conform to the expectations and norms of society without critically reflecting on their own existence. In everyday life, we often lose ourselves in routine and distractions, living according to the dictates of the "they" (what Heidegger called Das Man—the anonymous "one" or "they").

• Authenticity, on the other hand, involves confronting the reality of one's own existence, including the inevitability of death, and living in a way that reflects an understanding of one's individual freedom and responsibility. To live authentically is to own one's choices and act in accordance with a deeper awareness of one's own Being.

6. Being-toward-Death: One of Heidegger's most significant contributions to existential philosophy is his exploration of Being-toward-Death. Heidegger argued that an authentic understanding of life requires an acknowledgment of death. Death is not just an event that happens at the end of life; it is an ever-present possibility that shapes how we live. By confronting death, individuals can come to terms with their own finitude and live more authentically, rather than avoiding or

denying this aspect of their existence.

7. Temporality and Time: In Being and Time, Heidegger emphasized the importance of temporality in understanding human existence. For Heidegger, human beings are fundamentally temporal creatures, always existing in the context of time. Our sense of the past, present, and future plays a crucial role in how we understand ourselves and the world. Time is not an abstract, objective measure, but something that is intimately tied to our experience of Being. He described human existence as being oriented toward the future (anticipation of possibilities), connected to the past (which shapes who we are), and situated in the present.

8. The Question of Technology: Later in his career, Heidegger became concerned with the impact of modern technology on human life and the world. In works like The Question Concerning Technology (1954), Heidegger argued that technology reveals the world in a way that treats everything—including nature and human beings—as resources to be exploited and manipulated. This technological mode of revealing, which he called enframing(Gestell), limits our ability to experience the world in other, more authentic ways. Heidegger was not opposed to technology itself, but to the mindset it promotes, which reduces everything to its utility.

9. The Clearing (Lichtung) and Truth: Heidegger reinterpreted the concept of truth as unconcealment (aletheia), drawing on ancient Greek philosophy. He described truth as a process of things coming into the "clearing"(Lichtung), where they are revealed or disclosed. For Heidegger, truth is not just about correspondence between statements and facts, but about how beings reveal themselves to us. This concept is tied to his understanding of Being as something that emerges or becomes apparent, rather than something static and fixed.

Jean-Paul Sartre (1905–1980) was a French philosopher, playwright, novelist, political activist, and one of the leading figures of existentialism and phenomenology in the 20th century. Born in Paris, Sartre studied philosophy at the École Normale Supérieure, where he developed a deep interest in the works of philosophers like Hegel, Husserl, and Heidegger. Sartre's existentialist philosophy, as expressed in his major works such as Being and Nothingness (1943) and Existentialism Is a Humanism (1946), as well as his novels like Nausea (1938) and The Roads to Freedom series, left a profound mark on both philosophical and literary thought. He also became famous for his activism, particularly his involvement in Marxist and socialist movements, and his outspoken criticism of French colonialism and the Soviet Union.

Sartre received the Nobel Prize in Literature in 1964, but he famously declined it, stating that he did not want to be institutionalized by such an award. Sartre had a lifelong intellectual and personal partnership with fellow philosopher Simone de Beauvoir, and together they became prominent figures in Parisian intellectual and political life.

Key Aspects of Sartre's Philosophy:

1. Existence Precedes Essence: One of Sartre's most famous existentialist slogans is "existence precedes essence."This means that, unlike objects or tools that have a predefined essence (or purpose), human beings exist first and then define themselves through their choices and actions. Sartre rejected the idea that humans are born with a predetermined nature or purpose. Instead, he argued that individuals are radically free and must create their own essence or meaning through how they live. This leads to the responsibility of shaping one's own identity and destiny.

- Essence refers to the defining characteristics or purpose of an object or being.

- Existence refers to the fact of being or living.

2. According to Sartre, we are not born with any particular essence or purpose. Humans must define who they are through their actions and choices, giving them both freedom and responsibility.

3. Radical Freedom and Responsibility: Central to Sartre's philosophy is the notion of radical freedom. He believed that individuals have absolute freedom to choose their actions and shape their lives, but with this freedom comes radical responsibility. Since there are no predefined values or rules to guide us, we are entirely responsible for our choices. This responsibility can be overwhelming, leading to feelings of anxiety or anguish—the existential realization that we are alone in determining our path in a world without inherent meaning. Sartre argued that many people try to avoid the burden of freedom by denying it or by conforming to societal norms and expectations, a behavior he called bad faith (mauvaise foi). Bad faith occurs when individuals deceive themselves into thinking that they are not free and that their actions are determined by external forces such as societal roles, religious dictates, or other people.

4. Nothingness and Consciousness: In his major philosophical work Being and Nothingness (1943), Sartre distinguishes between two types of being:

- Being-in-itself: This refers to the being of objects or things that simply exist without consciousness, like a rock or a tree. They are self-contained and have a fixed essence.

- Being-for-itself: This refers to the being of conscious, self-aware individuals. Unlike objects, human beings are aware of their own existence and are not bound by a fixed essence. They are defined by their freedom and capacity for self-reflection.

5. Sartre introduces the concept of nothingness (néant) to explain human consciousness. He argued that human beings have the ability to negate or distance themselves from their current state of being, which allows them to envision future possibilities and alternative courses of action. This power of negation creates a gap between what we are and what we can be, giving rise to human freedom.

6. Bad Faith (Mauvaise Foi): Sartre's concept of bad faith is central to his existentialism. It refers to the human tendency to deny our own freedom and responsibility by hiding behind societal roles, external pressures, or deterministic beliefs. For example, a person might claim that they have no choice but to follow societal rules or the demands of others, when in fact they are avoiding the responsibility of making a choice for themselves.Bad faith involves self-deception—pretending that we are not free to act differently when, in fact, we are. Sartre believed that this is a common way in which people avoid confronting the anxiety that comes with freedom and responsibility. Living in bad faith means refusing to acknowledge one's own freedom, which leads to inauthentic existence.

7. Authenticity: In contrast to bad faith, authenticity is the recognition and acceptance of one's radical freedom and the responsibility that comes with it. To live authentically, according to Sartre, is to fully embrace one's freedom and create meaning through deliberate choices and actions. This requires individuals to face their existential angst and acknowledge that their life is defined by the choices they make,

even in the absence of any predetermined essence or values.

8. Being-for-Others: Sartre explored the complex relationships between individuals in his concept of Being-for-Others. He argued that we are not only conscious of ourselves but also aware of how others perceive us. This creates a dynamic tension, as other people's perceptions can shape or limit how we see ourselves. Sartre illustrated this idea famously through his example of the gaze, where being observed by another person causes us to become self-conscious and aware of ourselves as objects in their view. This interaction between self and others is characterized by conflict and struggle. Sartre argued that human relationships are often marked by attempts to dominate or control how we are seen by others, and vice versa. In his play No Exit (1944), Sartre famously summed up this idea with the line "Hell is other people" (L'enfer, c'est les autres), reflecting the tension that arises when we are subject to the judgments of others.

9. Atheistic Existentialism: Sartre's existentialism is often described as atheistic. He rejected the existence of a divine creator or any pre-established order to the universe. In his view, without God, humans are left to create their own meaning in an indifferent and often absurd world. This realization leads to existential angst, as individuals come to terms with the freedom and responsibility of living without external guidance or purpose. Sartre argued that we must face the "absurd" nature of existence and the fact that life has no inherent meaning, but this realization also opens the door to genuine freedom.

10. Commitment and Political Activism: Sartre was deeply involved in political and social causes throughout his life. He believed that existential freedom and responsibility extend beyond personal choices to the social and political realm.

His existentialist philosophy led him to engage in activism, where he championed the causes of workers, decolonization, and socialism. Sartre supported Marxism, though he critiqued the authoritarian aspects of Soviet communism. In his later works, Sartre developed the concept of "engagement" or "commitment", arguing that individuals must take responsibility not only for their own lives but also for the world they live in. His philosophy became increasingly focused on the collective struggle for freedom and justice, particularly in opposition to colonialism and oppression.

Philosopher	Edmund Husserl	Martin Heidegger	Jean-Paul Satre
Key Focus	Consciousness and the structures of experience	Being and existence (ontology)	Human freedom and responsibility in an absurd world
Method/ Approach	Phenomenological reduction (bracketing) to describe the essences of experience	Existential phenomenology focusing on Dasein and our relationship to Being	Existential phenomenology applied to human freedom, ethics, and meaning-making
Key Concepts	Intentionality, Epoché, Noesis/ Noema	Being-in-the-World, Dasein, Authenticity, Being-toward-Death	Existence precedes essence, Radical freedom, Bad faith, Being-for-Itself
Contribution	Founder of phenomenology; focus on epistemology and the structures of consciousness	Shifted phenomenology to ontology and existential analysis; focused on human finitude and authenticity	Developed a human-centered existentialism focused on freedom and responsibility; ethics of creating one's own values

- Husserl employed the epoché, a method of bracketing external assumptions to examine the essence of subjective experience.

- Heidegger rejected the bracketing approach and instead used existential phenomenology to examine how we live in the world, focusing on Being-in-the-World.

- Sartre adopted existential phenomenology but focused more on freedom, responsibility, and ethics, applying it to human choices and social relationships.

Cognition and Neuroscience

Daniel Dennett (b. 1942) is an American philosopher, cognitive scientist, and one of the most influential thinkers in the philosophy of mind, particularly in the areas of consciousness, free will, and artificial intelligence. Dennett is a leading proponent of scientific materialism and naturalism, advocating that the mind and consciousness can be fully explained in terms of physical processes, particularly those of the brain. He has written extensively on topics like the nature of consciousness, evolution, and the philosophy of religion, and his work often crosses disciplinary boundaries into neuroscience and psychology.

Dennett was born in Boston, Massachusetts, and received his Ph.D. from Oxford University under the supervision of the renowned philosopher Gilbert Ryle. He has held academic positions at Tufts University, where he is currently co-director of the Center for Cognitive Studies. Some of his most notable works include Consciousness Explained (1991), Darwin's Dangerous Idea (1995), Freedom Evolves (2003), and Breaking the Spell (2006).

Key Aspects of Daniel Dennett's Philosophy:

1. Consciousness as an Illusion (or Illusionism): Dennett is best known for his materialist and functionalist account of consciousness. In Consciousness Explained (1991), Dennett argues against the idea that consciousness is a mysterious, immaterial phenomenon. Instead, he views consciousness as a product of physical processes in the brain, which arise from the interaction of neural networks. Dennett famously argues that what we think of as consciousness is a kind of illusion created by various cognitive processes working together in the brain.

• Multiple Drafts Model: Dennett proposes the Multiple Drafts Model of consciousness, which rejects the notion of a central "Cartesian theater" where everything comes together into a unified experience. Instead, he argues that consciousness is the result of parallel processing in the brain, where various mental activities take place without a single point of conscious control. According to this view, our sense of a unified, conscious self is an emergent illusion produced by the brain's information-processing systems.

• Consciousness as a User-Illusion: Dennett likens consciousness to a user interface—a simplified representation of the brain's internal processes that helps us interact with the world but doesn't directly reflect the underlying reality. He argues that consciousness is not a "special substance" but a cognitive construct that allows humans to make sense of their complex mental lives.

2. Eliminative Materialism and Functionalism: Dennett is often associated with eliminative materialism, the view that common-sense concepts like "belief" and "desire" might eventually be eliminated from scientific accounts of the mind

in favor of more precise neuroscientific terms. However, he is more accurately described as a functionalist, meaning he believes that mental states are defined by their functions or roles in cognitive systems, rather than by any intrinsic properties.

- Intentional Stance: Dennett introduced the concept of the intentional stance, a strategy for understanding and predicting the behavior of complex systems (like humans or AI) by treating them as if they have beliefsand desires. While Dennett acknowledges that beliefs and desires are useful constructs, he argues that they are ultimately reducible to brain processes and that their utility comes from their predictive power rather than their ontological reality.

3. Critique of Cartesian Dualism: A central theme in Dennett's work is his rejection of Cartesian dualism, the view that the mind and body are separate substances. He dismisses the idea of an immaterial "soul" or "mind" that exists independently of the brain. For Dennett, all mental phenomena can be explained in terms of neurobiology and information processing. He argues that the persistence of dualistic thinking in popular and philosophical discussions about consciousness stems from misunderstandings about the brain's complexity and how consciousness emerges from it.

4. Free Will and Determinism: In Freedom Evolves (2003), Dennett argues for a compatibilist view of free will, which reconciles human freedom with a deterministic view of the universe. He believes that free will doesn't require the existence of a non-physical soul or an undetermined, indeterministic universe. Instead, free will can be understood in terms of complex cognitive processes that have evolved to allow humans to deliberate, plan, and act with self-control.

- Degrees of Freedom: Dennett asserts that human beings are still morally responsible agents, even if their actions are determined by physical laws, because our brain structures have evolved to make decisions based on complex reasoning. In this sense, humans have more degrees of freedom than other animals or simple machines, allowing us to make meaningful choices that are shaped by our goals, reasoning, and desires.

5. Darwinian Evolution and the Mind: Dennett's book Darwin's Dangerous Idea (1995) explores the far-reaching implications of Darwinian evolution not just for biology, but for philosophy, morality, and even consciousness. He argues that natural selection is a powerful explanatory tool that can account for the complexity of life and mind without invoking supernatural causes or "skyhooks" (magical interventions from outside the natural world). Instead, evolution operates through cranes—natural processes that gradually build complexity through small, incremental steps.

- Mind as Evolved Phenomenon: Dennett emphasizes that the human mind, like all biological features, evolved through natural selection. He argues that our cognitive capacities, including consciousness, are the result of evolutionary pressures and can be fully explained in biological and evolutionary terms.

6. Philosophy of Religion: Dennett is also known for his critical stance on religion, particularly in his book Breaking the Spell (2006), in which he examines religious belief through the lens of cognitive science and evolutionary biology. He argues that religion is a natural phenomenon, shaped by evolutionary forces that made human societies more cohesive. However, Dennett is critical of religious claims that are based on supernatural explanations, which he sees as incompatible with scientific naturalism.

• Memes and Cultural Evolution: Dennett uses Richard Dawkins' concept of memes (ideas that replicate and spread like genes) to explain how religious beliefs might evolve and persist in human cultures. He suggests that religious memes survive not because they are true, but because they are effective at spreading within populations.

7. Artificial Intelligence and Consciousness: Dennett has been a vocal participant in debates about artificial intelligence (AI) and the possibility of machine consciousness. He is skeptical of the idea that AI systems, as currently developed, possess consciousness in any meaningful sense. However, he argues that future AI systems could be conscious in a functionalist sense if they exhibit the right kinds of cognitive processes. For Dennett, consciousness is not an all-or-nothing phenomenon but may come in degrees, depending on the complexity and organization of a system's information processing.

• Consciousness in Machines: Dennett has argued that if machines become complex enough to emulate the cognitive functions of human brains, it's possible they could develop forms of awareness or experience, though this would depend on the architecture of their cognitive systems. However, he is clear that subjective experience (what it feels like to be conscious) is not something reserved exclusively for biological organisms.

Influence and Legacy:

1. Impact on Cognitive Science and Philosophy of Mind: Dennett's work has been influential in shaping modern debates about the nature of consciousness and the mind-body problem. His functionalism and materialistapproach have made him a central figure in the philosophy of mind, particularly

in discussions about the role of the brain in producing consciousness and how we should understand mental states.

2. Debates on Consciousness: Dennett's critique of Cartesian materialism and his insistence that consciousness is not a unified phenomenon have been important in challenging traditional views about the mind. His Multiple Drafts Model of consciousness has inspired debate and discussion among philosophers, neuroscientists, and cognitive scientists, particularly around the question of whether subjective experience is a coherent, continuous stream or an emergent product of brain processes.

3. Public Intellectual and Advocate for Science: Dennett is well known as a public intellectual, advocating for the scientific worldview and engaging in public debates about religion, evolution, and consciousness. His books and lectures have helped bring complex philosophical ideas to a broader audience, and he is often seen as one of the key figures in promoting secularism and naturalism.

4. Free Will and Moral Responsibility: Dennett's compatibilist view of free will has been influential in philosophical discussions about determinism and moral responsibility. His approach, which focuses on the degrees of freedom and the capacity for deliberation that humans possess, provides a middle ground between hard determinism and libertarian free will.

David Chalmers (b. 1966) is an Australian philosopher and cognitive scientist, best known for his work on the philosophy of mind and consciousness. He is one of the leading contemporary figures in the study of consciousness, particularly in addressing the "hard problem" of consciousness, a term he coined to distinguish between the easier problems of understanding cognitive functions and the deeper question of how and why we have subjective experiences (qualia). Chalmers' work has significantly influenced discussions in philosophy, neuroscience, and artificial intelligence.

Chalmers was born in Sydney, Australia, and pursued his undergraduate studies at the University of Adelaide before earning his Ph.D. in philosophy and cognitive science at Indiana University under the supervision of Douglas Hofstadter, a prominent thinker in cognitive science and artificial intelligence. He has held academic positions at the University of California, Santa Cruz, New York University, and the Australian National University. Chalmers is also co-director of the Center for Mind, Brain and Consciousness at NYU.

He is the author of several important works in philosophy, including The Conscious Mind: In Search of a Fundamental Theory (1996), where he elaborates on his key ideas about the nature of consciousness and dualism.

Key Aspects of David Chalmers' Philosophy:

1. The Hard Problem of Consciousness: Chalmers is best known for introducing the distinction between the "easy" problems and the "hard problem" of consciousness.

   • Easy Problems: These refer to the scientific and functional questions of how the brain processes information, governs behavior, and performs cognitive functions like perception, memory, and learning. These problems, while complex, are theoretically solvable through empirical investigation.

   • Hard Problem: The hard problem, in contrast, deals with the subjective, qualitative aspect of experience, or phenomenal consciousness. This is the question of why and how physical processes in the brain give rise to qualia—the raw, subjective experience of "what it feels like" to see red, feel pain, or taste chocolate. Chalmers argues that physical explanations alone cannot account for these subjective experiences, and he believes that consciousness poses a unique challenge that cannot be easily reduced to brain processes.

2. Philosophical Dualism: In tackling the hard problem, Chalmers defends a form of property dualism. He suggests that while the physical world operates according to natural laws, consciousness involves non-physical properties that cannot be fully explained by material processes. Unlike substance dualism (the idea that mind and matter are fundamentally separate substances, as in Descartes' philosophy), Chalmers' property dualism holds that consciousness is a non-physical aspect of reality, but it still arises from physical systems like the brain. Chalmers proposes that consciousness could be a fundamental property of the universe, akin to space, time, or mass. This position, known as panpsychism, posits that some form of consciousness or experience may be a basic feature of all matter, suggesting that even elementary particles might have proto-conscious properties.

3. Consciousness as Fundamental: Chalmers argues for the possibility that consciousness is a fundamental feature of reality, much like space and time. He suggests that consciousness cannot be reduced to more basic physical components but might instead be a basic building block of the universe. This view challenges the mainstream materialist perspective in cognitive science and philosophy of mind, which holds that consciousness arises from physical processes and can eventually be explained by neuroscience.

4. Philosophical Zombies and Thought Experiments: Chalmers is also known for his use of thought experiments, par-

ticularly the idea of philosophical zombies. A philosophical zombie is a hypothetical being that is physically identical to a normal human being but lacks conscious experience. It behaves exactly as a conscious person would, but there is no subjective awareness or "what it is like" to be that being. Chalmers uses this thought experiment to argue that consciousness cannot be fully explained by physical processes alone, since it is conceivable that a being could have all the same physical characteristics as a conscious human without having conscious experience.

5. The Extended Mind Thesis: Chalmers, along with philosopher Andy Clark, co-authored a famous paper titled The Extended Mind (1998), in which they argue that cognitive processes can extend beyond the brain to include external devices, tools, and the environment. According to the extended mind thesis, objects like notebooks, smartphones, or other external aids can become part of the cognitive process when they are integrated into our mental functioning. This challenges traditional views of the mind as being confined to the brain, suggesting that cognition can extend into the world through the interaction with external objects.

6. Artificial Intelligence and Consciousness: Chalmers has also contributed to discussions about artificial intelligence (AI) and the possibility of machine consciousness. He has explored the philosophical implications of whether machines, such as highly advanced AI, could ever become conscious. While he acknowledges that machines could perform cognitive functions, the hard problem of consciousness raises the question of whether they could ever have subjective experiences or consciousness in the same way humans do. Chalmers has been involved in debates about the future of AI, including the ethical concerns around creating poten-

tially conscious machines.

7. Virtual Reality and the Nature of Reality: In more recent work, Chalmers has explored the implications of virtual reality and simulated worlds for our understanding of consciousness and reality. In his book Reality+(2022), he argues that virtual realities could be as meaningful and "real" as physical realities, provided they offer genuine subjective experiences. This raises questions about what it means for something to be real and whether experiences in a simulated world hold the same value as those in the physical world.

Influence and Legacy:

1. Revitalizing the Philosophy of Consciousness: Chalmers' work on the hard problem of consciousness has sparked renewed interest in the philosophical study of consciousness, bringing attention to the limits of purely physical explanations in accounting for subjective experience. His challenges to reductive materialism have influenced debates in philosophy, neuroscience, and cognitive science.

2. Debates on Artificial Intelligence and Mind: Chalmers' engagement with AI and the extended mind thesis has had significant influence on contemporary discussions about the nature of cognition, the boundaries of the mind, and the potential for machine consciousness.

3. Panpsychism and Non-reductive Approaches: Chalmers' advocacy for panpsychism and property dualism has opened up new ways of thinking about consciousness as a fundamental property of reality. His ideas are part of a broader movement toward non-reductive approaches to the mind, which reject the idea that consciousness can be fully explained by neuroscience alone.

Glossary of Eastern Philosophy

The Upanishads

The Upanishads are a collection of ancient Indian philosophical texts that form the core teachings of Vedanta, a spiritual philosophy that underlies much of Hindu thought. They are part of the Vedas, the oldest and most authoritative scriptures in Hinduism, specifically forming the concluding part, known as the Vedanta ("the end of the Vedas"). The word "Upanishad" translates to "sitting near," implying the transmission of knowledge from teacher to student, often in a personal and contemplative setting. The Upanishads were composed between approximately 800 BCE and 200 BCE.

Main Philosophy of the Upanishads:

The central theme of the Upanishads revolves around understanding the nature of ultimate reality (Brahman), the self (Atman), and the relationship between the two. Key ideas include the unity of all existence, the illusory nature of the material world, and the goal of spiritual liberation (Moksha). Here are some key aspects of Upanishadic philosophy:

1. Brahman is the ultimate, unchanging reality in the universe, the source of everything, and the essence of all beings. It is described as formless, infinite, and eternal. The Upanishads emphasize that Brahman is not a personal god but the cosmic principle that pervades all existence.

2. Atman is the individual self or soul. The Upanishads teach that the true nature of every individual is the Atman, which is eternal and identical with Brahman. This leads to the famous realization expressed as "Tat Tvam Asi" ("That Thou Art"), meaning that the individual self is, in its essence,

identical to the universal Brahman.

3. Maya: It refers to the illusion or veil that conceals the true nature of reality, causing individuals to see the material world as separate and distinct from Brahman. The Upanishads teach that overcoming Maya through knowledge (Jnana) leads to Moksha (liberation).

4. Moksha: This a is the ultimate goal in the Upanishads: liberation from the cycle of birth and death (Samsara) and union with Brahman. It is achieved through self-realization and the knowledge that the Atman is identical to Brahman.

5. Karma and Rebirth: The concept of karma (the law of cause and effect) and rebirth (Samsara) plays an important role in Upanishadic philosophy. The soul, or Atman, goes through cycles of birth and death, with each life being shaped by the karma accumulated in previous lives. Moksha ends this cycle.

6. Self-Knowledge: The Upanishads emphasize the pursuit of self-knowledge (Atma Jnana) as the means to realize the unity of Atman and Brahman. This realization is said to lead to inner peace, liberation, and freedom from suffering.

7. Non-Dualism (Advaita): Many Upanishads advocate a non-dualistic (Advaita) understanding of reality, where the apparent duality of subject and object, or self and other, is seen as an illusion. The highest truth is the realization of the oneness of all existence in Brahman.

The Upanishads represent the culmination of Vedic philosophy and mark a shift from ritualistic practices to inward spiritual inquiry. They explore profound metaphysical questions about the nature of reality, the self, and the universe, offering a path toward self-realization and liberation.

Shad Darshanas

The six major schools of Indian philosophy, also known as the "Shad-Darshanas" ("six views" or "six philosophies"), offer diverse perspectives on metaphysics, epistemology, ethics, and spirituality. These schools fall under the umbrella of orthodox (Astika) philosophies, meaning they accept the authority of the Vedas. While their interpretations differ, they share a commitment to understanding the nature of reality, the self, and liberation (Moksha). Each of these schools has had a profound influence on Indian thought and, in more recent times, Western philosophy as well.

1. Nyaya (Logic and Epistemology)

Major Tenets:

- Epistemology: The Nyaya school focuses on logic and the theory of knowledge (Pramana). It recognizes four valid sources of knowledge: perception (Pratyaksha), inference (Anumana), comparison (Upamana), and testimony (Sabda).

- Realism: Nyaya asserts that the world exists independently of our perceptions and that knowledge is the accurate apprehension of objects as they truly are.

- God: Later Nyaya texts introduced a concept of God (Ishvara) as the cause of the universe.

- Liberation (Moksha): Liberation is achieved through true knowledge, particularly the knowledge of the self as distinct from the body, mind, and senses.

Nyaya's rigorous system of logic influenced other schools of Indian philosophy, particularly Vedanta and Mimamsa. Its focus on reason and debate contributed to the intellectual tradi-

tions of ancient India.

2. Vaisheshika (Atomism)

Major Tenets:

• Atomism: Vaisheshika is a form of realism and is known for its atomic theory. It posits that the universe is made up of eternal, indivisible atoms (paramanu), which combine to form matter.

• Categories (Padarthas): Vaisheshika classifies all things into six or seven categories, including substance (Dravya), quality (Guna), action (Karma), universal (Samanya), particularity (Vishesha), and inherence (Samavaya).

• Causality: Vaisheshika holds a theory of causality where effects are seen as real transformations of causes.

• Liberation: Like Nyaya, Vaisheshika seeks liberation through knowledge, particularly knowledge of the self as distinct from the body.

Vaisheshika had a strong influence on the development of Indian metaphysics, particularly with its atomic theory. It later merged with the Nyaya school due to their similar emphasis on realism and epistemology.

3. Samkhya (Dualism)

Major Tenets:

• Dualism: Samkhya is a dualistic philosophy that posits two fundamental realities: Purusha (consciousness) and Prakriti (matter or nature). Purusha is the passive, eternal, conscious self, while Prakriti is the active, dynamic source of the material world.

• Evolution of the Universe: The interaction between Purusha and Prakriti leads to the evolution of the universe, giving rise to the mind, senses, and elements.

• Three Gunas: Prakriti operates through three fundamental qualities or modes: Sattva (goodness, balance), Rajas (passion, activity), and Tamas (ignorance, inertia).

• Liberation: Liberation (Moksha) is achieved by recognizing the distinction between Purusha and Prakriti and becoming free from the attachments that arise from identifying with Prakriti.

Impact:Samkhya had a profound influence on Yoga and Vedanta schools, particularly the concept of dualism and the theory of the three Gunas. It also shaped early Buddhist and Jain metaphysical views.Its theory of the Gunas has influenced modern psychology and holistic health practices.

4. Yoga Darshana (Spiritual Discipline)

Major Tenets:

• Integration of Mind and Body: The Yoga school is closely aligned with Samkhya but focuses on practical methods for achieving liberation through meditation, ethical discipline, and control of the mind and body.

• Eightfold Path (Ashtanga): The path of Yoga, as described by Patanjali, consists of eight limbs: Yama (ethical restraints), Niyama (observances), Asana (postures), Pranayama (breath control), Pratyahara (withdrawal of the senses), Dharana (concentration), Dhyana (meditation), and Samadhi (absorption or union with the divine).

• Purusha and Prakriti: Like Samkhya, Yoga acknowledges the dualism of Purusha (consciousness) and Prakriti (matter). However, Yoga emphasizes the practices needed to realize this distinction and free the self from bondage to matter.

Yoga Sutras by Patanjali: The primary text of classical Yoga philosophy, outlining the practical steps to achieve self-realization and liberation.

Yoga has deeply influenced Indian spirituality and is one of the most widely practiced spiritual traditions. It has influenced various schools of Hinduism and Buddhism, particularly in their meditative practices.

In Western Philosophy and Culture, Yoga, especially in its modern postural form (Hatha Yoga), has become a global phenomenon, influencing physical health, mindfulness practices, and spiritual well-being. Philosophically, the integration of mind and body in Yoga has influenced holistic approaches to psychology and wellness.

5. Mimamsa (Ritual and Dharma)

Major Tenets:

- Dharma and Ritual: The Mimamsa school focuses on the correct interpretation of the Vedas, particularly the Brahmanas, and emphasizes the importance of Vedic rituals in maintaining cosmic order (Rta) and personal dharma (duty). Unlike other schools, Mimamsa does not focus on liberation (Moksha) but on fulfilling one's dharma through ritual action.

- Epistemology: Mimamsa emphasizes the eternal nature of the Vedas and holds that they are infallible. It recognizes six valid means of knowledge, with Vedic testimony being central.

- Non-Theism: Classical Mimamsa does not promote the

concept of God (Ishvara) and holds that the Vedic rituals are self-sufficient in maintaining cosmic order.

Impact on Eastern Philosophy: Mimamsa had a significant impact on the development of Hindu law and the interpretation of the Vedas. Its influence can be seen in the later development of the Vedanta school, particularly in its epistemology.

6. Vedanta

Major Tenets:

- Brahman and Atman: Vedanta is the culmination of the Vedic philosophy and centers on the teachings of the Upanishads. It emphasizes the identity of Brahman (the ultimate reality) and Atman (the individual self), and teaches that realizing this unity leads to liberation (Moksha).

Three Different Schools of Vedanta:

- Advaita Vedanta (Non-dualism): Founded by Adi Shankaracharya, this school teaches that Brahman alone is real, and the world of multiplicity is an illusion (Maya). The goal is to realize that Atman and Brahman are one and the same.

- Vishishtadvaita (Qualified Non-dualism): Founded by Ramanuja, this school teaches that Brahman is the ultimate reality but that individual souls and the material world are real and dependent on Brahman. The goal is union with Brahman, but souls retain their distinct identities.

- Dvaita (Dualism): Founded by Madhvacharya, Dvaita maintains a strict distinction between the individual soul (Atman) and Brahman (God), rejecting non-dualism. It emphasizes devotion (Bhakti) to a personal God.

Vedanta is the most influential school in Indian philosophy, shaping Hindu religious and philosophical thought. It deeply influenced the Bhakti movement, modern Indian spirituality, and leaders like Swami Vivekananda.

In Western Philosophy, Vedanta, particularly Advaita Vedanta, attracted Western philosophers and writers such as Arthur Schopenhauer and Aldous Huxley. Vedanta's non-dualistic teachings also influenced transcendentalistslike Ralph Waldo Emerson and Henry David Thoreau.

Adi Shankaracharya (circa 788–820 CE) was a highly influential Indian philosopher and theologian who consolidated the doctrine of Advaita Vedanta (non-dualism). His teachings and writings played a crucial role in reviving Hinduism in the face of growing influence from rival philosophies such as Buddhism and Jainism. Shankara is best known for his efforts to synthesize and systematize the philosophy of the Upanishads, Bhagavad Gita, and Brahma Sutras, forming the core of the Advaita Vedanta tradition.

Shankaracharya traveled extensively across the Indian subcontinent, establishing monasteries (mathas) and debating with scholars of other philosophical traditions. His teachings continue to influence Indian spiritual and philosophical thought, and his monastic institutions still play an important role in Hindu society.

Philosophy of Shankaracharya (Advaita Vedanta):

Shankaracharya's philosophy of Advaita Vedanta revolves around the idea of non-dualism, asserting the fundamental unity of Brahman (the ultimate reality) and Atman (the individual soul). His interpretation of the Upanishads and other sacred texts presents a vision of reality where:

1. Brahman is the absolute reality, formless, infinite, and

unchanging. It is the source and essence of the universe, transcending time, space, and causality.

2. Atman (the individual self) is identical to Brahman. The belief that the self is separate from the ultimate reality is an illusion caused by Maya (ignorance or illusion).

3. Maya: Shankara introduced the concept of Maya, which creates the illusion of duality and separation. Maya is responsible for the material world appearing as real, even though it is transient and impermanent. It veils the true nature of Brahman, making it seem as though there is a distinction between the self (Atman) and the world.

4. Non-duality (Advaita): Shankara's core teaching is that "Brahma Satyam, Jagat Mithya, Jivo Brahmaiva Na Parah", meaning "Brahman alone is real, the world is an illusion, and the individual soul is not different from Brahman." Thus, the ultimate goal of life is to realize the non-dual nature of existence, which leads to liberation (Moksha).

5. Moksha (Liberation): According to Shankara, liberation is attained not through rituals or external practices but through self-realization—the direct and experiential knowledge of the unity of Atman and Brahman. This knowledge removes ignorance and dissolves the illusion of duality.

6. Jivanmukti: Shankara emphasized the concept of Jivanmukti, or liberation while living, which suggests that one can attain enlightenment and freedom from the cycle of rebirth (Samsara) in this life itself, through realization of the non-dual nature of the self and Brahman.

Contribution and Legacy:

1. Revival of Hinduism: Shankaracharya played a crucial role in the revival of Vedic philosophy in the face of de-

clining Hindu practices and the rise of other competing traditions such as Buddhism and Jainism. His teachings reasserted the primacy of the Vedas and Vedanta as the highest knowledge.

2. Advaita Vedanta: Shankaracharya is considered the most important proponent of Advaita Vedanta, which became one of the dominant schools of Hindu philosophy. His interpretation of the Upanishads and Brahma Sutras established Advaita Vedanta as a complete and systematic spiritual philosophy.

3. Monastic Institutions: Shankara established four mathas (monastic centers) in different regions of India—Sringeri, Dwaraka, Puri, and Badrinath—to preserve and propagate Advaita Vedanta. These mathas remain important centers of learning and spiritual practice to this day.

4. Philosophical Debates: Shankaracharya engaged in debates with other schools of Indian philosophy, such as Buddhism, Mimamsa, Samkhya, and Nyaya, refuting their doctrines and establishing the supremacy of Advaita Vedanta. His debates helped shape the intellectual landscape of Indian philosophy and reinforced the Vedic worldview.

5. Influence on Later Thinkers: Shankaracharya's work deeply influenced later Vedanta philosophers like Ramana Maharshi, Swami Vivekananda, and Ramakrishna Paramahamsa, as well as modern spiritual movements like the Theosophical Society. His philosophy also attracted the interest of Western philosophers such as Arthur Schopenhauer, who saw parallels between Advaita Vedanta and Western metaphysical thought.

6. Synthesis of Jnana, Bhakti, and Karma: Though Shankara is primarily known for his emphasis on Jnana Yoga(the path

of knowledge), he did not dismiss the importance of Bhakti (devotion) and Karma Yoga (selfless action). He taught that these paths, when practiced with the right understanding, could lead to the same realization of non-duality.

The three great philosophers Adi Shankaracharya, Ramanuja, and Madhvacharya are the foremost exponents of Vedanta, a school of Indian philosophy that interprets the teachings of the Upanishads, Bhagavad Gita, and Brahma Sutras.

While all three sought to explain the nature of Brahman (the ultimate reality) and Atman (the individual self) through Vedanta, their interpretations differ significantly, particularly in the relationship between Brahman and Atman, the nature of the world, and the path to liberation (Moksha). Shankaracharya is known for Advaita Vedanta (non-dualism), Ramanuja for Vishishtadvaita Vedanta (qualified non-dualism), and Madhvacharya for Dvaita Vedanta(dualism).

Comparison of the Three Vedantic Philosophies:

Aspect	Shankaracharya (Advaita)	Ramanuja (Vishishtadvaita)	Madhvacharya (Dvaita)
Nature of Brahman	Nirguna Brahman (without attributes), formless, absolute reality	Saguna Brahman (with attributes), personal God (Vishnu)	Saguna Brahman (personal God, Vishnu), distinct from the world and souls
Relationship Between Brahman and Atman	Non-dualism: Brahman and Atman are identical; Atman is Brahman	Qualified non-dualism: Atman is distinct but inseparably connected to Brahman, like a body to the soul	Dualism: Brahman (God) and Atman (individual self) are completely distinct
Nature of the World	Mithya (illusion), a product of Maya	Real but dependent on Brahman	Real and eternally distinct from Brahman
Path to Liberation (moksha)	Jnana (knowledge): Realization of the unity of Atman and Brahman	Bhakti (devotion) and grace: Union with Brahman while retaining individuality	Bhakti (devotion) and grace: Eternal separation from Brahman but bliss in God's presence
Moksha	Merging of Atman with Brahman, no individuality remains	Union with Brahman, but the soul retains individuality	Eternal distinction: The soul remains separate from Brahman and enjoys bliss
View on God	View on God Brahman is impersonal, not worshiped as a deity	Brahman is personal, usually identified with Vishnu	Brahman is a personal God, specifically Vishnu, distinct from souls and the world

Patanjali

Patanjali is a revered figure in Indian philosophy, traditionally credited with composing the Yoga Sutras, a foundational text on Raja Yoga or the science of meditation. While little is known about Patanjali's life, he is often thought to have lived around the 2nd century BCE, though some scholars argue for later dates, possibly between the 4th and 5th centuries CE. In Indian tradition, Patanjali is sometimes linked to the Patanjali who wrote commentaries on Sanskrit grammar (Mahabhashya), though whether these two Patanjalis are the same person is still debated.

Patanjali's Yoga Sutras is a concise and systematic presentation of the practices and philosophy of Yoga, combining both practical techniques and metaphysical insights. The text has been enormously influential, not only in the development of Yoga philosophy but also in various Hindu and Buddhist meditative traditions.

Philosophy of the Yoga Sutras:

The Yoga Sutras of Patanjali is a foundational text of Raja Yoga, which emphasizes meditation, ethical discipline, and mental control. It outlines an eightfold path (Ashtanga Yoga) for attaining spiritual liberation (Moksha) through the discipline of mind and body. Patanjali defines Yoga as the cessation of the fluctuations of the mind (chitta vritti nirodha), leading to the realization of the true self, or Purusha.

Key concepts of Patanjali's Yoga philosophy include:

1. Chitta (Mind): The mind is a composite of different functions—intellect, ego, and sensory perception—and is subject to constant fluctuations (vrittis).

2. Purusha (Self): Purusha is the pure, conscious self, distinct from Prakriti (nature or matter). The goal of Yoga is for Pu-

rusha to recognize its true nature, free from identification with the mind or body.

3. Prakriti (Nature): Prakriti is the material world, including the mind and senses. It is governed by the interplay of the three gunas (Sattva, Rajas, and Tamas), which create the illusion of individual identity.

4. Ashtanga Yoga (Eightfold Path): The core practice of Patanjali's system, which includes ethical disciplines, physical postures, breath control, and meditation techniques to achieve mental clarity and spiritual awakening.

The Yoga Sutras are divided into four chapters, each focusing on different aspects of the practice and philosophy of Yoga. The only yoga mentioned in this text is Kriya Yoga.

Impact of the Yoga Sutras on the Western Worldview:

1. Introduction of Yoga as a Spiritual and Physical Discipline: The Yoga Sutras were first introduced to the West through Swami Vivekananda in the late 19th century, particularly in his talks on Raja Yoga. Vivekananda's teachings helped demystify Indian spirituality for Western audiences, presenting Yoga as both a practical philosophy and a spiritual discipline for achieving mental clarity and personal growth.

Over time, Yoga became popular in the West, first as a spiritual practice and later as a physical discipline. The spread of Hatha Yoga in the 20th century, with its focus on postures (Asanas) and breath control (Pranayama), derived its philosophical foundation from Patanjali's Yoga Sutras, even though the physical aspects were emphasized more in the West.

2. Mind-Body Connection and Holistic Health: The Yoga Sutras' emphasis on controlling the mind and senses, maintaining ethical conduct, and balancing mental and physical health has influ-

enced modern approaches to well-being and holistic health.

In the 20th century, Yoga began to be viewed as a tool for managing stress, improving physical fitness, and enhancing mental clarity. The focus on Pranayama (breath control), Asanas (postures), and meditation is seen as part of a broader mind-body connection that is essential to personal health.

Yoga practices based on Patanjali's system have been integrated into psychological therapies, mindfulness training, and wellness programs, helping individuals manage stress, anxiety, and emotional well-being.

3. Influence on Western Psychology: Carl Jung, a pioneer in modern psychology, was significantly influenced by Indian thought, including the Yoga Sutras. He compared Samadhi to states of individuation and self-realization, key concepts in his psychological theory. Jung also saw Patanjali's emphasis on the transformation of consciousness as analogous to the journey of psychological growth.

Modern psychological practices, particularly mindfulness meditation and cognitive-behavioral therapies, have been influenced by the techniques outlined in the Yoga Sutras for quieting the mind and developing inner awareness.

4. Popularization of Meditation and Mindfulness: Dharana (concentration), Dhyana (meditation), and Samadhi (absorption) have become central to the popularization of meditation and mindfulness in the West. These practices, inspired by the Yoga Sutras, are used in various settings—from clinical therapy to corporate stress management—as methods for cultivating focus, reducing anxiety, and achieving mental clarity.

The mindfulness movement, which has taken root in Western psychology, incorporates many elements found in Patanjali's system, such as the focus on present moment awareness and the non-reactive observation of thoughts.

5. Spiritual Philosophy and Personal Growth: In the 20th century, Western thinkers and spiritual seekers found in the Yoga Sutras a valuable source of spiritual philosophy and a practical path for personal growth. This is evident in the works of Aldous Huxley, Joseph Campbell, and Jiddu Krishnamurti, who integrated elements of Patanjali's teachings into their writings on self-realization and spiritual development.

The rise of New Age spirituality in the West has also been shaped by Patanjali's emphasis on self-discipline, mental clarity, and the transcendence of egoic desires. The practice of Yoga became a key element in the New Age quest for spiritual enlightenment.

6. Influence on Science and Medicine: Modern neuroscience and psychology have shown increasing interest in how practices outlined in the Yoga Sutras—such as meditation and breath control—affect the brain and mental health. Studies have shown that meditation can positively influence cognitive function, emotional regulation, and stress reduction.

The mindfulness movement in Western healthcare, which is rooted in Indian meditative traditions, has been validated by scientific research showing that techniques like Dhyana (meditation) and Pranayama (breath control) can reduce symptoms of anxiety, depression, and chronic pain.

7. Global Spread of Hatha Yoga: Though Patanjali's focus was on Raja Yoga, his text laid the philosophical groundwork for the development of Hatha Yoga, which emphasizes physical postures and breath control. This form of Yoga, particularly through teachers like B.K.S. Iyengar and Pattabhi Jois, became extremely popular in the West in the 20th century.

Western Yoga studios, often centered on the physical aspects of Yoga, still trace their philosophical heritage to the Yoga Sutras, which have informed the broader understanding of Yoga as a comprehensive system for personal transformation and mental discipline.

The Sufi Tradition

Sufism is a mystical and spiritual tradition within Islam that emphasizes the inward search for God and aims for direct personal experience of the Divine. The Sufi path (known as Tariqa) focuses on the purification of the heart, self-discipline, love, and the remembrance of God (Dhikr). Sufism is not a separate sect of Islam but rather a dimension of Islamic spirituality that seeks to deepen the individual's connection with God through inner transformation and devotion.

The roots of Sufism can be traced back to the early days of Islam in the 7th century, though it developed more formally over the next few centuries. Sufis often follow the inner teachings of the Qur'an and Hadith and seek to live according to the highest spiritual ideals of Islam. Sufism has produced some of the most revered and influential scholars, poets, and mystics in Islamic history, and its practices have profoundly shaped Islamic culture and spirituality.

Philosophy of Sufism:

The philosophy of Sufism centers on the idea of Tawhid (the Oneness of God), not just as a theological doctrine, but as a mystical reality to be experienced in the heart of the seeker. Sufis believe that every soul is on a journey toward God and that by purifying oneself of worldly attachments and ego, one can come closer to realizing the Divine Presence in all things.

Nyingma tradition of Vajrayana

The Nyingma school, also known as the Nyingmapa, is the oldest of the four major schools of Tibetan Buddhism, originating in the 8th century CE. The name "Nyingma" means "ancient" in Tibetan, and the school traces its teachings to the legendary figure Padmasambhava, or Guru Rinpoche, who is believed to have introduced Vajrayana Buddhism to Tibet during the reign of King Trisong Detsen.

The Nyingma tradition is distinguished by its emphasis on the Dzogchen teachings, which focus on realizing the primordial, natural state of mind—an awareness that transcends conceptual thought. The school places importance on a mystical approach to enlightenment, with the practice of meditation, mantra recitation, and esoteric rituals central to its path.

Nyingmapa doctrine is deeply rooted in the early Tantras, many of which were hidden as "terma" (treasures) by Guru Rinpoche and later discovered by tertons (treasure-revealers). These treasures are considered vital for the preservation and renewal of the teachings.

Unlike other Tibetan Buddhist schools, the Nyingma does not have a rigid monastic hierarchy. While it includes monasteries and monks, the school also places great importance on lay practitioners and yogis who often live as householders while pursuing intense spiritual practice.

Key figures in the Nyingma tradition include Longchenpa, Jigme Lingpa, and contemporary teachers such as Dilgo Khyentse Rinpoche. Today, the Nyingma school continues to be an influential force in Tibetan Buddhism, known for its rich tantric and philosophical heritage.

Dzogchen, often translated as "Great Perfection," is a highly advanced and esoteric practice within the Nyingma school of Tibetan Buddhism. It focuses on realizing the nature of the mind and attaining a state of non-dual awareness that transcends ordinary conceptualization. The ultimate goal of Dzogchen is to realize the intrinsic, primordial state of being, which is pure awareness or rigpa.

Core Philosophy of Dzogchen

1. Primordial Purity (Kadak): The foundational belief in Dzogchen is that all beings possess an innate, pristine awareness from the beginning. This "primordial purity" refers to the original state of the mind, which is free from obscurations, suffering, and duality. It is unconditioned, timeless, and beyond the reach of ordinary thoughts or emotions. Kadak emphasizes that this true nature of mind is always present, but remains obscured by ignorance and mental afflictions.

2. Spontaneous Presence (Lhundrup): Despite its primordial purity, the nature of the mind is not a passive or empty void. It is inherently luminous and manifest, meaning it naturally gives rise to the display of phenomena. This is referred to as "spontaneous presence," signifying that all appearances—thoughts, emotions, sensory experiences—are an expression of the mind's intrinsic awareness. Realizing this allows practitioners to see that all phenomena are non-dual with the mind.

3. Non-Duality (Advaya): Dzogchen teaches that the mind and the external world are not separate; they are aspects of the same primordial awareness. The dualistic separation between subject (self) and object (other) is an illusion created by conceptual thought. The aim of Dzogchen practice is to transcend this duality and directly experience the non--conceptual, non-dual nature of reality.

4. Rigpa (Pure Awareness): The key to Dzogchen practice is

realizing rigpa, the clear, unobstructed awareness that is the essence of the mind. Rigpa is not something that is created or developed; rather, it is recognized through direct experience. Once rigpa is recognized, the practitioner remains in a state of effortless, natural awareness.

5. Natural Liberation: Dzogchen emphasizes that liberation (or enlightenment) is not something that needs to be achieved through effortful striving. Instead, it is a matter of recognizing the already present nature of mind. This recognition allows the practitioner to be "naturally liberated" from the bonds of samsara (the cycle of birth and death) without having to engage in elaborate practices or rituals.

Dzogchen Teachings

Dzogchen teachings are usually divided into three categories or series:

1. Semde (Mind Series): These teachings focus on recognizing the nature of the mind. They guide practitioners to understand that the mind, in its essence, is empty and beyond dualistic concepts. The aim is to experience the mind's pure awareness through meditation practices that strip away distractions and attachments to mental phenomena.

2. Longde (Space Series): The Space Series emphasizes the experience of spaciousness in the mind. Practitioners learn to rest in the vast openness of their awareness, allowing all thoughts and experiences to arise and dissolve naturally without attachment or aversion. This spaciousness reflects the unbounded, non-conceptual nature of the mind.

3. Menngagde (Secret Instruction Series): The most esoteric and direct of Dzogchen teachings, the Secret Instruction Series provides practices that directly introduce the practitioner to the experience of rigpa. These teachings often involve profound meditative techniques and pith instructions

given by a qualified master. The goal is to break through the subtle layers of conceptuality and experience rigpa directly.

Dzogchen emphasizes non-conceptual meditation, which is free from effort and striving. Unlike analytical or concentration-based meditations, Dzogchen meditation involves relaxing into the natural state of mind without trying to control thoughts, emotions, or sensations. The key is to remain in the state of pure awareness, recognizing all phenomena as expressions of the mind's inherent luminosity.

Ultimate Goal of Dzogchen Practice

The ultimate goal of Dzogchen is realization of Buddhahood, which means fully awakening to the true nature of reality and the self. In Dzogchen, this is the direct and experiential recognition of rigpa, leading to the dissolution of all dualistic delusions. The practitioner is liberated from samsara and abides in a state of perfect wisdom and compassion, embodying the enlightened qualities of a Buddha.

In summary, Dzogchen provides a profound and direct path to realizing the nature of mind and attaining enlightenment. It requires devotion to a qualified teacher, a strong foundation in preliminary practices, and the ability to recognize and stabilize rigpa through the guidance of a master.

Gorakshanath and the Nath Tradition

Gorakshanath (also known as Gorakhnath) was a legendary yogi and saint, traditionally considered to have lived between the 9th and 12th centuries CE, though his exact dates are uncertain. He is one of the most important figures in the Nath tradition, a sect of ascetics that emphasized Hatha Yoga, meditation, and spiritual discipline as means to liberation (Moksha). Gorakshanath is believed to have been a disciple of the famous Matsyendranath, the founder of the Nath tradition, and is credited with organizing and systematizing the teachings of the Naths into a coherent spiritual path.

Gorakshanath's teachings are a synthesis of Shaivism, Tantra, Hatha Yoga, and Raja Yoga, blending asceticism with practical yogic techniques for physical and spiritual transformation. His influence extended beyond his own lifetime through the Nath yogis and other spiritual lineages in India, including various Sufi, Bhakti, and Sikh traditions. Gorakshanath is venerated in North India, Nepal, and Tibet, and his teachings have deeply influenced the Hatha Yoga practices that are widespread today.

He is considered an immortal (Mahasiddha) in many traditions and is said to have achieved spiritual immortality through his mastery of Yoga and Siddhi powers (supernatural accomplishments). His spiritual legacy is preserved in the Gorakhnath Math in Gorakhpur, Uttar Pradesh, which continues to be a significant center of Nath Yoga and spiritual practice.

Impact of Gorakshanath on Indian Thought and Life:

Gorakshanath's impact on Indian spiritual thought is immense, particularly through his teachings, disciples, and the various traditions that trace their lineage to him. His influence spans several fields, from Yoga to Tantra, Shaivism, and Bhakti, and his legacy continues through his many direct and indirect disciples.

1. Revival and Systematization of Hatha Yoga:

• Gorakshanath is credited with the formalization of Hatha Yoga, a path of Yoga that emphasizes physical postures (Asanas), breath control (Pranayama), and energy channels (Nadis) to purify the body and mind. His works on Hatha Yoga are foundational to what became known as Hatha Yoga Pradipika and other classical Hatha Yoga texts.

• His teachings focus on bodily discipline as a means to spiritual awakening, and many of the physical practices that are now widespread in modern Yoga originated from the Nath Yogis under Gorakshanath's influence. Goraksha Shataka, attributed to him, is an early text on Hatha Yoga, outlining its basic principles.

• The Nath Yogis, following Gorakshanath, were known for their mastery over prana (life force) and kundalini energy, which are central elements in Hatha Yoga. Gorakshanath's synthesis of Yoga and Tantric practices made a significant contribution to Indian spirituality by providing practical methods for spiritual liberation that could be followed by ascetics and householders alike.

2. Influence on Shaivism:

• Gorakshanath was a devout follower of Lord Shiva, and the Nath tradition that he led is closely aligned with Shaivism. His teachings emphasize the worship of Shiva in the form of Adinath (the primordial yogi) and integrate Shaiva philosophy with yogic practices.

• The Nath Yogis, through their emphasis on meditation, self-discipline, and renunciation, contributed to the Shaiva ascetic traditions that are still prevalent in India today. Gorakshanath's emphasis on direct spiritual experience through meditation and yogic discipline resonates with the non-dualistic and mystical aspects of Shaiva Siddhanta and Kashmir Shaivism.

3. Tantric Influences:

• Gorakshanath's teachings are deeply rooted in Tantra, particularly the Kaula tradition of Tantra, which combines esoteric practices with yogic disciplines. His integration of Tantric rituals, along with Yoga, provided a path to transcendence that was accessible to householders and ascetics alike.

• His philosophy involved the control of the body's energies through yogic techniques like Pranayama, Bandhas (energy locks), and Mudras (gestures). These practices were designed to awaken Kundalini Shakti and facilitate spiritual liberation, emphasizing the divine within the body.

4. Bhakti Movement:

• Although Gorakshanath is primarily associated with asceticism, his teachings also had an influence on the emerging Bhakti movement, particularly in North India. The Nath Yogis did not strictly adhere to caste distinctions and rejected the formalism of ritualistic Hinduism, which resonated with the egalitarian spirit of Bhakti.

• Kabir, one of the most prominent Bhakti poets, is often linked to the Nath tradition. Kabir's teachings on the unity of God and his rejection of both Hindu and Muslim orthodoxy share affinities with Gorakshanath's emphasis on inner spiritual practice over external ritual. While Gorakshanath focused on yogic discipline, many of his indirect disciples emphasized devotion to the divine within.

5. Sikhism and Influence on Guru Nanak:

• Gorakshanath's teachings also had an indirect influence on Sikhism through the Nath Yogis' emphasis on direct spiritual experience, internal discipline, and rejection of ritualistic religion. Guru Nanak, the founder of Sikhism, had interactions with Nath Yogis, and while Sikhism diverged from their ascetic practices, the focus on internal devotion and the rejection of caste and formalism echo some of Gorakshanath's values.

• Guru Nanak's Universalism and emphasis on a direct connection to God can be seen as a reflection of the Nath Yogis' non-sectarian approach, which embraced spiritual practices beyond religious orthodoxy.

6. Impact on Sufi Mysticism:

• The Nath Yogis, under Gorakshanath's influence, interacted with Sufi mystics in medieval India. These interactions led to a mutual exchange of ideas on asceticism, mysticism, and the nature of the divine. The emphasis on inner experience, meditation, and detachment from worldly concerns is a common thread between Nath Yogis and Sufi mystics.

• This exchange helped bridge the gap between Hindu and Muslim spiritual traditions, contributing to a syncretic spiritual environment in medieval India. The Nath Yogis' teachings provided a framework for interfaith dialogue and spiritual inquiry that transcended religious boundaries.

7. Formation of Nath Lineages:

• Gorakshanath's teachings spread through direct disciples and lineages that carried his message across India, Nepal, and even Tibet. The Nath Yogis became a significant religious and spiritual group, and several Nath temples and monasteries were established in his name, with the Gorakhnath Math in Uttar Pradesh being the most prominent.

- The Nath tradition remains influential in yoga, meditation, and tantra practices today, and many yogic techniques associated with Kundalini awakening and Pranayama can be traced back to Gorakshanath's teachings.

8. Influence on Modern Yoga:

- Gorakshanath's teachings on Hatha Yoga have been a major influence on modern Yoga practices. Many of the postures, breath control techniques, and meditative practices that are taught in Yoga schools around the world have their roots in the Nath tradition and were either introduced or popularized by Gorakshanath and his disciples.

- Figures like Swami Vivekananda and Swami Sivananda helped spread Yoga to the West, and while they focused on Raja Yoga and Vedanta, the physical and meditative aspects of Yoga that gained global popularity were rooted in the Hatha Yoga practices of Gorakshanath and the Nath yogis.

The Nath yogic tradition is a major Shaiva sub-tradition of spiritual practice in India that emphasizes Hatha Yoga, meditation, and the quest for spiritual liberation (Moksha) through direct inner experience. It is believed to have originated between the 9th and 12th centuries CE with Matsyendranath and Gorakshanath, and its influence has spread widely across India, Nepal, and Tibet. The Nath tradition is characterized by its blend of Shaivism, Tantra, and Yoga, and it emphasizes the importance of mastering the body, breath, and mind to achieve higher states of consciousness.

The Nath Sampradaya (tradition) is a lineage of yogis who follow the teachings and practices of their spiritual forebears, particularly Matsyendranath and Gorakshanath. It has had a profound impact on Indian spirituality, the practice of Hatha Yoga, and even on other spiritual traditions, such as Sikhism, Bhakti, and Sufi mysticism.

History of the Nath Yogic Tradition:

Origins and Development:

The Nath tradition is believed to have originated as a synthesis of earlier Shaiva ascetic traditions, Tantra, and Buddhist Vajrayana practices. The early Naths were Shaiva ascetics, deeply influenced by the non-dualistic Shaivism of Kashmir and the yogic practices prevalent in Tantric Buddhism.

1. Matsyendranath (c. 9th–10th century CE):

Matsyendranath is traditionally regarded as the founder of the Nath tradition. He is also revered in Tantric Buddhist Vajrayana as Minanatha. Matsyendranath is credited with reviving and systematizing Tantric and yogic practices. According to legend, he learned the secrets of Yoga from Lord Shiva himself while Shiva was instructing his consort Parvati.

Matsyendranath's teachings emphasized the awakening of Kundalini energy through yogic practices. He is also associated with early Hatha Yoga practices and is considered one of the 84 Mahasiddhas (spiritual adepts) in Indian and Tibetan Buddhist traditions.

2. Gorakshanath (c. 10th–12th century CE):

Gorakshanath, a disciple of Matsyendranath, is regarded as the most important figure in the Nath tradition. He systematized the teachings of the Naths and codified their practices, especially focusing on Hatha Yoga, which he saw as a means of achieving spiritual enlightenment through control of the body, mind, and breath.

Gorakshanath's influence is far-reaching, and he is venerated as an immortal saint (Mahasiddha) in Indian and Tibetan spiritual traditions. His emphasis on self-discipline, detachment, and yogic practices formed the foundation of what became known as the Hatha Yoga tradition.

3. Expansion and Spread:

The Nath tradition quickly spread across North India, Nepal, and Tibet, with Nath Yogis establishing monasteries and centers of learning. These yogis were known for their austere practices and were often itinerant ascetics who engaged in deep meditation and breath control techniques to awaken spiritual powers.

Nath yogis became influential not only within Shaivism but also interacted with other spiritual movements, including the Sufi mystics, Buddhists, and the emerging Bhakti movement.

Key Historical Developments:

- Interaction with Other Traditions: Nath Yogis often interacted with Sufi saints and Bhakti poets, leading to a mutual exchange of ideas. Nath teachings on direct spiritual experience influenced early Sikhism and figures like Kabir, who rejected both Hindu and Muslim orthodoxy in favor of an inner spiritual path.

- Esoteric Practices and Alchemy: Nath Yogis were known for their Tantric and alchemical practices. They believed in the transmutation of the body through Yoga, and some texts attributed to the Naths discuss physical immortality and mastery over the elements.

- Nath Influence in Hatha Yoga: The Nath yogis, particularly

Gorakshanath, are credited with formalizing the system of Hatha Yoga. The Nath school's focus on Asanas (physical postures), Pranayama (breath control), Mudras (hand gestures), and Bandhas (energy locks) became central to later developments in Yoga.

Kashmir Shaivism is a non-dualistic tradition of Shaiva philosophy that originated in the Kashmir Valley around the 8th century CE. It represents a profound and intricate system of metaphysics, spiritual practice, and mysticism that seeks to explain the nature of reality and the self. The tradition is sometimes also referred to as Trika Shaivism because of its emphasis on the triadic nature of reality, focusing on three primary principles: Shiva (the ultimate reality), Shakti (the dynamic energy), and Nara (the individual soul).

Historical Background

Kashmir Shaivism developed between the 8th and 12th centuries CE, a period when Kashmir was a major cultural and intellectual hub. During this time, it emerged as a powerful alternative to Advaita Vedanta, the non-dual philosophy of the South Indian philosopher Adi Shankaracharya. While both traditions are non--dualistic, Kashmir Shaivism focuses on Shiva and Shakti as the ultimate reality and creative force, while Advaita Vedanta centers on Brahman as the singular, formless absolute.

The tradition drew from earlier Shaiva and Tantric schools, such as the Shaiva Siddhanta and Kaula schools, incorporating their practices and philosophies into a cohesive, sophisticated metaphysical framework.

Philosophy of Kashmir Shaivism

The philosophical foundation of Kashmir Shaivism is non-dualism (Advaita), but it differs from Advaita Vedanta in significant ways. Instead of viewing the world as maya (illusion), Kashmir Shaivism asserts that everything is a manifestation of Shiva, the supreme consciousness, who is both immanent and transcendent.

Key Tenets:

1. Shiva as Ultimate Reality: Shiva is both the ultimate reality and the dynamic, creative power behind the universe. He is both the unmanifest and manifest, the cause and the effect, pure consciousness and its active expression.

2. Spanda (Divine Vibration): The universe is seen as a constant flow of energy or vibration, referred to as spanda. This vibration is the pulsation of Shiva, through which the material world comes into existence. Everything that exists, whether material or immaterial, is a form of this vibratory energy.

3. Recognition (Pratyabhijna): The central theme of Kashmir Shaivism is self-recognition or pratyabhijna, the realization that the individual soul (jiva) is not different from Shiva, the universal consciousness. The ignorance or avidya that veils this truth is dispelled through spiritual practice and knowledge, leading to liberation (moksha).

4. Shakti (Dynamic Power of Shiva): Shiva's creative power is represented by Shakti, his feminine aspect. Shakti is responsible for the manifestation of the universe and all phenomena, and the interplay between Shiva and Shakti is central to the philosophy. They are inseparable, representing the stillness of consciousness (Shiva) and the dynamism of creation (Shakti).

5. The 36 Tattvas: The cosmology of Kashmir Shaivism includes a hierarchy of 36 tattvas, or principles, which map

out the process of creation from pure consciousness (Shiva) to the material world. These tattvas encompass everything from the highest spiritual realities to the most gross physical elements. Spiritual evolution is seen as a process of ascending through these tattvas, shedding layers of ignorance and limitation.

6. Liberation in This Life (Jivanmukti): Kashmir Shaivism emphasizes the possibility of attaining liberation while still living in the physical body. This concept, known as jivanmukti, holds that through spiritual practice, one can realize their identity with Shiva and live in a state of blissful freedom from the limitations of ego and duality.

Mahavatar Babaji

Mahavatar Babaji is a legendary and mysterious figure in the Kriya Yoga tradition, revered as an immortal yogi who is believed to have played a crucial role in the spiritual evolution of humanity. Babaji is said to be an ascended master and an avatar, a divine incarnation who has taken a physical form to guide humanity toward enlightenment. He is associated with the revival and transmission of Kriya Yoga, an ancient yogic technique designed to accelerate spiritual progress through the control of prana (life force) and meditation.

The most well-known accounts of Babaji come from Paramahansa Yogananda's Autobiography of a Yogi, published in 1946, where Babaji is depicted as an eternal and ageless master who has lived in the Himalayas for centuries, perhaps millennia, overseeing the spiritual evolution of humanity. According to Yogananda and other sources, Babaji continues to exist in a physical body, though he is able to dematerialize and manifest at will, working behind the scenes to assist the progress of those on the spiritual path.

Life and Legend of Mahavatar Babaji:

Babaji is often referred to as a Mahavatar, meaning a "great incarnation" or a divine being who appears on Earth to aid in the spiritual evolution of humanity. The term "avatar" in Hindu philosophy refers to a divine incarnation, usually of Vishnu, but in Babaji's case, it signifies his role as a direct manifestation of the divine, not tied to any particular deity.

The historical details of Babaji's birth, early life, or physical origins are largely unknown and remain shrouded in mystery. There are no specific records of his birth or death, and his life is described more in terms of his spiritual impact rather than personal biographical details. The accounts of Babaji's existence come primarily from oral traditions and testimonies of direct disciples and realized yogis who claim to have encountered him.

1. Immortality: Babaji is said to have achieved immortality through mastery of the Kriya Yoga techniques and spiritual realization, transcending the limitations of the physical body. He is believed to be living in the Himalayas with a small group of advanced disciples, where he continues his work of guiding the evolution of consciousness on Earth.

2. The Silent Guardian: Despite his great spiritual power, Babaji is portrayed as a silent guardian of humanity, working anonymously and without seeking recognition. His role is not to create a religion or sect but to revive and protect the eternal teachings of Yoga and Sanatana Dharma (the eternal way), ensuring that the knowledge of spiritual liberation is preserved and made accessible to sincere seekers.

3. Revelation to Lahiri Mahasaya: Babaji became widely known to the world through his revelation to Lahiri Ma-

hasaya, a householder yogi in the 19th century, who revived the practice of Kriya Yoga under Babaji's direct guidance. According to Yogananda's account, Babaji appeared to Lahiri Mahasaya in the Himalayan hills, initiated him into the advanced techniques of Kriya Yoga, and instructed him to spread this powerful spiritual practice to the world. This event marked the beginning of Kriya Yoga's revival and its subsequent spread across India and the world.

4. Paramahansa Yogananda's Introduction of Babaji: The most prominent introduction of Babaji to the West came through Paramahansa Yogananda's Autobiography of a Yogi. In this work, Babaji is described as an ageless, ever-youthful saint who works with other enlightened masters (such as Jesus Christ) to guide humanity toward spiritual evolution. Yogananda presents Babaji as the guiding force behind the lineage of Kriya Yoga, which includes Lahiri Mahasaya, Sri Yukteswar, and Yogananda himself.

5. Association with Lord Shiva: In many accounts, Babaji is seen as an incarnation or manifestation of Lord Shiva, the cosmic yogi and ascetic who represents the force of transformation and dissolution. Babaji is sometimes called Shiva Goraksha Babaji, linking him to Gorakshanath, the founder of the Nath yogi tradition and another great yogi who achieved immortality through yogic practices.

Babaji's teachings are primarily transmitted through the practice of Kriya Yoga, a specific system of spiritual techniques that aims to accelerate spiritual evolution by controlling the life force (prana) and awakening the Kundalini energy within the body. His philosophy reflects the non-sectarian and universal principles of Sanatana Dharma, emphasizing self-realization, direct experience of God, and inner transformation over external rituals or dogma.

Key Tenets of Babaji's Philosophy as revealed to Gurunath

1. Kriya Yoga is the central practice that Babaji has revived for modern times. It involves a series of techniques that regulate the flow of prana (life energy) in the body, harmonizing the breath and mind, which leads to spiritual awakening. Kriya Yoga is a direct method to purify the mind and nervous system, enabling the practitioner to reach higher states of consciousness and ultimately attain self-realization.

   • The Kriya Yoga techniques are rooted in the ancient Patanjali's Yoga Sutras and incorporate Pranayama(breath control), meditation, and mantra repetition. These practices are designed to accelerate the evolution of consciousness and deepen the seeker's awareness of their unity with the Divine.

2. Unity of Religions: Babaji's teachings transcend specific religious boundaries. He is often described as a master who embraces all religions, viewing them as different paths to the same truth. Shiva-Goraksha-Babaji is said to work to promote spiritual unity and uplift humanity. The unity of religions is a key element of Babaji's philosophy, emphasizing that the essence of all spiritual traditions is the same – the realization of the Divine Self.

3. Self-Realization: A core teaching of Babaji is the goal of self-realization, or the direct experience of the self as a manifestation of the Divine. Through the practice of Kriya Yoga and meditation, the seeker can transcend the ego and body consciousness to experience the eternal nature of the soul, which is one with Brahman (the ultimate reality).

4. Non-Attachment and Inner Renunciation:Babaji's teachings emphasize inner renunciation rather than outward asceticism. He teaches that one can live in the world, fulfill worldly re-

sponsibilities, and still achieve liberation, provided one remains inwardly detached from desires and ego attachments. This aligns with the Bhagavad Gita's teaching of karma yoga—acting without attachment to the fruits of action.

5. Guru-Disciple Relationship: In Babaji's tradition, the guru-disciple relationship is of paramount importance. The transmission of spiritual knowledge and awakening through the guidance of a realized master (guru) is seen as essential for spiritual progress. Babaji himself plays the role of the eternal guru, offering guidance to those who are sincerely devoted to the spiritual path.

6. Service to Humanity:Though Babaji is often depicted as a reclusive yogi, his service to humanity is a fundamental aspect of his mission. He is said to work tirelessly behind the scenes to assist the spiritual evolution of individuals and the collective consciousness of humanity. Babaji encourages selfless service (karma yoga) as a means of purifying the heart and cultivating humility.

Kriya Yoga: The Core Practice

Kriya Yoga, as taught by Mahavatar Babaji, is a form of Raja Yoga (the yoga of mental control) that involves specific techniques for controlling the breath, calming the mind, and awakening Kundalini energy. The goal of Kriya Yoga is to unite the individual soul (Atman) with the Universal Consciousness (Brahman/Paramshiva), leading to the direct experience of God.

Key Components of Kriya Yoga:

1. Pranayama (Breath Control):Kriya Yoga teaches the control of breath to calm the nervous system and focus the mind. By harmonizing the breath with the spinal energy centers

(chakras), practitioners can awaken Kundalini, the dormant spiritual energy within the body, and move it upward through the spine.

2. Meditation: Through focused meditation techniques, the practitioner learns to silence the mind and concentrate on the inner light and sound. This helps to dissolve the ego and awaken to the divine presence within.

3. Mantra Repetition (Japa): Mantras (sacred sounds) are often used in Kriya Yoga to still the mind and invoke spiritual energy. Repeating these mantras helps to cleanse the mind of distractions and attune the consciousness to higher vibrations.

4. Direct Perception of God: Kriya Yoga leads to direct perception of God through inner experience, rather than through intellectual study or external rituals. This direct experience is seen as the highest form of spiritual knowledge, leading to self-realization.

Babaji's Impact on Indian and Global Spirituality:

1. Influence on Kriya Yoga Lineage: Babaji is considered the source of the Kriya Yoga lineage that was passed down through Lahiri Mahasaya, Sri Yukteswar, and Paramahansa Yogananda. Yogananda's efforts to spread Kriya Yoga to the West in the early 20th century introduced millions of people to Babaji's teachings, making Kriya Yoga one of the most widely practiced forms of spiritual discipline today.

2. Integration of Eastern and Western Mysticism: Through Yogananda and modern spiritual Masters such as Yogiraj Gurunath Siddhanath, Babaji's teachings have bridged Eastern and Western mystical traditions. His association with figures

like Jesus Christ in Yogananda's account shows Babaji's influence in promoting a universal spiritual path that transcends cultural and religious boundaries.

3. Inspiration for Yogis and Spiritual Seekers: Babaji has inspired countless spiritual seekers, yogis, and teachers who continue to practice and spread the techniques of Kriya Yoga. His life serves as an example of spiritual mastery and immortality, encouraging practitioners to pursue the highest goals of yoga and spiritual evolution.

4. Modern Yoga Movements: Babaji's legacy has also influenced the broader Yoga movement, particularly through the emphasis on Hatha Yoga, Raja Yoga, and Kundalini awakening. Babaji's teachings helped shape the modern understanding of Yoga as both a spiritual practice and a method for physical and mental well-being.

Mahavatar Babaji is one of the most revered and enigmatic figures in modern spirituality, known for his role in reviving Kriya Yoga and guiding the spiritual evolution of humanity. Though he remains a mysterious and transcendent figure, his influence is felt through the Kriya Yoga lineage, which continues to transform the lives of countless seekers. Babaji's teachings emphasize self-realization, non-sectarian spirituality, and the direct experience of God through the practices of Yoga and meditation. His presence in both Eastern and Western spiritual traditions represents a universal call to awaken to the divine potential within all beings and to live in harmony with the highest spiritual ideals.

His direct disciple, Yogiraj Gurunath Siddhanath has revealed how this enigmatic Mahavatar has been guiding humanity's spiritual evolution since the dawn of intelligent life on Earth. Gurunath has shown that Babaji has often appeared as different Masters such as the Mahasiddha Gorakshanath to directly influence the flow of spiritual instruction.

More Books By Rudra Shivananda

The Teachings of Bhagavad Gita for the Householder Yogi

According to the author, the Bhagavad Gita is a handbook for those on the path of Self-Realization, especially that of the integrated Kriya Yoga, He has taken the teachings and applied them to help the modern day householder yogi.

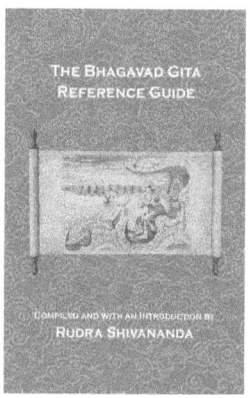

The Bhagavad Gita Reference Guide

The Gita has inspired and influenced Western thought since the first translation over two hundred years ago. Poets, philosophers, thinkers, and scientists have attested to its wisdom and life-changing impact.

It is the most translated Indian spiritual classic.

In this guide, the following useful reference material has been included:

    An introduction and analysis of the English translations of the Gita
    A few verses from 25 translations are provided for the reader's own comparison
    Traditional Gita Dhyanam (meditations) and Gita Mahatmyam (chants in praise of the Gita)
    The Gita Chalisa - forty selected verses traditionally considered the core teachings of the Gita
    The Gitartha Samgraha of Yamunacharya
    The ten key verses from the Advaita perspective
    The eighteen verse summary from Kashmiri Shaivism
    The epithets used for Lord Krishna and Arjuna
    A complete translation of the Gita from Swami Swarupananda
    A detailed bibliography of English translations

Transformed By The Presence

An illuminating chronicle of the author's journey from a spiritual seeker in a quest for immortality to a yogic practitioner guided towards Self-Realization and then flowing into an awakening to serve humanity as one's larger self through the role of a spiritual teacher. He takes us from his childhood in the British colony of Hong Kong to the eclectic mystic movements in California and the mystery shrouded spiritual realm of India, on this path of self-actualization.

The highlights of the Rudra Shivananda's accounts are the enlightening experiences he shares of his spiritual Master, the unique Himalayan Grandmaster, Yogiraj SatGurunath Siddhanath. These surreal experiences correspond to his transformational breakthroughs in higher consciousness that lead to a satisfying, joyful and meaningful life.

Rudra also shares with the reader the many different spiritual paths that he explored in his journey before meeting his Master. His insights into these spiritual disciplines are helpful to the seekers and practitioners who are still unsure of their life paths.

As a spiritual teacher himself, Rudra offers guidance on the many issues that may effect those sincere students who have shared their questions and doubts with him over the years.

Practical Nada Yoga For Self Realization

The timeless discipline of Nada Yoga has been given a renewed interpretation based on the practical experiences of the author. Rudra Shivananda provides his insights as well as practical guidance in successfully engaging on this spiritual path that leads to higher states of consciousness and to Self-Realization.

Nada is the term given to the subtle inner sounds in our deepest awareness of the cosmic Hum of the Universal Matrix. In various cultures, it has been praised as the "Music of the Spheres," the Shabda, the Sound of Creation, or the voice of the Divine: The Universal unstruck sound we seek. The vibration guides us to our core - Rudra Shivananda helps the reader to navigate the theoretical and practical aspects of reconnecting with our superconscious states.

Howling From The High Heavens

Rudra Shivananda is a well-known teacher (Acharya) of Kriya Yoga who is established in living a spiritual life in the material world. He shares his insights and experiences in a thought-provoking and impactful way through the medium of poetic verses and art forms. His purpose is to point the way to Self-Realization from various perspectives gained during his own amazing journey. He strives to move us beyond our comfortable boundaries to broader and more profound vistas of reality.

Living A Spiritual Life In A Material World

Seekers on the path of Self-Realization are soon trapped by the many pitfalls along the journey. Spiritual practices should develop the wisdom mind and lead the soul to one's True Nature or Spirit, but interacting with the demands and desires of the material world often causes the strengthening of the ego instead. When the practitioner tries to dissociate from the material world, apathy and depression results.

In order to balance the spiritual life within the matrix of materiality, it is useful for the practitioner to develop within a model that encompasses both facets. This book provides the reader with inspiration and guidance along the path to navigate the treacherous waters along the river of your soul journey towards the source of Self.

In Light Of Kriya Yoga

Suitable for all those interested in expanding their awareness and how to live their lives joyfully. The author speaks from his experiential realization and connects current events with ancient teachings as well as applying parables to lives' dilemmas. He gives thought provoking and unique interpretations on topics such as: Living spiritually in a material world; do you need a Guru? liberation; Self-Realization; karma; dharma; samadhi; devotion and grace; how to develop concentration and meditation; why do good people do bad things? plus many other mysteries of spirituality. An inspirational and trustworthy companion for all those seeking to raise their consciousness to ever higher levels.

Practical Mantra Yoga

In modern times, the use of mantras has become popularized, but their reputed powers have been waning due to the proliferation of 'fast-food' mentality among those eager to grasp at results. The author, Rudra Shivananda, has tapped into the traditional mantra programs through his yogic lineage of the Siddhanath Parampara. He has re-introduced an effective graded program of three levels for attaining higher consciousness through the discipline of Mantra Yoga, one of the true and tried spiritual paths for Self-Realization.

The three levels for this practical mantra program consist of mind transformation, unity consciousness and Self-Realization. Each level is described in detail and the appropriate mantras introduced.

Breathe Better Live Longer

Hundreds of scientific studies have shown that the use of breathing techniques can help treat difficult health problems such as depression, anxiety, asthma, high blood pressure and gastrointestinal maladies. This book is a wellness program that will be helpful for preventing many health problems among young people and to heal many of the problems affecting older people.

The techniques in this program were chosen because they will show rapid if not immediate results with the investment of a short duration of practice.

Books By Rudra Shivananda

Chakra selfHealing by the Power of Om
Yoga of Purification and Transformation
Surya Yoga - Healing by Solar Power
Breathe Like Your Life Depends On It
In Light of Kriya Yoga
Healing Postures of the 18 Siddhas
Insight and Guidance for Spiritual Seekers
Practical Mantra Yoga
Breathe Better Live Longer
Superconsciousness By Practical Nada Yoga
Living A Spiritual Life In A Material World
Howling From The High Heavens
The Bhagavad Gita Reference Guide
Transformed by the Presence
Teachings of the Bhagavad Gita for the Householder Yogi
Philosophy of the Himalayan Master

website: www.rudrashivananda.com
blog: www.sanatanamitra.com
www.youtube.com/user/KriyaNathYogi

About the Author

Rudra Shivananda, a disciple of the Himalayan GrandMaster Yogiraj Gurunath Siddhanath, is dedicated to the service of humanity through the furthering of human awareness and spiritual evolution. He teaches that the only lasting way to bring happiness into one's life is by a consistent practice of awareness and transformation. He has developed healing programs utilizing the energy centers [Chakras] and Prana Energy techniques through breath.

Rudra Shivananda is committed to spreading the message of his Master: "Earth Peace through Self Peace". He teaches this message of World and Individual Peace through the practice of Kriya Yoga. As a student and teacher of yoga for more than 50 years, he is trained as an Acharya or Spiritual Preceptor in the Indian Nath Tradition, closely associated with the Siddha tradition. He lives in the San Francisco Bay area, and has given initiations and workshops in USA, Ireland, England, Japan, Spain, Brazil, Russia, Singapore, Malaysia, Hong Kong, India, Australia, Canada and Estonia.

www.ingramcontent.com/pod-product-compliance
Lightning Source LLC
Chambersburg PA
CBHW040723240426
43666CB00045B/2906